150 BC

BY DAVE ARMITAGE

CLOUGHIE
THE INSIDE STORIES

Hot Air Publishing Ltd

A CIP catalogue record for this book is available from the British Library.

ISBN 978-0-9552466-2-3

Published by

Hot Air Publishing Ltd,
10 Marigold Court,
Red Lake, Telford,
Shropshire TF1 5ZN

DEDICATION

To Brian Clough and Peter Taylor
- for all the joy you gave so many

Many of the people I interviewed stressed the important part
Peter Taylor played in one of football's true success stories.
Following Peter's sudden death in 1990, Brian himself
more readily acknowledged his mate's legacy and
was desperately sad the pair of them had never
patched up their long-standing differences.

*'I never imagined Peter dying at all. I wish he hadn't.
I wish he was still around and that we were together
talking the way we used to and going to football
matches and telling one another that
we'd have done it better!'*

*'I do so wish our relationship, so special and
successful, hadn't soured.
Whoever said: 'Never go to sleep on an
argument' was right.'*

CONTENTS

ACKNOWLEDGEMENTS

Special thanks to all the people who so kindly helped with
this book, not least all the contributors.
Huge thanks to Phil Shaw, Ian Edwards and Peter Lansley for their efforts.
Also, I am indebted to Steve Mitchell of the Nottingham Evening Post
and Steve Nicholson of the Derby Evening Telegraph.
A big thank you to both of those publications and
Express Newspapers for the help they gave in
providing pictures for this book.

*Visit the Nottingham Evening Post Brian Clough
picture archive at:
www.thisisnottingham.co.uk*

Typography by Alison Smith, Justified Design - 01952 246174

Printed by TJ International Ltd, Padstow, Cornwall PL28 8RW

THE CHAIRMAN OF THE BOARD

The more I think about Cloughie's admiration for Frank Sinatra, the less it surprises me.

Just like his hero, when Clough was in full swing he made it all look so darned effortless.

He was The Chairman of the Board even if Cloughie would have struggled with any acknowledgement containing such words.

They were peas from the same pod – just kids from modest upbringings who went on to scale the heights. Sometimes they bit off more than they could chew. But more, much more than this, they did it their way. And when they were in their pomp, it all looked so simple.

For Old Blue Eyes read Old Big 'Ead. When it came to football he was King of the Hill, Top of the Heap.

Both were capable of showing a thousand-and-one different personalities. Difficult? Yes. Headstrong? Most certainly. For every act of pig-headed rudeness, they were capable of astonishing acts of generosity and kindness. Both were dynamic and gave off auras of astonishing self-confidence. They were brash, unconventional, obstinate, infuriating, outrageously candid, forthright, outspoken, funny, charming and agreeable, all in one maverick package. But most of all they were good. They were very good indeed. And what's more, they knew it. Like another of his great heroes – Muhammad Ali – Clough delivered brilliant one-liners like lightning jabs.

The premise for writing this book was to try and give those fascinated with Clough a unique insight into what made him tick through the eyes of those who crossed his path. How well did I know him? Well, it's difficult to say. I was a visitor to his house at his invitation on a few occasions and as the Daily Star's Midlands Sports Reporter had the privilege of getting into his inner sanctum at Nottingham Forest and watch him hold court on too many occasions to count. Yes, he could be difficult, downright infuriating at times, but when I was made redundant by the Sunday Mirror in the mid - 1990s, Cloughie made a point of contacting me offering an in-depth interview 'to make yourself a few bob.' This was the time when Clough commanded £1,000 for a big interview – and invariably gave it away to buy wheelchairs for disabled youngsters.

I even had sweet peas growing in his garden (see Chapter One) but how well anyone really knew him, I am not sure at all. I was asked recently if I liked Clough. The answer – a resounding 'yes' but qualified by times when he could have you tearing your hair out in frustration. But this collection of stories isn't being done on 'the man who knew him best' basis. Of course I knew him, but more importantly, I came into regular contact with players, staff at the club, and, of course, journalists. Here, I am the collator of a bunch of stories that have been, up to now, largely in the private domain of those concerned. However, the players, journalists, and assorted friends interviewed hopefully make for a fascinating cocktail and a unique insight into what made Brian Howard Clough box-office.

He was very funny. A couple of the recent books about him just didn't convey that at all. When journalists or players start recalling Clough stories either among themselves or to pals in a pub, they are sure things. People have made careers out of after-dinner speeches where he is the main subject. Everyone who ever met him has a tale. Late into the night in bars and press rooms all around the world, I've entertained and been entertained by Cloughie tales. When you bump into his former players, they inevitably tell a story of something left-of-centre that he had done. Compiling them into some sort of collection just made total sense. At the risk of being self-indulgent, the first couple are mine, if only to let the reader realise that, on the odd occasion, I was privileged to get closer than most. After that, they follow in a staccato Clough-style – like bullets spraying from a machine gun. They are not arranged in any particular order of time or importance. Some subjects have more than one tale to tell. And you know, the funny thing is, that when the idea first came to me to compile the book, the original title was 100 BC. Even then there was a nagging worry that collecting a century of tales of sufficient entertainment value might be pushing it. How many people lend themselves to one hundred anecdotes? Not many. Yet, from early on, it became clear my main problem would be running over. And so it became 125 BC, then 150 BC before I really had to call a halt. Invariably, the subject of my questions rattled off two or three stories concerning the Life of Brian. That alone says more about the man as a subject than I ever could. Yet I still take this opportunity to apologise to those I was still unable to accommodate.

I found him fascinating – and I found him funny. I also cursed him on more than the odd occasion. That's what you got – take it or leave it. The other distinguishing factor about him was that his outrageously honest, no-nonsense views seemed to stretch him across boundaries of club or place. He was a genuine cult hero. Whether in Scotland, Liverpool, Manchester, Devon or in some foreign bar – everyone was receptive to a Clough story.

As a point of reference, for the purposes of this book I will most frequently refer to him affectionately as 'Cloughie' because that's how I talk about him now. I wouldn't have been so bold to address him so informally.

'I'll give you fucking Cloughie!' would no doubt have been his reply. I called him Mr Clough in the first instance until instructed to call him Brian. That was his preferred stance with mostly everyone. Lady Di could have brought a smile to his face by calling him Cloughie, but to lesser mortals there was still a certain protocol. Now, to refer to him just as Clough is far too harsh, while Brian can seem overly familiar. Cloughie is a term which just sits easier in cold type or in chatter over a pint.

Was he, like Ali, The Greatest? I suspect he was. The argument will always rage on. Personally, I think he might well have been, if only because he took two provincial clubs – Derby County and Nottingham Forest to the title - then conquered Europe with Forest. The fact that he then went on to win the European Cup twice just for good measure was little short of astonishing. Almost forgotten is the fact that he took Derby to the European Cup semi-finals where they were cheated out of it. His CV is impressive but imagine winning the European Cup with two different provincial sides. That really would have put the debate beyond any doubt. People will have their standpoint and there can never be a definitive conclusion. Perhaps it was best summed up by the man himself when he famously observed: 'I'm not sure if I'm the best manager in the business, but I'm in the top one'

One thing is for sure – he is sorely missed. He believed in the beautiful game being played as beautifully as was possible and remained uncompromising in that belief. He abhorred cheats on and off the pitch. He despised crooks and conmen. He saw himself, rightly or wrongly, as a footballing Robin Hood.

Even those who had no allegiance to Forest or Derby, invariably acknowledge that his belligerent approach to the cynical side of football could give a warm glow. He liked his sides to play football. To call it simple football would be doing him and his teams a disservice, though his philosophy shone through when he said: 'Football should be like a golf swing – the more you try and complicate it, the harder it gets.'

Like Sinatra, he was an entertainer who made it look God-given. It probably was. When he was centre stage, which is where he liked to be, he was magnificent. And just like Old Blue Eyes, Old Big 'Ead could silence a room merely by walking into it.

There was a magic about him and if I could pay him any lasting tribute, I just hope some of that stardust shines through in the pages of this book.

The contributors to this unique collection are as varied as they are fascinating. Only one thing can I guarantee - I spoke to EVERY single one who appears in this book personally. Not one story has been taken from press cuttings. There are many of his players – some who got on with him, others who didn't. And in the following pages you will find accounts from his gardener and his secretary and, yes, even a whole host of 'shithouse' journalists. Don't be fooled by the oft-voiced notion that he didn't like us. He detested many, but some of them like Vince Wilson were lifelong friends. Former Sun columnist John Sadler was also very close and the man who was his ghost-writer for his autobiography, as was Nottingham journalist John Lawson. I thank them all for contributing.

Thanks to everyone who gave up just a small piece of their memories and hopefully they make for a memorable collection for the rest of the world to enjoy.

DAVE ARMITAGE

CLOUGHIE: MOMENTS IN TIME

1935: Born 31 March, Middlesbrough

1951: Signs pro forms for Middlesbrough and goes on to score 197 goals in 213 league games for the club.

1959: Makes his two appearances for England v Wales(a) and Sweden(h).

1961: Signs for Sunderland for fee of £42,000 and scores 54 goals in 61 league games.

1962: Injures cruciate ligaments in collision with Bury goalkeeper on Boxing Day.

1964: Brief comeback but forced to retire through injury.

1965: Becomes youngest manager in Football League, aged 30, when he takes over at Hartlepool. Peter Taylor becomes his assistant.

1967: Takes over as manager at Derby County.

1969: Derby win Second Division title.

1972: Derby become First Division champions.

1973: Resigns after row with board and joins Brighton.

1974: Ill-fated 44 day spell at Leeds United.

1975: Joins Nottingham Forest as new boss.

1976: Taylor joins him.

1977: Forest win promotion and Clough interviewed for England job.

1978: Forest win League and League Cup. Named Manager of the Year.

1979: Forest win European Cup beating Swedish side Malmo 1-0 in Munich. Win League Cup with win over Southampton. Makes Trevor Francis Britain's first £1m player.

1980: Forest keep European Cup with 1-0 win over Hamburg in Madrid.

1989: Forest win League Cup with win over Luton Town.

1990: Forest retain League Cup with win over Oldham.

1991: Forest get to FA Cup final but lose to Tottenham. Clough awarded OBE.

1993: Receives Freedom of City of Nottingham. Announces his retirement shortly before Forest's relegation.

2002: Has liver transplant.

2003: Receives Freedom of Derby.

2004: Dies, 20 September, aged 69.

2008: Statue unveiled in Nottingham in acknowledgement of his achievements.

Author DAVE ARMITAGE gets the ball rolling with this story of how a surprise gift for Cloughie prompted a typically unpredictable reaction. Dave, who works for the Daily Star, has been a national newspaper sports writer for over 25 years.

1

PEAS OFFERING

THE AUTHOR

I once spent a couple of quid and really made an impression with Cloughie – more so than if I'd stuffed a hundred pounds in his hand. He was strange that way. Financially set up for life and proud of it, there wasn't too much you could give him which would capture his imagination for more than thirty seconds. You could have bought him something quite expensive and though he would have thanked you, I'm sure on many occasions he would have been suspicious of the motives. My 'gift' was a tiny impulsive thing he still mentioned to me years later. It was never actually intended that way . . .

It would have been the mid-80s and I'd been to the magnificent Shrewsbury Flower Show. Strolling past the various exhibits, I spotted a sweet pea called 'Brian Clough.' Behind each vase were small, unspectacular packets of seeds. There was no picture on them, just the name rather crudely stamped on them. I can't even remember how much they were but I thought I'd get a couple of packets and give them to him when I was next at the City Ground. If they were a pound each it's as much as they were.

Knowing what kind of reaction you would get from Cloughie about anything was always tricky. If he was in a particularly pig-headed mood, even an act of generosity, no matter how small, could be considered risky. There was always the ridicule factor with him and there weren't many who could hit back with a neatly delivered put-down.

Anyway, I recall seeing him at the ground and saying something like: 'I've brought you something I think you'll like.'

'Have you now? It had better be good because I'm loaded, you know,' he replied. Suddenly it didn't seem such a good idea. How excited did I expect him to be about a couple of packets of sweet peas? I was now on edge as I went to the red Ford Cortina on the car park and leant over into the glove compartment. I came back and dropped them on the desk in front of him. This could go spectacularly wrong. If he thought it was just a crummy attempt to gain any kind of favour, he'd just as likely toss 'em in the bin. I dropped the packets in front of him and as they landed on the desk, it was clear his attention had been caught

'Hey are they what I think they are?' he said fingering the small brown packets.

'What do you think they are?'

'Are they sweet peas?'

'Yep.'

'Well, bugger me. I haven't seen any of these for years,' he said.

'Told you, you might be interested,' I said, getting slightly bolder.

'Well . . . there's a funny story about these. Well, thank you. Very kind.'

Cloughie went on to tell of how he'd been approached by a nurseryman some years ago and asked if he would allow a new sweet pea to be named after him. Cloughie was suitably honoured and went to see the new variety and the man responsible.

'They're beautiful you know. He used to send me some but whether he died or lost my address I don't know, but I haven't seen them for ages.'

Months later, I'd forgotten all about them when Cloughie bounded across the car park by Forest's Jubilee Club and came up to me.

'Hey shithouse. My missus was talking about you this morning!'

I must have looked startled. 'Yes. You know those sweet peas you gave me? Well, she's grown them all up the back of our house and they are absolutely beautiful.'

'Oh right, nice one.'

'Yes, our Barbara said 'You ought to ask that nice young man around to come and see them now they're out.'

Wow, for the briefest of moments, I quite possibly thought I'd cracked it. An invitation to the house . . .

'Hey 'I told her,' I'm not having shithouse reporters up at my house. But thanks very much anyway!'

Typical Cloughie – build someone up then knock him straight back down. It was a weapon he used to stunning effect.

❝ . . . You don't put snowdrops in the ground and expect them to come up the next month. It's the same with football teams - you have to nurture them ❞

*The author recounts a story when Cloughie,
at his mischievous best, just happened to let slip
how he had hatched a cunning plan to nobble
GRAEME SHARP, one of the top strikers in the country.*

2

GET SHARP

AUTHOR & GRAEME SHARP

Cloughie's instinctive ability to excite, shock and grab a back page headline was unrivalled. And on May 11, 1985, the few of us lucky enough to be in his office witnessed him in action getting his message across in the media, long before Max Clifford earned a fortune at it.

After games, a select few of the national press guys used to hang around in the hope that Cloughie would be in a good mood and invite us in. It was totally hit and miss and, to be honest, I'd say that for every time we did get the nod, there were probably three or four occasions when we just hung around in the car park only to eventually abandon any hopes of catching him. Maybe time has massaged my memory – perhaps the blowout rate was higher. Whatever, the fact is I spent a lot of time hanging around car parks at Cloughie's expense. It's not something you'd do for any other manager. When you got Brian, if only for five minutes, he was inevitably in fantastic form.

Sometimes he'd call us in just to be sociable and we'd have a couple of Scotches and have a chat.

'Hey, come on in – but we're not working,' he'd sometimes say. No one dared get a notebook out when you were in Clough's office, unless you'd been told otherwise, so if he was going off on one, it was sometimes confusing as to whether he was happy for it to go in the paper. Generally, we got by, working out for ourselves what was for public consumption and what wasn't.

That particular day, Forest had played the newly-crowned champions Everton who had rested a number of big-name players including Andy Gray, Peter Reid and leading goalscorer Graeme Sharp. That wasn't too surprising really. Everton were going for glory on three fronts – they had won the title a few days earlier, were playing Rapid Vienna in the European Cup Winners' Cup final in a few days, before playing Manchester United in the FA Cup final on the Saturday. To say they were very much the team of the moment would be an understatement.

Anyway, Forest beat Howard Kendall's under-strength side 1-0 and afterwards, as we loitered around outside the corridor, we got the nod from

Cloughie's secretary Carole that we could go in for a drink.

I considered myself very fortunate to be included in this 'select' group which comprised Midlands-based reporters who had built a relationship with Clough from his days at Derby and then as his Forest side had travelled all over Europe.

Although I got on pretty well with him, I was the youngster of a group that had clocked up some miles with Clough. On this particular day there was Ray Matts of the Daily Mail, John Wragg from the Daily Express, David Moore from the Mirror and the late and much missed Roger Duckworth from The Sun. 'Rodg' was a jovial, cheery-faced guy who Cloughie genuinely had a soft spot for.

'Hey Rodg, you do make me laugh,' he'd often say.

Clough's office was just about big enough to accommodate half-a-dozen or so and we arranged our chairs accordingly and, with notebooks firmly wedged in pockets, said 'cheers' as Clough poured out a few tumblers of Scotch.

Very matter-of-factly, he dropped something into the conversation which seemed to be of little or no importance at the time. Pretty soon, we'd be praying we'd had our notebooks out and taking down every line! No problem . . . Clough knew that too.

So, as he sat holding court with his trademark green rugby top on, he said: 'Hey, did anyone see me go to the Everton bench before the game?'

A couple of us must have nodded or grunted, acknowledging that he had been spotted stooping into the Everton dug-out and having a word with someone. An old friend perhaps? Not likely.

'Ask me why!' he roared mischievously.

'Why Brian?' I recall Rodg saying, chortling at the absurdity of it.

'Hey, I'll tell you why. I told that boy Sharp that I was really sorry he wasn't playing today because I'd ordered my players to break his leg – just like he broke Gary Mills' leg up at Goodison.'

Silence . . . glances exchanged, eyebrows raised, but no one dared say anything. Had Clough really just said that? Bear in mind Sharp was a huge name, whose bagful of goals had been a massive reason behind Everton's phenomenal success this season.

'Yep,' he continued, absolutely determined not to let the matter drop.

'I even told my nipper Nige – our No 9 – to follow him around and break his leg if he got the chance. Hey and my bairn is only knee high to a grasshopper while that big sod is well over six foot.'

Gasps from a group not easily shocked . . .

'What did he say?' one of us asked.

'Not a lot he could say. I just said I was sorry he wasn't playing and I fucking well told him why as well.'

Cloughie had clearly wanted to get this off his chest. It was potentially explosive stuff, but we hadn't a clue whether it was 'on the record' or just Cloughie making a point within the confines of the four walls. Imagine that in print – a big name manager like

Clough openly admitting that he'd told his players to try and break the leg of one of the very best strikers in the league. Even if he hadn't meant it literally, it was still cracking stuff.

Just for the record, it must be said that while Clough had the major hump with Sharp about the challenge which broke Mills' leg, there is nothing to suggest that there was any malice in the tackle at all.

Clough left his office for a while and we all looked at each other gobsmacked. Fucking hell! Was that rant for our consumption or was he just getting it off his chest but not wanting a word of it to appear in public? This was tricky because any misreading of the situation and we'd not only land Clough in massive bother with the FA but probably sever our relationship with him for ever.

The plan of attack was devised. We would get Jolly Roger to pop down the corridor and see if he could merely enquire where we stood with this. Cloughie had often remarked that he never said anything off the record, unless he made it absolutely clear that it was. Then grey areas like this arose. . . Fucking hell, who would be a reporter in the Court of King Clough? Rodg nipped out and had a quick look around, but couldn't find him. This was a nightmare. Clough would often just disappear into the night.

We sat there, debating the issue. I remember being in there for a good 15 minutes, on the premise of finishing our drinks, but actually deciding on if - and how – to pursue this. It was a great story. But it wouldn't be quite so great if it proved to be our last! We carry the story, Cloughie gets hauled before the FA and fined and we burn our bridges big-time. On the other hand Cloughie, the most media-savvy guy in the world, drops a nugget in our laps because he wants to make a point and we ignore it like a bunch of lemons.

We examined the evidence. Clough had asked us in and deliberately asked us to ask him why he'd gone to the dugout. And . . . he'd gone off on one because he'd clearly got a major bee in his bonnet about what had happened to Mills. But suddenly our deliberations came to a halt as Clough popped his head through the office door.

'Goodnight lads.'

Before one of us could say: 'Er . . . Brian?'

'Hey, and I want to see some of that fucking stuff in the papers on Monday morning! Tara.'

Point made.

Such is the life of a sportswriter that I now regularly bump into Graeme in his capacity as a radio broadcaster. We've had a laugh about this particular story on a few occasions and he can offer a nice twist to it as he gives his account of their meeting . . .

I remember the incident well! Who wouldn't? In fact there's a slight twist to it at the end from my perspective, as you'll discover. Needless to say it was the inimitable Brian Clough who ended up having the final say, despite my best efforts.

Our boss Howard Kendall had decided to rest a number of our lads with the huge match against Rapid Vienna just a few days away. I was one of a small band of players given a breather.

We even went out in Nottingham the night before because we had been told we wouldn't be required. If I'd known Cloughie was such a big fan of mine at the time, I'd have invited him along!

The background, as explained, was that I had caught Mills in a challenge and the unfortunate consequence was that he ended up with a broken leg.

It was just a challenge – one of those things that happens in football occasionally. It was regrettable, but something of an unfortunate occupational hazard. Cloughie clearly wasn't happy though.

A few of us were sitting in the dugout watching the lads warm up when Clough in his famous green jumper stopped and he peered in at us.

"Young man, I'm really sorry you're not playing today,' he said, jabbing his finger in my direction.

'Why's that then?' I said

'Because I would have got my son Nigel to kick you. In fact, I'd have ordered him to kick you.'

'Your son?' I said with a grin, like I was going to be really worried about that. Andy Gray looked at me and you could tell from our reactions that we thought Cloughie was off his trolley.

Who was he to poke his head in at us and come out out with this sort of stuff? He wasn't about to stop his tirade either.

'Yes, my nipper. I'd have got him to break your leg, just like you broke Gary's leg up at your fucking place.'

'Yeah right. Whatever you say.'

Andy, myself and the lads couldn't believe what was happening. It was just such a surreal moment.

'Anyway, really sorry you're not playing young man.'

'Hey, I'm sorry too but the reason I'm not is because I've got a European Cup Winners' Cup final in a few days time,' I declared, rather proudly.

I thought that was a pretty good way to shut Cloughie up, but still he managed to trump it.

'I know you have and I sincerely wish you all the very best young man,' he said offering me his hand.

We shook hands and off he went to the Forest bench. I think he was just making a point about something that had obviously upset him, even though there was certainly nothing deliberate on my part.

To this day I still find him a fascinating character. The fact that he shook my hand and wished me well after informing me in no uncertain terms that he'd like to have put 'a hit' on me.

❛ **That Jose Mourinho's got a lot to say for himself. He reminds me of what I was like at his age - but I was better looking** ❜

3

SHILTS' SPANISH ISLAND

VIV ANDERSON

Can anyone imagine the sight of the world's greatest goalkeeper practising in the middle of a Spanish traffic island on the afternoon before the European Cup final? Hard to believe? Absolutely. I certainly thought so when I received a call in Madrid to ask me why the hell Peter Shilton was throwing himself around on a traffic roundabout in the city.

My friend assured me he wasn't winding me up. He'd seen the legendary Shilts being put through his paces with cars and mopeds flying past and wondered if the sangria had got to him.

'It's news to me,' I assured him as I took the call at our hotel. We were in Madrid to defend our European Cup crown against Kevin Keegan's Hamburg.

When Shilts returned he confirmed that although Cloughie had told the players to relax, he really wanted to do some training and the only place near-by was a totally unsuitable clay tennis court.

So Jimmy Gordon and Peter Taylor had found a traffic island with grass on it, a few palm trees too I'm led to believe, and gave Shilts his workout there after clearing away any offending bits of rubble and bricks.

That to me was vintage Clough. Would anyone else have allowed such a thing? What people must have thought as they walked past is anyone's guess.

Shilton takes up the story, revealing: 'I couldn't train on the tennis court so I asked the gaffer if some alternative arrangements could be made.

'He asked me to follow Peter. The only bit of grass we could find was this roundabout near the city centre. It was fairly quiet, but a few cars came past beeping their horns! So that's where I had to train and I ended up having one of the best games for the club in that final.'

❛ Some idiots say my players live in fear of me. It's just that they know where they stand with me - that's the difference ❜

*Clough's warm side is revealed here in a touching tale from
his trusty lieutenant ALAN HILL. The former goalkeeper
was Clough's companion on the infamous Pennine Walk when
the Forest boss learned he'd lost John Robertson to Derby.*

4

GOLDEN GESTURE

ALAN HILL

One of my fondest memories of Brian was when I recall something that happened in the summer of 1983. I was with him on a four-day charity walk on the Pennines. That walk has gone down in history as the one on which he heard that his old mate Peter Taylor had signed John Robertson and sparked the acrimonious break-up of one of the game's greatest ever partnerships. But I'll remember it for something completely different.

I can't remember exactly how we came to be on the walk but Brian was raising some money to buy an electric wheelchair for a young girl who lived in West Bridgford near the Forest ground.

Anyway, we had stopped to have a drink in this lovely little pub along the way when this small boy comes up to Brian and says: 'Hey, look it's Cloughie!'

'Mr Clough to you,' he corrected him.

'Hey Mr Clough, would you do me a favour?'

'If I can.'

'Would you mind if I went and got my grandad and brought him to see you?'

'Where is he?' asked Brian.

'Just down the road. Can I go and get him?'

'Aye, all right then. Run along with ya,' came the reply.

A little while later the lad returned, carefully steering his grandad who was quite clearly blind.

'Watch the step grandad,' he said.

'Watch it there grandad, there's some cow muck,' the boy continued, gently getting the old fella towards us.

'Right, if you put your hand out grandad, you can shake Brian Clough's hand,' the lad said.

The gaffer, clearly touched, moved towards the old man and gave him a massive hug.

'I idolise thee,' the man said in a thick Yorkshire accent. 'You don't know how much this means to me.'

The gaffer was quite moved and assured him the pleasure was all his.

'You've made my day and that takes some doing because it's a special one for me today.'

'How come?'

'It's my golden wedding.'

'Where's your good lady?' he asked.

'She's just down at the house.

The next thing I knew, we were making our way down to the old fella's house.

I'll tell you what, we had the warmest welcome you could ever imagine and word spread that the gaffer was around.

I kid you not, we were there for hours, having a cup of tea and some cake and by the time we left, I reckon half the village had been through the house, staring on in disbelief at Cloughie's kindness in giving one old couple a golden wedding day they'd never forget!

❛ We don't like the French and they don't like us, but they picked a plum out with that Wenger bloke - *on Arsenal topping Nottingham Forest's 42-match unbeaten run* ❜

When Cloughie splashed out £175,000 for COLIN TODD it smashed the British transfer record. But the brilliant defender proved a superb acquisition, helping Derby to two titles and winning 27 England caps in the process.

5

BET YOU GET GRIEF

COLIN TODD

I received a phone call at home one afternoon asking me to report to the gaffer's office and to bring my wife Jenny with me. What on earth could it be? As we made our way there, we couldn't help but try to work out what could have prompted such a request. Perhaps I'd won an award and they wanted to tell me first rather than hear it second hand.

'Come in.' The gaffer and Peter Taylor summoned us in and then the mystery began to unravel in quite dramatic fashion. Well, it was pretty dramatic for me, I can assure you.

'Have you any idea why you are here?' I was asked.

'No, boss.'

'You sure?'

'Yes boss.'

'You can't think of any reason why I should have you in here then?'

'Not really. Have I won the Player of the Year award?'

'Player of the Year award?' Clough said in a perplexed tone.

'Player of the Year award?' he repeated a couple of octaves higher and looking even more bemused.

'No it's not that. You have a prob-lem, don't you?' he said looking me full in the eye.

'No, I don't think so,' I assured him.

'Over the road,' he said, pointing in the general direction of the bookmakers just across the way.

'It's come to our notice that you owe the bookies some money and you are in a bit of trouble,' the boss continued.

Bit of trouble? Master of the understatement. I looked at the wife and realised that I was going to be.

'Well?'

'Yes,' I muttered, absolutely petrified.

'Right, well if we hear any more of anything like this and you will be kicked out of this club,' I was told.

This was Clough and Taylor at their very best. Their method was that if they had just collared me privately it wouldn't have meant anything. I could have sloped off and got it sorted without any recriminations. As it was, I got another bollocking the minute I'd walked out of the office door!

It did the trick. I owe them for that, even though I probably couldn't have appreciated it right at that moment.

The funny thing was that the debt was mysteriously cleared. From that day on I was scared to even look at the racing pages in the papers for fear of one of them catching me.

It had shaken me rigid that they had found out and I owe it to them that I'm not ruined.

❛ Don't walk on my pitch with your high heels on. Mind you, they go with your earrings
- to a bunch of fashion-conscious opposition players ❜

Sports writer DAVE HARRISON became close to Cloughie during his two years ghost-writing the manager's column for the News of the World. Here he recalls how a brush with royalty made for a lovely story.

6

HEAVEN SCENT

DAVE HARRISON

In the week following Lady Diana's tragic death in 1997, there was barely a column inch spare for anything other than copy that had a slant on The People's Princess.

The sports pages weren't exempt, with coverage of her funeral on Saturday, September 7, taking over virtually the entire paper.

Working for the biggest selling Sunday newspaper in the world meant that to get anything in the News of the World that was to appear the following morning, you would have to come up with something special.

I had an idea because I remembered how captivated Brian Clough had been when he was introduced to her just prior to his only FA Cup final appearance six years earlier.

Nottingham Forest were playing Spurs and when Lady Di was introduced to the teams before the big game, I recalled that she'd stopped and spoken to him for a good minute or so, which was unusual.

Perhaps it wasn't that unusual given that he had a big rosette on proclaiming ' World's Greatest Grandad,' but I decided to drop in on him and see if I could come up with a nice story.

I drove to his house where his wife Barbara answered the door and informed me that Brian was out in the garden.

I went around the back and ventured into the Clough garden that was truly magnificent and noticed him sitting there. He spotted me.

'Hey shithouse. What do you want?' he exclaimed.

I told him the purpose of my visit and you could tell Diana's death still hadn't properly registered with him.

'You met her. What was she like?' I asked.

'Breathe in,' he said.

'What?'

'Take a really deep breath in and smell my garden,' he said. I breathed in.

'You want to know what she was like – well that's what she was like,' Clough said his eyes moist.

'You see that butterfly?' he continued.

'Yeah.'

'Well, that's what she was like. And they crushed her, you know. They bloody well crushed her.'

It was typical Cloughie. He had that knack of summing things up so succinctly and the fragrance from his garden was the only way he could find to describe his briefest of meetings with probably the most famous woman in the world.

'I'll tell you what. She made such an impression that I couldn't get her out of my mind for the first 20 minutes of the game. Hey, she probably cost us the Cup final.'

❛ I didn't blame him for going to Italy, but I made him buy a house for his mam and dad. It was the first they'd owned - they deserved it
- *on Des Walker's move to Juventus* ❜

Age was no barrier for GARY MILLS. He was regularly bawled out while playing for Forest's reserves at just 14. But it all paid off when he won a European Cup winner's medal just four years later.

7

FOR GOD'S SAKE - GO

GARY MILLS

One of the funniest things I can remember from my days at Forest came at the time when the gaffer and Justin Fashanu weren't seeing eye-to-eye. Cloughie had forked out £1m for Fash to bring him from Norwich and it was a move that just hadn't come off for a variety of reasons. Things had broken down so much that the gaffer famously had Fash 'arrested' and taken away from the training ground. Needless to say, their relationship wasn't the best by this time. Norwich had come back in for him and the gaffer, seeing a possible solution to the problem, had told Fash to go away and think about it.

I was sitting in the boss's office at the City Ground with Colin Walsh when whatever it was we had been discussing was interrupted by a knock on the door.

Normally the gaffer didn't take too kindly to being interrupted, but whether he'd had a phone call or was just expecting Fash, he gave a welcoming 'come in' when he heard the polite knock on the door. It was Fash – a born-again Christian with a soft voice but with the physique of a professional boxer.

He had done some boxing when he was younger and made for quite an imposing figure as he entered the room to inform the manager of his thoughts on making the switch back to Carrow Road.

'What can I do for you?' said the boss.

'Well, gaffer, I've had a think about it and I've even had a chat with God and the fact of the matter is that God has told me that I shouldn't move back to Norwich.'

Myself and Walshy just kept our council and awaited the gaffer's reply, which was delivered quickly and with maximum impact.

'Now listen to me Justin, there's only one God in Nottingham – and he thinks you should go back to Norwich."

❛ How would I have handled Eric Cantona after that kung fu kick? I'd have cut his balls off ❜

National sports writer DAVID MOORE went all over the world with Clough in over 30 years covering Midlands football for the Daily Mirror. Here he recalls the great lengths the manager went to in a bid to exact some kind of revenge.

8

HOME TRUTHS

DAVID MOORE

When Churchill described the old Soviet Union as 'a riddle wrapped in a mystery inside an enigma,' he could so easily have been talking about himself - or one Brian Howard Clough. I was not alone in enjoying an oft tempestuous relationship with Brian, a man I still consider to be a genius, albeit flawed. Our paths crossed frequently as you would expect from someone who covered the Midlands area for a national newspaper for the thick end of 30 years. Add to that the fact that my family home, an integral to this particular story, was just down the road from The Elms – the Cloughs' grand country house.

The Elms is a superb piece of prime property sat back from the road in the beautiful village of Quarndon. It was right opposite the cricket club and sat back some 30 yards, protected by large trees at the front.

Quarndon is perched on a hill and from the back of Cloughie's house you would be treated to a spectacular view over the Derwent Valley. The village looked down, somewhat appropriately, on Duffield, where my ex-wife and I lived in a nice bungalow.

Anyway, enough. My sports editor was planning a double-page spread on Clough for which I had to supply the words and because it was something to do with his wealth, they wanted me to arrange a picture of his house. The picture was duly arranged and taken by someone we used locally and appeared quite prominently in the Mirror.

Clough went ballistic and let me know in no uncertain terms that he was beside himself with rage. He regarded the picture of his family home as a gross intrusion of his privacy and what really set him off was that it had been taken from a little way down his drive to get around the problem of it being obscured by the trees.

'You've been down my drive, shithouse,' screamed Clough on seeing me a day or two later.

'Brian . . .'

'You've been down my drive.'

'I haven't been anywhere near your drive, Brian.'

'Well, your shithouse photographer has. It's a good job I wasn't in. I'd have set the bloody dog on him!'

Clough's dog was a beautiful golden retriever called Del who had the admirable quality of generally not giving a toss what instructions his master barked out. Few got away with such an indifferent attitude. They say every dog has his day . . . and so Cloughie quickly found a way to exact his revenge on The Mirror, or, perhaps more precisely, me.

A few days after the article had appeared, something unusual caught my attention as I looked out of the window at home. I saw a freelance photographer of my acquaintance who appeared to be taking a picture of my house. It crossed my mind that maybe he was doing something for a local estate agents and so I didn't attach any importance to it at the time.

It wasn't until I went to my village post office and then the newsagents in Duffield that what I thought I'd seen fitted into place.

There, clearly posted for all to see, was a picture of my bungalow with accompanying words to the effect of that if anyone felt like invading my privacy in the way my newspaper had invaded his, then this is where David Moore lives. Signed: Brian Clough.

Obviously he thought he'd taught me a lesson, especially when at Forest's next game, I found a further picture of my house in the match programme! Needless to say, no one came knocking my door, but I suppose Cloughie felt he'd got his own back and made his point in his own inimitable way.

‘ I've lost to a team that sounds like a firm of solicitors - *on Brighton's 4-0 FA Cup defeat to amateurs Walton and Hersham* **’**

9

THE DAY THE MUSIC DIED

MARK CROSSLEY

Vinnie Jones and his pals got more than they bargained for the day they tried to ruffle Cloughie's feathers. Vinnie's Wimbledon boys had built a reputation for not giving a toss and their alternative way of approaching the game had earned them the name of The Crazy Gang.

They were unconventional and went against the grain with a lot of people with their roughhouse style of play and devil-may-care, no-nonsense approach to the game.

Don't get me wrong, they could play a bit too, but they weren't averse to playing mind-games themselves to try and get under the opposition's skin. They were certainly different. They prided themselves on bossing people about – but they hadn't banked on rais-ing the hackles of the man who was bossed by no one – Clough.

When it came to mind games, Cloughie was the master and he wasn't about to get a lesson in them from a bunch of players who hardly sub-scribed to his way of playing football.

The gaffer prided himself on having players who tried to play football the proper way and all his teams had a much-admired ethic of never arguing with referees. Vinnie, Lawrie Sanchez and the like probably thought we were a bunch of softies they could easily put the frighteners on. They hadn't counted on the boss.

We were in the home dressing room preparing for a match against Vinnie and his crew and there was an almighty din coming from down the corridor. They had introduced the practice of playing really loud music in the dressing room just prior to games to really get them in the mood for battle. Crazy Gang? It was more like Kool and the Gang and the gaffer was having none of it. I'm guessing that there was more than just a little bit of letting the opposition know just who was in town and what to expect. The place was rocking. The walls were banging and it sounded like a nightclub had opened just down the corridor.

Cloughie was more Sinatra than Stone Roses, more Matt Monro than Motorhead. This was testing his patience to the full. Big mistake.

'What the fuck's that racket?' the gaffer said to Alan Hill.

'They've got one of those ghetto-blasters on.'

'Ghettoblasters? Well go and ask them nicely to turn it down.' Hilly disappeared after knocking on the away dressing room and asking them if they'd be kind enough to turn it down a bit.

The story goes that Vinnie answered the door in his pants and agreed that they would. Down it went – for about a minute. Then the volume was cranked up again.

'Hilly, did you ask them to turn it down?' asked the gaffer.

'Yes.'

'Right well go back and this time say please!'

As players, we were all up the corridor, intrigued as to what was happening, but couldn't actually see proceedings. Apparently Vinnie has answered the door again to go face-to-face with the slightly harassed Hilly.

'Our gaffer has asked me to ask you if you could turn that thing down please?'

The music went down for a very little while before it started booming out again. Cloughie hit the roof.

'I'll show the bastards,' he growled, storming out of our dressing room in the direction of Vinnie and Co.

And apparently he waltzed straight past the self-styled soccer hardnut, picked up the ghettoblaster and silenced the lot of 'em.

'Now turn it up!' Cloughie bellowed dropping the ghettoblaster onto the tiled floor, smashing it to pieces.

Wimbledon star TERRY PHE-LAN was in the dressing room that day and reveals his take on an extraordinary encounter:

Hey, we might have been known as The Crazy Gang who didn't suck up to anyone but when The Master comes in and says he's not happy, even we listened.

You don't mess with Cloughie and when we realised that he wasn't having the loud music at any price, he got it sorted.

If I remember rightly, I think Vinnie just started laughing and kind of held his hands outstretched as if to say 'What was all that about?' Even Vinnie didn't say much to Mr Clough. He owned the place!

Cloughie didn't care – he was bigger and better than Wimbledon and he wasn't having us dictating what happened on his patch. It was quite funny really because he was a real gentleman about it all but made it quite clear he just wasn't having it.

As I recall, we'd been asked to turn it down and obviously we hadn't gone along with the request. Then this legendary figure came in, tracksuit bottoms and the famous green top and took matters into his own hands.

I seem to think he gave the ghetto-blaster a kick actually, but I know it got a proper whack as he went on about wanting some peace and quiet without all the racket that was coming from our dressing room.

He got what he wanted. I'm not sure whether Vinnie turned it down or it no longer worked after taking a belting from Cloughie but, either way up, he got his way.

Looking back it was just incredible

to see him that close up because he didn't give a toss about our reputation. This was his place, the place where he ruled and he wasn't having it.

And guess what . . . he got his way. We might have had a fearsome reputation, but even we didn't want any trouble.

6 What is the point of giving you the ball when there's a genius out on the left wing?
- to Martin O'Neill on the playing merits of John Robertson **9**

Clough went to extraordinary lengths to pip Everton to the signing of ARCHIE GEMMILL. The brilliant midfielder went on to win three league titles along with 43 Scotland caps and was later Clough's assistant.

10

SLEEP ON IT

ARCHIE GEMMILL

Brian Clough slept at my house and had breakfast the next morning rather than let me wriggle off the hook and sign for Everton. It ended up being one of the best decisions of my life but I was just trying to get him out of my hair. The guy just wouldn't take no for an answer.

I had more or less agreed to join Everton when my Preston boss Alan Ball Snr said they had received a bid from Derby County. He asked me what I thought and I told him I wasn't in the least bit interested. I'd kind of made my mind up that I would go to Everton.

I was only a young lad at the time and eventually was persuaded that there would be no harm in meeting him. We arranged a rendezvous at a pub in Blackburn. The conversation was a bit cool and even though he told me that if I joined Derby I'd be a regular in the Scotland side, I wasn't taking a great deal of interest. Then Mr Clough started to cast his spell . . . I can remember exactly how he got inside my head by suggesting that my first team prospects at Goodison weren't good.

'Howard, Kendall, Alan Ball, Colin Harvey . . . you won't get a kick in that team son.'

Alan Ball Snr got wind of what was happening and motioned to me to go to the gents' toilets. We were standing there in the urinals and he urged me not to get doing anything hastily.

Peter Taylor realised something was afoot and came in saying: 'If you think this lad's going to any other place than Derby, you shouldn't be in management!'

Things were getting a bit tied up and the upshot was that I went home, closely followed by Cloughie. Everton had been on the phone and begged me not to sign for anyone else.

Eventually Clough said: 'What are you going to do?'

'I need to sleep on it,' I assured him.

'Right, well I'm not leaving until you sign,' he said.

'You're leaving,' I said.

'Right, I'll sleep in the car then,' he countered.

My wife Betty was heavily pregnant at the time and didn't really like him at all. She had seen him on TV and thought he'd got far too much to say for himself! But somehow he ended up staying the night at the house.

He came down in the morning in boxer shorts and a vest and ended up having a cooked breakfast. And, yes, I agreed to sign even though it was for less money than Everton were offering.

Clough's incentives were a colour TV and my front room carpeting. Once he'd got to me, there was no way he was going to let me escape. How could I have known that I would end up working under him until the day he retired?

This story is rather bizarre given the circumstances surrounding me eventually agreeing to sign for him and my good wife's understandable misgivings about him.

As I said near the start, she was heavily pregnant at the time but how could any of us have known that the baby she was carrying would one day go on to play under Brian Clough at Nottingham Forest!

Our son Scot was signed up by Cloughie, just like his old man, and played there for nine years. He went on to be a Scotland international too.

But the co-incidence stretches even farther. From Forest he went to Everton, the club I would have joined but for Clough kipping down at my house and refusing to move and also enjoyed a spell at my old club Preston on loan.

* * *

FOOTNOTE: Archie's career ended up taking in three league titles but arguably his most famous moment came for Scotland in the 1978 World Cup when he scored a goal generally acknowledged as one of the greatest of all time.

Scotland needed to beat Holland by three goals to qualify for the next stages of the competition and were 2-1 up when Gemmill played a superb one-two with Kenny Dalglish before jinking past three defenders before shooting home.

It's a goal which achieved even greater fame when featured in cult film Trainspotting when Tommy finishes having sex with Lizzie and groans joyfully: 'I haven't felt that good since Archie Gemmill scored against Holland in 1978!'

6 Champagne socialist? Of course I am, but the difference between me and a good Tory is that he keeps his money while I share mine about a bit 9

A League title and UEFA Cup winner with Liverpool already, LARRY LLOYD'S best years were still to come when he became a pivotal part of the great Forest teams that won two European Cups and the League Championship.

11

HORRIBLE BASTARD

LARRY LLOYD

Clough thought I was a bastard and didn't mind telling anyone who cared to listen. He was one of the few blokes who could call you something like that and get away with it! Not just because he was your boss, but because he told you he meant it as a compliment . . .

I'd broken my foot in two places and was going to be out of the reckoning for at least six weeks. The gaffer immediately signed David Needham from Queens Park Rangers. I wasn't best pleased about that and – surprise, surprise – decided to confront Cloughie about what was going on. It was a bad move on my part in more ways than one because the gaffer not only had an aversion to me, but he hated crutches. Whether it was because his own career was cruelly cut short by injury I don't know, but he didn't particularly want to see injured players.

So anyway, Billy Big Bollocks here decided to go in and see him seeking some clarification on exactly where I fitted into this equation.

'So how do I stand?' I asked.

'Badly! Now get out of my office and don't come back until you've got rid of those crutches!' he screamed.

Fucking hell. There was just no winning with him and as he had so gleefully pointed out I hadn't a leg to stand on until I could get myself back in contention.

Needham had played really well in my absence and it was a while before I eventually got a reserve game under my belt and was ready to be at least considered for a return. David's form, and the fact that he was a bit younger than me, made me a little nervous. We'd beaten Manchester United 4-0 (happy days!) and beat Bury 3-0 away with him in the side. No matter how much Cloughie and I clashed when that team sheet was pinned up on the Friday it was always 'No5 - Lloyd.' Whatever his private feelings about me, he never let it get in the way of picking the team. He respected me for my ability and attitude on the pitch and I respected him.

Anyway, the team sheet is pinned up and, even a little to my surprise, it's 'No5 – Lloyd.' I looked across at Needham and he was crushed. He was just staring at the floor.

Clough decided words of comfort were needed.

'Hey, David. You are a lovely lad and I couldn't have asked more from you. I can't fault you. You've not put a foot wrong and you've done everything I've asked of you. You've every right to feel a bit hard done to . . .

'Like I said, you've been a model pro since I signed you. You're polite, well dressed and you can play too. You are welcome in my house any time young man. In fact David, if my daughter was looking for a young man to bring home and say she was marrying, you would fit the bill . . .

'You're that nice and that's why you're not in the team,' he said, turning around and pointing that famous finger right in my direction.

'I need a bastard – and that's him over there. You're not a fucking horrible bastard like him.'

I was ready to jump up and say my piece on whether Cloughie had the right to question my parentage, when he pre-empted my move and addressed the startled dressing room.

'Hey . . . it's a compliment. You are a big horrible bastard!'

6 **Can you imagine any other profession where NOT doing something makes you better at it? It's ridiculous. A pianist learns to play by spending hours at the keyboard** - *on players being asked to run around, rather than practice with the ball* 9

A member of Forest's European Cup winning team of 1979, TONY WOODCOCK moved to Cologne the following summer and thus missed the successful defence a year later. He then became an Arsenal legend in a glitttering career which saw him pick up 42 England caps.

12

BAWL BOY

TONY WOODCOCK

Cloughie would shout and yell at me so much when I was playing for Forest's reserves, it just ended up driving me mad. The thing was that while screaming and bawling certainly might help some players, I found it just put me off so much I struggled to concentrate.

I plucked up the courage to ask him if I could have a word with him. He asked me what was the matter.

'Gaffer, all I want to say is that every time you come to watch the games and you start bellowing and ranting at me isn't helping. You're frightening me to death.'

'I thought it might motivate you a bit,' he replied.

'Well, I find it has the opposite effect. I just can't play,' I assured him.

'Ah well, you can't win 'em all,' he observed and just walked off. It was his way of saying that I should stop grumbling and just get on with it.

I was forever knocking his door and forever getting knocked back. One day I went in and dared tell him that I wasn't happy playing on the left hand side.

'Where do you want to play?' he asked.

'Well, I sort of see myself as playing just behind the front two,' I dared say to him.

'Do you now? Well, you know what that suggests to me?'

'No.'

'That just proves to me that you're too lazy to play up front and not brave enough to play in midfield!'

You could never get the better of him as I found out in one of the most frequently told stories among the Forest players of the time. I know Martin O'Neill and Robbo never tire of hearing this one.

I was playing well for the reserves and hoping I was catching the eye of the gaffer. We went up to Newcastle for a game the one day and I had a three-day growth after deciding to have a break from shaving.

John Sheridan, the reserve team coach, said: 'You'd better be good because that'll get back to the gaffer,' pointing at my stubble.

Anyway, I scored a great goal, played pretty well, I thought, and we won. Obviously, because it was such a long trip, we got back late on the

Saturday night. We were told we didn't have to come back in until Tuesday. Or so I thought . . .

I received a message that the gaffer wanted to see me on the Monday – 9am sharp. I had to catch two buses to get in to the City Ground – happy days! I knocked on the door and waited.

'Come in.'

'You wanted to see me gaffer.'

'That's right. Tell me about Saturday.'

'Oh, I was given a free role and . . .'

Cloughie put on his best bemused look, which I must say he was excellent at and began wagging that famous finger.

'Hey, I'm not talking about the game. I'm talking about your face!'

'What?'

'Why have you got that stuff growing on your face?'

'I just wanted to be a little bit different,' I said.

'Do you now? Well, young man, if you really want to be different, score me a hat-trick on Saturday. And score me one not just Saturday but every week. That's different,' he roared.

6 **Don Revie's Leeds perfected harassing referees. Any time a free kick was given against them, you couldn't see the poor ref for white shirts** 9

Snapped up for £2,000 from part-time football, carpet fitter GARRY BIRTLES went on to win the European Cup and three England caps. Signed by Manchester United for £1.25m, he now works in the media.

13

STOP THE BUS

GARRY BIRTLES

Thanks to the gaffer I must be the only person who set off on a journey to Kuwait and only managed to get a mile. To be fair, I was moaning and cursing when the team bus suddenly came to a halt and Cloughie decided it would be best for all concerned if I got off! It was bizarre and that was only the half of it. He then flagged down a stranger in a car and asked if he'd be kind enough to take me back to the ground. You've guessed . . . . the guy did. It could only happen with Cloughie, but nothing he did ever really surprised me.

What had happened was, the club had arranged an exhibition match in Kuwait. No one hated the travelling more than the gaffer but because cash was so tight, Forest took advantage of blank weekends in the season by playing lucrative friendly games.

I couldn't have played anyway because I was injured. None of the players were happy about it, but I envisaged being well out of it and in the pub for a nice couple of pints come Sunday lunch time. To my horror, I was told to report to the ground at 9am anyway, injured or not. I was fuming.

I got on the coach and the gaffer was late as usual. I was grumbling away at the back of the bus. Like I said, we'd probably only gone a mile or so, when the gaffer strides up to the back and says: 'Right Gaz, out with it. What's wrong?'

'Well, you're taking me halfway around the world for a match I can't play in and I honestly think I'd have been better staying here,' I replied.

'Son, you're quite right. Albert! Stop the bus,' he bellowed down to our trusty driver at the front.

The gaffer jumped out and virtually got in the road and flagged down a car. It was a Sunday morning, so the poor fella was probably going to church or something.

'Excuse me, would you be so kind as to take one of my footballers back to the ground?' asked Cloughie.

This bloke seemed transfixed, motioned me to come in and – to cut a long story short – I was in the pub by 12 congratulating myself and thinking of the lads still probably not quite at Heathrow!

That was a result for a start off, but what really made it a double whammy was the fact that the lads never got to Kuwait anyway.

The gaffer was a dreadful flyer at the best of times but when they aborted the first take-off, he ordered the stewardess to let the Forest party off.

She said she couldn't because they were on the runway, but Cloughie, being Cloughie, got himself and the lads off the plane anyway.

There were one or two envious glances from the lads when we reported back for training and they filled me in on the trip from hell.

6 Forget it! I don't want troublemakers; I don't want shithouses and I don't want an ugly sod like Kenny Burns littering up my football club - *on Peter Taylor's suggestion that they should sign Kenny Burns* **9**

Regarded as one of the true Celtic greats, DAVIE HAY reveals how the master psychologist got one over him in the cheekiest way possible as he was preparing his side for a massive European Cup clash in Glasgow.

14

LAST ORDERS PLEASE

DAVIE HAY

Brian Clough pulled off one of his greatest psychological master-strokes – right in my backyard. I don't think he knew exactly what he was doing – I *know* he did. And just for good measure, he executed it right there in my Glasgow pub.

I was manager of Celtic and we had drawn with Forest in our UEFA Cup Third Round, first leg clash at their place. I certainly didn't think we were home and dry, but it's fair to say that the general perception was that Celtic were as good as through. It was December, 1983 and the feeling was that they wouldn't fancy coming to our place in front of 60-odd thousand die-hard Celtic fans.

I had a pub called Davie Hay's just five minutes from Glasgow Airport and because he had been so fantastically hospitable to us in the first leg, I said in passing that he must have a drink with us when he was up.

Imagine my surprise when my brother-in-law Gerry rang me at the luxury hotel and spa where I was preparing with my team, to tell me that Cloughie and all his players were in the bar having a drink!

Gerry couldn't believe it – and I certainly couldn't. What the hell was he playing at, having a pint or two with all his players the night before such a massive game? I sensed what he was doing and all these years later I can't help thinking it was the masterstroke of a footballing genius. There he was, with all of his players in Forest track-suits, having a few beers and signing autographs for gobsmacked locals as if to say: 'We're pretty relaxed about it all.'

The locals couldn't believe it! You can imagine can't you – MY regulars all phoning their pals and saying: 'You'll never guess who's in here having a drink.'

I couldn't make it because we were shacked up in our traditional pre-European base at the Seamill Hydro Hotel. That didn't seem to bother Cloughie and the likes of Garry Birtles, Ian Bowyer and Kenny Swain who chose to do part of their big-match preparation in MY bar.

It really was an astonishing thing to do, and for me, underlines what a genius the man was. Word got out what had happened and it completely deflected the pressure off them. And guess what? Forest won 2-1 in front of 66,000 fans and left us crying in our beer. The punters in my pub were talking about it for years. It's gone down in Glasgow folklore.

The background to it was that when we had gone down for the first leg, it was November and really frosty and he had invited me over to have a look at the pitch and have a chat.

He was very pleasant indeed and when someone came in to say that my wife Catherine and my mother-in-law Margaret were outside, he insisted they came in to see him.

He made such a fuss of the pair of them that my missus was just charmed off her feet. We told him that we had a pub in Paisley, not five minutes from the airport. I didn't think any more of it, but he had clearly clocked it. I honestly didn't give the matter a second thought until I took that call from Gerry.

'You'll never guess who's just come in the pub, Davie,' he said.

'Only Brian Clough, Peter Taylor and his entire bloody team! There's a coachload of them. What do I do?'

I told him to serve them and pass on my regards and the more I thought about it, I couldn't help thinking what a canny bugger he was.

Clough had taken the time to find out where the pub was and how to get there and in a way, completely deflected the pressure off his team. It was like he was saying there was nothing to worry about.

I've got to say that I had total and utter respect for the man before our paths crossed. That certainly wasn't diminished from meeting him.

My wife and my mother-in-law were both absolutely won over by him. So in one fell swoop, my missus thinks he's one of the most charming men she's ever met, he's had a drink with all my regulars and then gone out in front of 66,000 Scots and knocked my team out of Europe.

And I still think he's great. Now that is genius.

❛You'll get it when you learn how to play with it properly - *on Peter Withe's request for match ball after scoring four goals against Ipswich* ❜

Respected BBC sports journalist PAT MURPHY built up a close relationship with Clough on mutual respect and their love of cricket. Pat ghosted Clough's last column for Match of the Day magazine shortly before he died.

15

SIMPLY THE BEST

PAT MURPHY

After a couple of decades jousting with him for the BBC before he packed up in 1993, I was lucky enough to get closer to him when the fires within him raged less. I collaborated with Brian in his monthly articles for Match of the Day magazine then FourFourTwo. He was the best subject I have ever worked with.

The pittance the magazines could afford didn't bother him at all. He relished the chance to dilate on the current game and its ills. His passion for football never left him, nor his love of other sports, melodic singers and his family. When our monthly deadline drew near, Brian was ready. There was always something he needed to get off his chest – pithily, wittily, with spades of common sense thrown in. Having enjoyed the privilege of watching many live football matches with him in his retirement, I can vouch for his acute insights, that uncanny knack of spotting something that is about to unfold in front of your untutored eyes. No wonder he was so brilliant at his job, if he was that sharp in his sixties.

Our meetings and phone calls stretched over hours and I'd always look forward to them. He never bothered with a watch – they were for unluckier mortals who had normality to deal with – and I had to cancel many other appointments because I was too busy enjoying myself. His wife, Barbara, would occasionally come into the lounge to tell him to stop shouting, and in vain Brian would protest that it was because he still felt strongly about something. Brian Clough didn't do lukewarm.

Our last conversation took place just four days before he died. My latest deadline was imminent and he had gone into hospital for some tests. I'd spent an afternoon at his home three weeks earlier, when we talked about Arsenal toppling the record of 42 unbeaten league matches he achieved at Nottingham Forest.

The interview he gave me for BBC Radio was his last and one of the best, for its gracious acknowledgement of Arsenal's style and Arsene Wenger's status as a manager. As usual, Cloughie's turn of phrase was characteristic – 'We don't like the French and they don't like us, but they pulled out a plum with this Wenger bloke' – and also defiant: 'At least I had a better goalkeeper with Peter Shilton, even if we had to pay him a lot.'

That day, Brian complained of a sore back and lay on the sofa throughout the interview. When I left, he was kind enough to say: 'I wasn't feeling owt special before you arrived, Patrick – but you've cheered me up.' The feeling was always mutual. His ability to raise the spirits of his players and make people feel special was something that set him aside from other managers.

He did it for me in the summer of 2002, when I'd been laid low by peritonitis and pneumonia. We were still doing our monthly column but I was housebound for two months of recuperation and feeling distinctly sorry for myself.

Brian rang me up and instead of his usual salty observations he spoke warmly and personally to me, avoiding all references to himself. When I came off the phone, I felt more cheerful, thinking: 'So that's how the bugger did it with his players!'

It was typical of Brian's kindness that he asked after my mother in our final conversation. He was in hospital, so was she – rising 90 and having suffered a heart attack. His last words to me were: 'Give your mam my love and tell her to get out of there as soon as she can. Hospitals aren't much fun.' She made it out, but Brian didn't.

And so when the most recognizable voice in football was finally stilled, successive generations of supporters from every club were stunned and then reflective. I was at the Edgbaston Cricket Ground, working for BBC Radio. I was inbetween interviews to preview the following day's match between England and Australia.

Knowing Brian's passion for cricket, it would have been an encounter he would have been looking forward to, watching every ball on his television at home. Instead that most idiosyncratic of men had breathed his last, felled by cancer, the disease that had claimed his adored mother 31 years earlier.

It was one of those JFK or Diana moments for the world of football. You always remember where you were when the news broke . . .

> **❛ I'm not saying he's thin and pale, but the maid in our hotel made his bed the other day and didn't realise he was still in it -** *on Forest player Brian Rice* ❜

31

Glaswegian hard man KENNY BURNS proved to be a Clough masterstroke after being signed for £150,000 in 1977. Burns proved to be one of the main men in leading Forest to the title and two European Cups.

16

GONE TO THE DOGS

KENNY BURNS

As I was having a flutter at the Perry Barr greyhound track that night, there was no way I could have known I was being watched. Unbeknown to me, Brian Clough had ordered his mate Peter Taylor to go undercover and monitor my every move to see just how much I was spending on my nights out at the dogs. Their concern could be seen as caring and thoughtful but for one thing . . . I wasn't even their player! I was at Birmingham and the pair of them had seen something about me that they liked. They wanted to sign me, but they weren't prepared to make a move until they'd found out more about a man with a rebellious reputation.

Clough and Taylor didn't mind someone having a bet. But had I gone to the dogs? That's what Taylor's special assignment was all about. As it happens I wasn't a big gambler. My team mate Paul Hendrie and me used to put £15 in each so we had a kitty of thirty quid to have a bet with. Small time stuff really but it's just something we really enjoyed doing. Anyway, Taylor dutifully reported back that he'd certainly seen nothing untoward

and that if I had any vices, gambling didn't appear to be one of them. They signed me and set me off on a career that was to be laden with trophies and some of the most fantastic days of my life.

But that story for me just shows the fantastic attention to detail Clough and Taylor had in those days. They wanted to know everything about you and left no stone unturned.

They had a lot of people scattered about the place who they trusted. They knew everything that happened in Nottingham. If you went to a nightclub, they knew where and when you'd been. So long as you weren't stupid they didn't care.

Birmingham was off their patch, but that didn't stop them putting me under close scrutiny to see just how I was getting my kicks and if I was chucking worrying amounts in the direction of the bookies.

I must have passed the test because they took me on and, I've got to say, it was a marriage made in heaven in many ways. Clough was the easiest manager I ever worked with. It was an absolute dream. Everything was so simple and the gaffer was so laid back it was untrue.

But you know, a lot of people who didn't know him reckon he was some kind of dictatorial bully who was always giving players a hard time. Nothing could be further from the truth. In my first season at Forest we played 75 games and only had a squad of 14 players so Clough made sure he got enough rest into us as he could.

We hardly did what you'd call conventional training. We had so much fun. We'd have five-a-side games and Cloughie would say: 'Right, today we'll play English v the Jocks' and things like that. I'll always remember one day, he said: 'Today lads, it's whites versus blacks!' Viv Anderson piped up that he was the only black player there.

'Hey, bad luck son,' said Cloughie with a huge grin. There was nothing racist about it, it was just the banter we all had and we had such a tight dressing room, it was unbelievable.

❛ I'm sure England's selection committee thought I'd want to run the whole damn show. They were shrewd then, because that's exactly what I would have done ❜

Teacher ANDY RICE saw the Clough children at his school but never thought he would play in a football match refereed by their famous dad. From the first whistle it promised to be fun and games . . .

17

JEEPERS KEEPERS

ANDY RICE

It's not often you can say you've played in a match refereed by the legendary Brian Clough, but I have . . . and the story gets much better than that.

I was a teacher at the Woodlands School in Allestree where Brian's three children were educated. It was a 1,000-pupil comprehensive school with a sixth form college, so his kids were definitely not afforded any kind of privileged education. I was actually an art teacher there and didn't have any of the three young Cloughs – Simon, Nigel and Elizabeth – in my class. That's not to say I didn't keep a careful eye on all of them coming through their secondary education and emerging the very level-headed, normal individuals they all are today.

Simon, the eldest, ran a Sunday soccer side called AC Hunters and I played for a local village team called Stanley. A lot of the Hunters team were Woodlands sixth formers – all pretty fit and athletic, while the average age of our side was probably late 30s.

We arrived for our fixture at their ground and as kick-off time approached it became apparent that we were missing one very important thing – a ref. Seeing Brian there in his trademark green top wasn't anything unusual because he was a regular on the sidelines at Hunters' games.

'If you're short, I'll ref it,' Brian said generously, prompting a few of us to look at each other in astonishment. It's perhaps testament to the man, that we all instinctively knew he wouldn't favour his son's side. That was just taken as read, in fact a few of us probably sensed that having Cloughie with the whistle might well work to our advantage! To be fair, it needed to . . .

After about 20 minutes, Hunters were running us ragged. They were like whippets and they were well in front when our lads started dishing out one or two heavy tackles.

There was nothing malicious. It was more desperation than anything else. If they were looking for any sympathy from the ref, they could certainly think again.

'Play on, it'll toughen you up,' barked the great man, brushing aside any appeals for some kind of protection.

But the funniest thing that happened and something I'll take to my grave was when we had a pot shot at goal that ended up going behind the nets and finished 30 or 40 yards away as happens with park football.

The Hunters keeper wasn't so much wasting time as just being a bit lethargic at retrieving the ball. Like most young fellas there was no particular sense of urgency about him.

I was standing on the half-way line when a green flash shot past me. It was an irate Cloughie, hurtling towards the keeper.

When he got to him, he barged him in the back and yelled to the startled youngster: 'Run after the ball, lad. Get a move on. There's 90 minutes in a game and you've just wasted two of them strolling after the ball.'

It was so funny and something that when you tell people they find it almost unbelievable. But that's the kind of man he was I think and was loved all the more for it.

He was a man of the people who loved his family and that shone through. But his determination to ensure they weren't treated differently is full credit to him.

I'll bet Simon must have cursed when he saw his dad taking the whistle because he would have known that his side could forget any notion of being handed some kind of advantage.

I know one thing. I didn't question any of his decisions!

❛ Don't worry too much about what to do, just give the ball to John Robertson and he'll do the rest
- to first £1m footballer Trevor Francis ❜

Don't mention 'greens' to former Forest defender
JIM McINALLY. Signed by Clough from Celtic
as a teenager, the youngster soon learned to do
as he was told - never mind the consequences

18

SPROUT OF ORDER

JIM McINALLY

It's Christmas, 1984 and while Bob Geldof is trying to feed the world, Brian Clough is feeding me Brussels sprouts. Honest to God, that Christmas Day is the first and last time I ever ate the darned things – and it was all down to an act of unbelievable generosity on the gaffer's part. Even so, to this day I can't help thinking there was just a hint of mischief about him watching me trying to gulp down whole sprouts without them touching the sides!

I had not long joined Forest from Celtic and whether it was my typically pasty, pale Scottish look that set the alarm bells ringing, I'm not sure, but Cloughie seemed to think I wasn't eating enough 'greens.'

He was spot on. I never ate them. I was 20 years old and had a pretty normal Glaswegian upbringing. For me, vegetables weren't really a massive part of my life. If steak was on the menu, I'd have it with chips. If chicken was being served, then chips were good with that too. Cabbage, sprouts and stuff like that weren't part of my particular culinary make-up – that is until Cloughie decided to take on the

role of an unlikely Delia Smith.

The gaffer plagued me to death about eating vegetables to such an extent that there became an almost bizarre ritual when we were having team meals on away trips.

No matter where I tried to sit to dodge him, Cloughie would always make sure he was sitting either opposite or next to me and it wouldn't be long before I'd hear him chuntering 'Eat your greens, son.'

He used to drive me mad . . . and he knew it. He was just making a point in his own unique way and I happened to be the one who was copping it. It became a standing joke among the lads that no matter where I tried to sit myself at the team table, Cloughie would end up either next to me or directly opposite.

I had only joined Forest in the summer and so I hadn't yet made permanent living arrangements. I was staying at The Balmoral Hotel in Nottingham when Cloughie showed a side of him that only the privileged few see. I hadn't really given it too much thought, but I was going to be spending Christmas on my own. With the heavy programme of games over the festive period, there would be no chance of nipping back to Glasgow to see my folks. To be perfectly honest I hadn't really given it too much consideration when Cloughie asked me if I'd like to come to his house and have Christmas lunch with his family. Actually, he didn't ask me - he told me!

'Hey, young man, you're coming to my house for Christmas. I don't want you being on your own.'

There's no way I would ever have refused, but as you can imagine, I was pretty scared to be honest. Cloughie's sheer presence could overwhelm you. I hadn't been there long but I'd seen seasoned pros, genuinely intimidated by him. There's an aura about the man. I'd seen him on the telly for years and he was up there with the greats. I don't mind admitting I was totally in awe of him. Now I was going around his house for Christmas lunch! And greens . . . . . plenty of them!

The gaffer had extended the same invitation to Steve Hodge because he was single as well and, like I say, it was one of the loveliest, kindest things you could do for anyone. And the thing that really surprised me was that he was very hands-on and, in the main, seemed to be in charge of the cooking arrangements. His wife Barbara, who is an absolutely wonderful lady, seemed to let him get on with it largely and I could see both her and Nigel Clough having a wee laugh when Cloughie started dishing out the vegetables.

It was like the scene from Cool Hand Luke where Paul Newman is wolfing down the eggs. I was gulping down whole sprouts trying to avoid chewing them and just when I thought I'd finished, Cloughie would pop a few more on my plate!

Needless to say, it was a really nice day and, with hindsight, I realise just how privileged I was to spend a smashing Christmas Day at home with one of soccer's true greats and his lovely family.

Mind you a sprout hasn't passed my lips since, whether the great man would have approved or not.

❛ It hurt a great deal but the FA knew I thought they were all as weak as piss-water - *on not getting the England job* **❜**

*Of all his players, JOHN ROBERTSON held a special place
in Clough's affections. And why not? Robbo set up the
goal which won the 1979 European Cup and grabbed
the winner a year later to retain the trophy.*

19

THE CONNECT 4 GANG

JOHN ROBERTSON

One of the most bizarre things that happened during all the glory days at Forest was the night of our second European Cup win over Hamburg in Madrid. The team hotel was at least 20 miles from where the wives, girlfriends and families were staying. Cloughie was in one of his pig-headed moods and absolutely refused to budge on frequent requests from his victorious players to meet up with their loved ones. I was one of a few players who kept on at him, but he was having none of it.

'Hey, we came here as a team and we go back to our hotel as a team,' he insisted. It really was ridiculous and I wasn't the only one who just couldn't believe he was serious. We'd asked him before the match and now after our finest hour we were begging him to relent. He still wasn't having it and on this particular occasion he really had stretched our patience to breaking point. There was only one thing for it - we decided to stage a breakout! Can you imagine it? Here we were, a bunch of top professional footballers who had just won Europe's biggest prize and we were having to hatch this cunning plan to get over to see our wives and families. But it's absolutely true. And the story gets even more bizarre.

So, a group of us plucked up the guts to slip away from the hotel, get a taxi and embark on a deadly secret mission to see our loved ones.

There was myself, Martin O'Neill, Frank Gray, Larry Lloyd and Kenny Burns, if my memory serves me right. Mission accomplished, it was only a few hours later that we had to think about getting ourselves back having, hopefully, not been missed.

We made sure we were back by about 7.30 in the morning and the funny thing that I'll always remember is that down in the bar/reception area, there were a few of the 'Connect 4' games you so often see in Spanish bars. They had managed to keep us amused for the odd hour over the previous three or four days anyway.

We all walked in, and arranged to get a few drinks served because we were well up for a few more. We still had our club blazers on. It was Peter Taylor who was the one to look out for because he was always the early riser.

As we'd thought, it wasn't long before Pete came down for breakfast. There we all were, good as gold, playing Connect 4.

'Now I've seen everything. I really can't believe you boys have been up all night playing that stupid game!'

Anyway, if he didn't believe it, he never said anything and we managed to get away with it.

We were just lads together. We thought it was a great stunt to do something like that and get away with it. There was never a dull moment with Cloughie around that's for sure.

It wasn't often we managed to pull the wool over his eyes and most of the time, we didn't need to anyway.

It was a funny thing with the gaffer because people still believe he ruled by fear and all that nonsense. It was actually quite the opposite. You just wanted to please him. That might sound a bit soppy, but it's the only way I can explain it. A lot of the other lads felt exactly the same way.

The thing with him was he was an absolute genius in simplicity. It makes me laugh when you see people coming up with all these complex theories about football. He wouldn't have any of that.

Cloughie was a great communicator. Once you got to know the things he wanted, things became as clear as crystal. He laid great emphasis on heading the ball and would look closely at players and how they did that. I don't know how I got away with it! I never thought there was that much importance to it, but he maintained you could gauge a player's bravery by his approach to heading. For example, he didn't like centre forwards just flicking it on to no-one – he felt there was an element of cowardice about that.

He had to trust his players and once he did he wouldn't be afraid to switch the way they operated. I can reveal one of the best ever examples of that – the 1980 European Cup final victory over Hamburg.

No one outside the camp really knows what happened on the tea-time before that game, but it was quite astonishing when you think about it. Cloughie and Taylor's original thinking was that they would try and attack them down the left because they felt Manny Kaltz was a bit of a weakness.

But at 5pm on the night of the match, just as we were all ready to tuck into some pre-match tea and toast, they changed everything. The pair of them suddenly decided that they would try something we hadn't even worked on in training.

Cloughie threw us all out when he said: 'Right listen, we're going to go five across the middle with Garry Birtles alone up front and young Gary Mills trying to get support to him.'

That was the first we heard of it. He just thought his players could take that on board at such short notice. That's where the trust came in. We were just a few hours away from the European Cup final and the tactics were completely changed around. It could have been an absolute disaster but we won 1-0.

And it was that trust that ends up forming such a bond between you.

People ask me if I was his favourite but it was more a case of I liked him and I think he liked me. He rescued my career, there's no shadow of a doubt in my mind about that. I was going nowhere. I had let myself go a bit and thought nobody cared about me – then Clough came in and showed a bit of faith in me.

If he hadn't come in at that stage, I think I'd have quite possibly drifted out of the game. He'd bollock me, don't worry about that, but he thought I was big enough to take it. He was a larger than life figure.

I've always felt that actually he could have been a scriptwriter or something like that because he had such a quick mind. He was phenomenally sharp. There was an intelligence and brightness about him that you really had to see close up to appreciate.

He'd often use me as the brunt of his jokes or smart remarks. Whether he was making fun of me being a scruff, or my smoking, or my weight, looking back I probably quite liked the attention. I really admired him.

When he shouted across to you on the pitch and made that sign of his where he made like a circle by touching the tip of his thumb with his forefinger and raising it aloft, it just made you feel ten feet tall.

But I honestly owe him so much because, like I said, if it hadn't been for him I definitely wouldn't have gone on to enjoy a career where I lifted the European Cup twice.

When I was a wee boy I wanted to be a footballer but never in your wildest dreams do you imagine you'll lift the trophy that players like Ferenc Puskas and Alfredo di Stefano have had in their hands.

I remember that 1960 final between Real Madrid and Eintracht Frankfurt and I was only about seven years old. It sticks with me. I'm certainly not saying I was their equal as a player but I did play my little part in history in that competition. How could you dream of ever doing that? Along came Brian Clough.

❛ We were unconventional to say the least, but boredom was something we wanted to avoid at all costs ❜

Derby Evening Telegraph sports writer GEORGE EDWARDS
knew Clough better than most. He not only covered
The Rams for his evening newspaper but was a neighbour -
and occasional drinking companion - of the Derby boss

20

MINE'S A DOUBLE

GEORGE EDWARDS

Try telling anyone that you've not had a lot to drink and explain how it came about that right there in front of you were two Brian Cloughs! To my right - Brian Clough. To my left Brian Clough. What a session that turned out to be but, believe it or not, I was seeing double long before the alcohol kicked in.

The fact that I eventually left the bar of The Midland Hotel at 6am and went straight to work, doesn't go anywhere near unravelling the matter fully either. Let me explain . . .

Mike Yarwood, the famous impressionist who was a household name with his own TV show in the 70s, was appearing at the Talk of the Midlands Club in Derby. He happened to be staying at The Midland Hotel in the city centre that was a favourite watering hole of ours.

Anyway, Brian and myself went in there for a few beers after a night match when Yarwood, who did a famous Clough impression, walked in with his manager.

Needless to say there were no introductions required on either part and Brian was hugely flattered as he watched Yarwood launch into an impression of him. God, he sounded more like Brian than Brian!

Yarwood was a top of the bill performer in those days – one of the most famous faces on the television in days when top shows could attract audiences of 15 million plus. Yarwood was among the elite performers of the day and was known nationwide for taking off Harold Wilson, Ted Heath, Prince Charles and, of course, Brian Clough.

'Hey, you're top of your profession – just like me!' Brian informed the master mimic. In a curious way he could be quite star struck. When I say that, I mean that he did quite enjoy the company of other famous people. Only the true superstars like Muhammad Ali or Frank Sinatra had him struggling for words. The rest, he just loved swapping stories with. People who think he just loved the sound of his own voice have got Brian all wrong. He was actually a remarkably good listener and I noticed that on numerous occasions. He wasn't just waiting for his turn to take over the conversation.

When Brian spoke, people listened. Not because he was loud, but because of who he was and the way he said things. He'd cut all the crap and just get straight to the point. Pearls of wisdom just tumbled from him.

On the subject of tumbling . . . if my memory serves me correctly, which it might not, Brian and Yarwood called it a day at around 4am, while I stayed on for a couple of hours with the entertainer's manager. I had real staying power in those days.

To say I was a little the worse for wear was a bit of an understatement. There wasn't a lot of point going home at such a ridiculous hour and I'm sure my wife wouldn't have been best pleased even though she knew where I was.

I made my way out of the hotel, managed to grab a cup of coffee in a futile bid to cancel out some of the night's excesses and made my way to the office.

That's one good thing about journalism. The whole point of being a good operator and being on the ball is to have a good relationship with your best contacts.

So what could be better than having a few pleasant sociable hours with the man who just happened to be one of the most famous managers in the country?

And just to top that, how about having a back up just in case the real Brian Clough decided he wasn't speaking to you! If you get into the office a little the worse for wear it's always handy to have an excuse and so mine was that I'd been in a bar until the early hours with Brian Clough and Mike Yarwood doing impressions of Brian Clough

Have you been drinking, George? Exactly.

❝ Can that young Wayne Rooney
live with all the hype?
If he's as thick as I think he is - yes! ❞

Incredibly, JOHN McGOVERN didn't start playing football until he was 15. But Clough spotted something and the midfielder went on to play for him at four different clubs and went on to lift the European Cup twice.

21

THE CHARMER

JOHN McGOVERN

If Brian Clough hadn't charmed my grandmother, chances are I would never have become a professional footballer. It's quite an incredible story really – particularly when you consider I didn't really play any proper football until I was 15 years old.

But Cloughie's legendary persuasive powers were at their very best and, as many people will vouch for, once he wants to sign someone, he's like a dog with a bone. He just won't let go! Once the gaffer had made his mind up on someone, he would go to any lengths to make sure he got what he wanted.

I went to a rugby school in Hartlepool – the Henry Smith Grammar – and little did the gaffer know the waves he was making trying to convince people I might have a future as a footballer.

I was captain of the rugby and cricket teams and the headmaster gave me a right rollocking for even considering the notion. He thought it disgraceful I should even be giving it any serious thought.

Peter Taylor had spotted me and famously said he wanted to lock the gates of the ground until he had got me. Once Peter had given me the thumbs up the rest was down to Cloughie.

He had one hell of a job persuading my mum Joyce because she wanted me to continue with my education. He came to the house every single day for a week and fortunately for him my grandma was down from Scotland and he managed to charm her.

I hadn't been playing the game long and had only just joined a local team – one season later I was making my debut for Hartlepool!

The first time I met Clough was at a trial match. I was a Rolling Stones fan and I had long hair.

'Stand up, get your shoulders back and get your hair cut' were virtually the first words he ever said to me.

My mum asked me how it was going and I told her I wasn't going to go there because the Bogeyman had arrived!

That was the start of my 14 years under Clough and he ended up signing me four times.

It could have been a unique grand slam of all five clubs he ever managed

. . . but all I got was the phone slam. Bang! Down went the receiver as the boss suffered the rare indignation of someone actually saying 'no' to him for once. I'm proud of the fact that Cloughie signed me four times in all – and it could so easily have been the full five. If I'd joined him at Brighton, which was the reason for his call, I'd have had the full set.

I was at Derby at the time and the gaffer and Peter Taylor had moved down to the South Coast to take charge at Brighton.

Cloughie phoned and said he wanted me to join them. I'd been with the bloke since I was 16 and thought the absolute world of him. But Brighton?

'You coming?'

'Gaffer, you're in the Third Division!'

Slam! He'd tossed the phone down in his temper, but he was soon back.

'I will make you captain.'

'Great, but you're still in the Third Division.'

Down went the phone again as even he realised his extraordinary powers of persuasion weren't going to work this time.

Playing in the Third Division was no use to me at that stage of my career and so, as it turned out, I passed on the chance to play for him with every club.

Still, I worked under him for 14 years which isn't too bad and over the years we became close. There was a great mutual respect there and I think he forgave me for turning him down just that once.

It turned out that if I was going to get in trouble with Clough for anything it would be for training too hard! If we had a free week Clough would say: 'I don't want to see you until Thursday and if you train I will fine you.'

I trained all year round. It's just the way I was. I could run for ever and loved keeping myself fit. Because of the manager's directive, I often used to go and do some running where nobody could see me – just so it never got back to him.

Imagine that – a player who was scared of the manager because he was putting in 'extra' work on his fitness. Clough believed fervently in getting rest into players.

There was no better example of that than the week before the 1980 European Cup final against Hamburg. Clough and Taylor took all the players to Majorca for the week before the game and the schedule was strict – no training, no curfews, just go and enjoy yourself! I did a bit because I knew what was best for me, but a lot of the lads just put their feet up and relaxed. If anyone had known, there would have been heavy betting on Kevin Keegan's team to beat us, but the rest is history. We ended up winning 1-0 to retain the European Cup. I can't imagine what might have been said if we had lost.

❝ You may have A' levels, but you're thick as a footballer - *to Martin O'Neill* **❞**

*The Clough player to emerge as the most successful manager
is undoubtedly MARTIN O'NEILL who followed up a
trophy-laden playing career by going on to prove he was
also a top boss with Leicester, Celtic and Aston Villa.*

22

SHIRT SWAP

MARTIN O'NEILL

I am in no doubt now that I had the privilege of working with the most charismatic football manager of the twentieth century. I have to admit that I didn't always appreciate it at the time.

He changed my outlook on football and on life. To say that we didn't always see eye to eye might be something of an understatement. On more than the odd occasion I informed him that I might as well way go back to university in Belfast and many is the time he offered to book my flight tickets.

A lot has been made of this thing that he thought I was a smartarse, but actually it was just something that he kind of liked to use. Believe you me, intellectually there wouldn't be many who could live with him.

I'm quite proud that I lived through it – from the very first day he walked through the door at Forest to the second European Cup win. I was there. I survived all the threats to send me back to university – or sometimes Siberia, dependent on how he felt.

I'm just thankful that I was given the opportunity to witness his genius close up. He was absolutely brilliant and also absolutely of his time. Just like George Best epitomised the 60s and was the Fifth Beatle and all that, so Clough struck a chord with everyone in the 70s. He was outspoken and outrageous. Everybody knew him.

He was on the TV all the time and bear in mind in those days, there were only a few channels and the big shows would get audiences of over 20 million. He was on Parkinson and Mike Yarwood did him too. Brian Clough was nationally known.

It's fair to say I didn't always share his viewpoint, especially when it concerned my footballing ability. I spent many a fruitless argument with him on this very subject.

One such time springs to mind when I was playing pretty much as a right winger but felt I would be better suited to playing in a central midfield role. I even had the temerity to venture into his office with this grand opinion in mind.

I had played a more central role for a few games because of injuries. I had done pretty well and the results had been good.

45

These were the days long before shirts had sponsors names all over them, let alone a player's name on the back. The numbering system for 'squads' was pretty simple back then – it was one-to-eleven plus one substitute.

Anyway, I went in to see him and told him that I'd really relish the chance of playing more in the middle and how well I thought I was suited to it. He had a question for me, which shouldn't have come as any surprise.

'Son, what can you do in there, that you can't do 15 yards further out?'

It was annoying because he was just being obnoxious. The game is totally different. It's a different picture completely and he knew it. He was being deliberately over-simplistic just to undermine my argument. I told him that I thought I could do things that were required in that position. I was strong on the ball. I could run . . .

'And what do you think you'd do there that Archie Gemmill can't do?' he said.

Before I could even think about defending myself, he quickly asked: 'So what number have you been wearing recently?'

'Seven, boss,' I replied.

'Right, we're playing Wolves on Saturday and I'll give you a choice if that's what you're looking for. . .'

I couldn't believe it. 'Choice?' The great man was actually about to offer me a choice. Wow, what choice is this he's going to offer me? I could feel my heart getting bigger by the second.

And so he continued: 'Right, you've got a choice. Do you want to play seven or twelve?'

I didn't bother him again.

❝ When Glenn Hoddle was going on about karma, I thought he'd arranged a friendly against a club side in Sri Lanka ❞

Big LARRY LLOYD reckons if Clough's genius was ever encapsulated in one masterstroke then his transformation of one player from rebellious firebrand to class act might just take the biscuit.

23

FIRST DEGREE BURNS

LARRY LLOYD

If anyone wants to see Cloughie's genius as a football manager and man-manager, they should look no further than Kenny Burns. I reckon his ego made him take a chance on a rough diamond who had built up a reputation as something of a wild man. Clough was so full of himself, he probably just felt that if anyone was going to polish that diamond, then there was no one better in the business than him. God, was he right!

Burns came to Forest as a centre-forward from Birmingham but was quickly converted to a central defender. I'd played against Kenny and he was a handful as a striker. When he turned up at Forest, we were all amazed. We hadn't got Burns down as his type of player.

It was always really funny to hear Cloughie refer to him as 'Kenneth.' Here was this snarling, wild-looking guy with no teeth and whenever the gaffer referred to him it was as 'Kenneth.'

When Kenny signed, some of the forwards at our place were understandably a bit worried, wondering who he'd been brought in to replace when Cloughie pointed in my direction and said: 'Go and play with big head there in defence.'

It was an absolute masterstroke. Kenny and me just clicked and for the next five years we ruled the roost, terrifying the opposition with intimidation, and a little brute force. Honestly, we were the most formidable of pairings at the time. Hey, and let's have it straight, we could play a bit too!

Only Cloughie could have come up with the transformation of Burns. It really was an astonishing piece of forward thinking. I didn't always get on with Cloughie. In fact, I didn't get on with him most of the time. But hats off to him on that one – he really got it spot on.

And the night that his intuition and nous really paid off came in Madrid's Bernabeu Stadium when Burns came face to face with superstar Kevin Keegan.

No one should have to go face-to-face with Kenny. There stood a man who fell out of the ugly tree and hit every branch on the way down. But he was a magnificent player and that night in Spain will go with me to the grave if only for my attempt to scare the shit out of Keegan in the tunnel.

I'd played with Kev for four years at Liverpool so exchanging 'pleasantries' in the tunnel wasn't something anyone would have found unusual.

'How you doing, little fella?' I said.

'Hiya, big man. How are you?' said Keegan.

'Great,' I said, leaning towards him just a little to indicate that I wanted to tell him something. I had a cunning plan . . .

'I've got to tell you something, mate – Burns' job tonight is to break you in two if ever you come near him. His one job is to kick the shit out of you!'

It was stiflingly hot that night but I didn't mind trying to give my old team mate something to make him sweat a bit. What happened next was sheer perfection of comic timing.

'If you don't believe me, just look at him,' I said turning and pointing to Kenny at the back of the line.

As luck would have it, Kenny was just removing his teeth and ramming some pink chewing gum in his mouth. It might just as well have been a piece of raw meat. Keegan's face was a classic.

Hamburg were a gifted side with plenty of flair, but we did what we did best and our true grit and hard work got us through that night. For all their efforts, they couldn't put one away. I clattered Keegan a couple of times that night but Burnsy was cruel.

He made four horrendous challenges on Keegan who eventually ended up playing deeper and deeper. We kept one of the world's true superstars quiet that night and when he did escape us the once, Peter Shilton pulled off a magnificent stop. John Robertson got the crucial winning goal – with his right foot – and then we put up a brick wall to try and keep Hamburg at bay. We were awesome, even if I do say so myself.

Yes, make no mistake, the transformation of Burns from wild rebel to European Cup winner was a truly remarkable piece of Clough magic.

❛ It's bullshit. A Rolls Royce is always a Rolls Royce and it's the same with the England strip. There's no need to mess about with it
- on garish new Admiral England kit ❜

*Legend of the Anfield bootroom RONNIE MORAN has filled
every role imaginable at Liverpool. Starting as a player,
he went on to become physio, coach, trainer and even
caretaker manager on a couple of occasions.*

24

HARD CASE

RONNIE MORAN

I must say, I liked Brian. We at Liverpool had some great tussles with his teams and we both wanted to win – make no mistake about that. But there was always a good handshake at the end and whenever he came to Anfield he'd always come into the Boot Room after the match.

In fact, it was tradition at Liverpool that we'd invite the visiting manager and staff for a drink and a chat after the game. I think a lot of them looked forward to going into the Boot Room.

I do have one outstanding memory of Brian in there . . . I can see him now perched on a big skip basket and not saying a word. He was just sipping his drink and listening.

People like our boss Bob Paisley, Joe Fagan, Tom Saunders and myself along with Brian's colleague Peter Taylor would be giving their opinions on the match that had just taken place – or on football matters in general.

But, in contrast to the public perception that he never shut up, Brian just sat there and said very little. He'd look, listen and probably learn. That was our thing too. Bill Shankly often used to say that you can learn some-thing from everyone – even the most stupid person you knew.

I think Brian must have believed that too. It's not a bad philosophy to have and it obviously worked for him, given his achievements in the game. But that's not to say we didn't have our flashpoints with him!

I remember one game we played at Forest. Jimmy Case turned in a first half performance that was typical Jimmy . . . hard, tough-tackling and totally committed.

As Jimmy walked off down the tunnel at half-time, Cloughie took a kick at him and to say that Jimmy was angry would be understating the case. He was furious that the home manager would do something like that – and I can't say that we were too happy about it either!

But I have to say, to Brian's credit, he came in our dressing room at the end of the game and offered his apologies. That was Brian, passionate and sometimes maybe over-passionate, but he was never too big to do the right thing.

I'll tell you something that does worry me very much and that's today's insistence that managers must have coaching qualifications and badges to do their job. Brian, just like Shanks and Bob Paisley, wouldn't be allowed to manage if they were forced to adhere to that directive so what kind of nonsense is that when much lesser people would be allowed to? There's no doubt in my mind that Brian is one of the greats.

❛ **Why is that a nation with the technology to put a television in my wrist watch can't grow some bloody grass in its Olympic Stadium** - *before 1981 World Club Championship in . . . Tokyo* ❜

Clough smashed the British transfer record when he made TREVOR FRANCIS the first £1m player. Payback time was just around the corner when the striker headed the winning goal in the 1979 European Cup in Munich.

25

THE £1m TEABOY

TREVOR FRANCIS

A Cloughie joke to the assembled press ended up with me rather unflatteringly being known as 'The £1m tea boy.' Good job that I took it for the joke it was – and actually got to realise that it was a compliment.

How it came about was that I was cup-tied for the 1979 League Cup final win over Southampton having not long been plastered all over the newspapers for being the first £1m footballer.

After the 3-2 win, the gaffer mischievously told the gathering of reporters that not only did he have a very good side, but a £1m tea boy as well. You can imagine – the press loved it even though it all got a little bit distorted. It sounded like he was cutting me down to size, but that wasn't really the case at all. He was making the point that no matter what a player cost, the club came first and I totally went along with that.

All the players got used to pouring the tea for everyone if they weren't in the side for any reason. It didn't matter whether it was Peter Shilton, myself or anyone. We were all part of the group and it was accepted that's the way it was. Brian was very strong on creating a very happy and harmonious dressing room.

I was very happy to pour the tea – in fact that's the way I wanted it. I didn't want to be seen as being precious so the tea-pouring duties were no bugbear to me. It was just the headlines of being Brian Clough's £1m tea boy which wore a bit thin after a while.

I didn't need pulling down a peg or two – Brian had made sure I wouldn't be getting ideas above my station the day I went to Nottingham to sign.

I was rather nervous at the thought of negotiating my transfer with him but when I got there, he was playing squash with Garry Birtles and kept me waiting for an hour! It was his way of playing the whole thing down.

He was good at that. In fact he was very, very good at what he did regardless. If he or Peter Taylor wanted to make a point they had a whole repertoire of ways to do it. No one should underestimate the part that Taylor played. The two of them were a tremendous double act playing one off against the other. Peter was very humorous and played a big part in their partnership.

An example of how that humour could sometimes defuse a situation was when I had shown a flash of temper and took it out on an office door! There had been a suggestion that perhaps I lacked aggression but I think I went a long to showing that wasn't the case when I stormed into Cloughie's office one day. I'd been damned annoyed about something and when I walked out, still less than satisfied, I slammed the door behind me.

Three or four days later I went to see them not knowing just what reaction I was going to get when Taylor said with a smile: 'Hang on a minute Trevor, the carpenter's just fixing the door you broke the other night!'

Their reaction completely floored me. They saw my anger as a positive form of aggression at last. They wanted to see that I passionately cared.

❛ I called Robbo the fat man, but give him the ball and he was an artist. He was the Picasso of our game - *on John Robertson* **❜**

Now it's goalkeeper MARK CROSSLEY'S turn to let us in on how his big debut game was kept secret from the one person who you might have expected to be the first to know - him!

26

DON'T WORRY SON

MARK CROSSLEY

I didn't exactly have much time to worry about being thrown in to make my debut against Liverpool – Cloughie saw to that! I was sweeping the corridors at the City Ground less than an hour before kick-off, oblivious to the fact that I was about to be tossed in for my first senior game against mighty Liverpool. I can't imagine what the gaffer's concerns were really! Kenny Dalglish's men included such names as Ian Rush, John Barnes, Peter Beardsley and John Aldridge – not that much for an untried teenage keeper to fret about . . .

It was a night game – October 26, 1988 – and the buzz from a crowd of around 30,000 was already starting to seep through into the inner sanctum of the ground.

I had been far too busily occupied doing apprentice duties to attach any significance to the fact that my boots had mysteriously gone missing. Something was going on backstage and I was quite deliberately the last to know. First-choice keeper Steve Sutton had fallen ill and with Hans Segers out on loan, I was to be handed the proverbial baptism of fire.

Clough had secretly called my mum and dad back home in Barnsley to tell them I was going to be making my debut and that he would treat them to a lovely meal at his expense, if they wanted to get down to see it. There was one condition – they weren't to tell me! It seemed that by this time I was the only one who hadn't a clue what was about to happen. The gaffer was concerned that if I had too long to think about things, it could affect me! How right could he have been? If ever anyone needed an example of a Cloughie masterstroke, then surely this was it. I had absolutely no idea what was going on – not a clue. It must have been 7pm when he popped his head around the door and I can remember exactly what he said to me.

'Hey shithead, come here. Come and get your boots on – you're playing tonight!'

My boots, which had mysteriously vanished during the day, were there under the peg with the goalkeeper's shirt on and in 45 minutes I would be out there.

My mum Sandra and dad Geoff were in the crowd and were probably more worried than me, after all they'd had more time to think about it!

We ended up winning the game 2-1 and Cloughie got all the lads to sign the match ball and presented it to me as a special memento.

It really had been a night to remember . . .

❛ Hey, Hitler only took half an hour to get through the place and he stopped for 20 minutes to have tea. The Dutch were waving him through
- on Holland (he loved the place) ❜

*Clough prided himself on sticking up for the underdog,
but in this moving story close friend ALAN HILL
shares a special moment when the master manager
rolled over and showed his soft underside.*

27

THE UNDERDOG

ALAN HILL

The gaffer was known as being something of a champion of the underdog and I saw that first hand on the day he decided to patch up a stand-off with his daughter Elizabeth.

We were sitting in the office one day when he said: 'I've fallen out with my daughter and I need to do something to get her back onside. She's always wanted a dog you know.'

He asked if there was anywhere local where he could go and have a look at some dogs. I admit to being a bit taken aback because he wasn't actually a massive fan of dogs at that time. In fact, to put it bluntly, he could never have been described as a dog lover in any way, shape or form. Anyway, we went out to a kennels not too far away where they had a number of nice dogs.

The fella who appeared to be in charge obviously recognised him and asked him if he was looking for anything in particular.

He nodded in the direction of some golden retriever pups.

'I quite like the look of those,' he said, pointing at a litter of gorgeous bundles of mischief.

'Good choice, they're lovely dogs. Good temperament. Intelligent. Excellent family dog,' the guy assured him.

'Which one's the runt?' he asked.

'That one there,' said the man looking somewhat perplexed.

'I'll have that one.'

'You don't want that one,' the man assured him. 'Have the best one. I'll sort you out the pick of the litter, Mr Clough.'

'Na, I'll have that one,' he said and wouldn't be deflected from his choice.

He bought a bed for it . . . the lot. But I remember smiling as we made our way back to his house. This man, who could knock you dead with one glance, looked into the dog's eyes lovingly and said: 'Hey, little fella, you don't realise just what a life you're going to have.'

❛ I'll talk to a player for 20 minutes and then we'll decide I was right after all ❜

Few got as close to Clough as former Sun columnist JOHN SADLER. No one wrote in Clough-speak better than him and it was to close friend John that he turned to when he wrote his autobiography Walking on Water.

28

GET OFF YOUR ARSE

JOHN SADLER

Basically, it means you're in my patch,' I said.

'It's your lucky day,' came the reply. Little did I know that might just turn out to be the truest thing he ever said to me. Brian and myself became great friends by a strange quirk of fate. There's no other way to describe it really. I was working for The Sun as a football reporter responsible for Yorkshire as my 'patch.' When a certain Brian Clough moved to Derby, someone on the desk in London decided that some seismic movement in the Earth's crust meant the Baseball Ground and surrounding area came under my jurisdiction. Brian Clough was that earthquake. Derby were just a middling kind of club, doing nothing of note, so the decision really wasn't seen as having too much of an impact on anyone. How wrong can you be!

I went to see him and introduced myself and he asked me if I'd like a drink.

'Coffee, please.'

'No problem. Right, sit down. What can I do for you?'

I explained that although I actually worked the Yorkshire beat, some geo-graphical quirk meant that news from the Baseball Ground was in my charge. He assured me it was my lucky day. He shuffled forwards in his seat and looked at me intently.

'Listen, I don't use telephones. I'm suspicious of telephones. If you are prepared to get off your arse and come and see me, then I promise you that in one hour, I will fill your newspaper for a week!'

It was a slight exaggeration ... but only just. Up to that point, I think it's fair to say Derby had been a nothing club. The Midlands-based reporters hadn't had too much reason to go there very often because the club just wasn't in the news. Boy, how was that about to change? I rose to the challenge of getting off my arse and going to see him and I'll bet within two or three weeks, they were all flocking over. He was absolutely phenomenal. I have to say that from those first meetings, I was lucky enough to chart his rise from close-up. I ended up 'ghosting' his column for The Sun for many years and ended up having the privilege of being asked to write his autobiography. I have to say – and I've been lucky enough to travel the world meeting top sports personalities and going to the biggest events – Brian was the most remarkable human being I've ever met.

Yes, he was bolshy, arrogant, pig-headed and a thousand-and-one other things. But he was also a very warm-hearted and charming man. The previous story about wanting the runt of the litter absolutely goes to the essence of the man. He was looking for something to take care of. He had an inherent hatred of anything that he saw as an injustice. It burned from deep within him.

He was once going home from training on the bus in his days as a young player and the driver went past an old lady at the bus stop. Cloughie shouted and rang the bell. The bus stopped and he got off to be told by the conductor 'This bus is full.'

'No it's not – she's getting on,' the young Clough insisted.

He promptly got off the bus, helped the old lady onto the bus and gave her his seat. That was typical of him from an early age. The closer I got to him the more I appreciated what a brilliant mind he had, even though he hadn't a qualification to his name. His knowledge of journalism and how it worked was quite stunning at times. He knew all the terms of the newspaper business and would often say things like 'Hey that's plenty of stuff there, but we need an intro don't we?'

You couldn't help but laugh. There was the biggest name in football, filling your notebook with absolutely terrific copy and he was desperate that WE got a great intro to the story. On one occasion when he did it, I laughed and said: 'Don't worry that's my job.'

'I know it's your job, but no one was ever the worse for a bit of help, you know.'

And he was right, as usual. Every time he opened his mouth he hit the button. You left his company with the problem of what you were going to have to leave out because it was all such good material.

That's why he was such a fantastic TV pundit all those years ago. He had opinions – and he wasn't shy in voicing them. That unmistakable voice of his and the piercing delivery of a line made him famous. Let us not forget Mike Yarwood, the country's top entertainer at the time, doing impressions of him because he was that popular and that distinctive.

The modern TV football experts can't hold a candle to Clough. He was the best. The rest are nowhere near. Listen to the current so-called pundits and they are total amateurs. They haven't a phrase between them. In the main they are absolutely useless. Cloughie was absolute television gold. He not only had big, bold opinions but he never ducked from saying the things that others were frightened to go near.

❛ I felt something worse than misery at Leeds. I was desolate ❜

Former TV executive JEFF FARMER was the Daily Mail's sports reporter on the Midlands beat when Clough decided to show the big-time London hacks that you can't beat a bit of local knowledge.

29

A TWIST IN THE TALE

JEFF FARMER

Brian Clough was a champion of the underdog. If ever he could give the underdog a fighting chance in a scrap, he would. That, along with his acute sense of loyalty, led to me being treated to one of the nights of my life back in 1980. Forest were playing Valencia in the second leg of their European Super Cup final. Cloughie's boys had won the European Cup while the Spanish outfit had won the European Cup Winners' Cup.

I was the Daily Mail's Midlands man who covered Forest on a day-to-day basis and had a good working relationship with both Cloughie and Peter Taylor. But as often happened when clubs progressed to major finals, Fleet Street's top writers and columnists became involved. Jeff Powell was my paper's No1 football writer and so it became a question of which of us, or both, went to Valencia for the game.

Let me stress this, first and foremost. Jeff has been a colleague and friend of mine for many years and there was no personal dispute over this. It's the sort of thing that crops up regularly in our business. It's not a thing of years gone by either – you can guarantee that when the likes of Manchester United and Chelsea have massive European ties, there's no shortage of reporters who could argue a claim as to why they should be there.

Anyway, in this particular instance our sports editor Tom Clarke took the view that it was a quiet week on other fronts and we should both go. After all, Jeff was the big-name No1 and I was the guy who covered Forest 52 weeks of the year.

I was feeling a bit of a spare part because Jeff was reporting on the game, so the rest of my colleagues from other papers like the Daily Express, Mirror etc decided they could make good use of me. Because they would be tight on time and busy getting their 'live' match reports over, it didn't take them too long to find gainful employment for me! I could be really useful to them by getting some quotes from the manager at the end and feeding them up to the Press Box.

We were staying at a lovely hotel about 10 miles outside of Valencia called the Monte Picayo. Funny how you remember these things! I decided to grab a quick word with Cloughie at the very first opportunity.

'Brian . . . I'm feeling a bit of a spare part here, so I've offered to do the quotes for all the lads. Is it okay if I get to you pretty quickly afterwards for a word?'

I could just tell that Cloughie was uneasy about what he would have considered the big-time Charlies from London coming in and treading on the toes of the reporters who had been doing the day-to-day stuff all year. This appealed to his sense of justice - and mischief, I suspect.

'Hey, I'll do better than that. Come and sit on the bench with us. You can watch the match with me and my mate (Peter Taylor) and my bairn (son Nigel).'

'Are you serious?'

'Hey, I've never been more serious in my life.'

'Can I do a piece on it?'

'That's why I'm asking you to sit there!'

I could just tell that this was Clough at his most mischievous. He was looking after one of his lads – me! He didn't want me not being able to justify a foreign trip to my boss in London – not that I had to. He was going to make sure I got something extra-special that was off-limits to anyone else.

You could have knocked me down with a feather. I told the rest of the boys that getting the quotes up to them quickly wouldn't be a problem . . . I was on the bench. They were more gobsmacked than me. I rang the office in London.

'Cloughie's asked me to sit on the bench and watch him and Peter Taylor in action close up.'

My boss Tom was incredulous and instantly congratulated me on what was going to be a stitched-on double page spread.

'Hey, if you're going to do it, you might as well do it properly. Come in the dressing room with us beforehand as well!' said Clough.

I sat there quietly and just watched. I was surprised how calm it all was. Cloughie and Taylor were acting like the renowned double act they were, but there was no ranting or raving. Clough was calm and assured, just telling the players to do their jobs.

'Hey, remember, you lot are the champions of Europe. Don't let the crowd get to you out there. Just remember, pass it to one of your mates.'

I was genuinely surprised how calm it was. I've been in football all my life and yet that night goes down as one of the most memorable of my life. To think I was sitting there with Clough, Taylor and a young Nigel Clough still takes some believing. But there was more to come . . .

Once the match kicked off, that's when they earned their money. They never shut up once during the whole game. Clough just bellowed out instruction after instruction.

'Get it down! Play it . . .' stuff like that which totally endorsed the footballing philosophy which had brought him so much success.

But Clough at his unpredictable and hilarious best was yet to come. Colin Walsh was playing on the flank right in front of the dugout when a Valencia defender clattered into him, sending him flying through the air. As the defender slid, he ended up following through and landing right at our feet. Cloughie grabbed hold of his boot and twisted his leg.

'You dirty fucking bastard!' he exclaimed. The guy's face was a picture. I don't think he could believe what he had just heard.

Anyway, needless to say, I supplied the boys with the quotes and ended up with a feature that was the envy of everyone. I felt not just pleased, but privileged.

To be given such an experience of seeing legendary figures working close up was like . . . well, like riding pillion with Lester Piggott around Tattenham Corner. It was an experience that money couldn't buy in the rare event of it ever being on offer.

❛ The only agent back then was James Bond and he only shafted women - not entire football clubs - *on the rise to prominence of football agents* **❜**

*Ex-England boss GRAHAM TAYLOR has fond
memories of Cloughie and recalls how he'll
never forget an astonishing offer put to him when
he was in charge at Watford.*

30

POCKET MAN

GRAHAM TAYLOR

Brian Clough prides himself on getting his man – but he missed out in an audacious attempt to get what would have been his biggest signing ever. Cloughie wanted Elton John, who was just about the biggest rock star in the world at the time – and went to extraordinary lengths to get him. Let me explain . . .

Elton was my chairman at Watford and we had just won promotion from the old Fourth Division. I took a late night phone call from Peter Taylor who asked me if I would be with the team training the following morning. I said I would and Taylor replied: 'My mucker wants a word with you.' Mucker was a term he often used instead of 'pal' to describe Brian. I didn't give it a lot more thought, though it was obviously something quite pressing.

Elton had just finished an eight-week tour of the United Kingdom, was absolutely knackered, and happened to be sitting in the office with me, when Brian called the next day.

'Now then, young man,' he said. 'I have a proposition to put to you. After 14 years of management, or whatever it was, my directors are giving me a testimonial.'

Forest had just won the title and Clough and Taylor were to be rewarded for a quite fantastic achievement.

'I just wondered if your big man would do a concert for us!'

Elton was just a few yards away and had clearly got the gist of what was being said and was mouthing: 'No, no, no' quietly, shaking his head at the same time.

'It'd be great if he could do it. We've got the Theatre Royal here in Nottingham which would . . .'

There was no way Brian could have known that Elton was right next to me as he tried his level best to swing it.

'I know he's wealthy and won't want any money so I've decided that what I will give you in return is two seats in my directors' box for a reserve game.'

'Two seats at a reserve game?' Was I really hearing him right? Surely this had to be some kind of game. Brian explained:

'I'll make sure every player who is available plays and you can have your pick of any three – and they'll cost you sod all!'

Only Cloughie could try and pull that one off. So this is the deal – he gets a superstar who could pack any arena in the world to play a benefit concert for nothing; we get two seats for a Forest reserve game! Vintage Cloughie.

The other big memory I have of him was, again, during my time at Watford. I'd taken my side to Forest and we had been battered 7-3 in a quite incredible game.

I was understandably a bit brassed off at the end and was in the dressing room ready to give them a right rol-locking. The theme of my ear-bashing was going to be something to the effect of that while scoring three goals away from home was admirable, it was sod all use to anyone if you let seven in at the other end!

I was fuming and just about to sound off when Cloughie comes into our dressing room and plants a big kiss on both of my cheeks.

'Fantastic,' he says. 'What a game, eh? Now that's what football is all about.'

I could see it from his point of view but if he could only be in my shoes for a few minutes, he'd see that the beauty of a free-flowing open game was slightly tarnished by the scoreline. I was going to give them a hammering, the very second he'd shut the dressing room door.

Brian proceeded to go to each of my players and give every one in turn a kiss on the cheek and compliment them on their wonderful display. I decided to wait until he'd finished. He kissed every single one of my players, gave me a hug and kissed me again before leaving.

I'm only guessing that I gave them the bollocking they deserved, but somehow, I suspect, the sting had been taken out of it!

He was a complete one-off.

❛ Real fame is when they spell your name right in Karachi and ordinary fame is when Mike Yarwood does an impression of you ❜

One unscheduled 'party' goes down as one of the big nights in Forest's history among the players who were there. Here, a few of them reveal just what happened on the eve of that big Wembley final.

31

ARE WE WORRIED?

VARIOUS

The night of Friday, March 16, 1979, is one etched in Nottingham Forest folklore, yet even some of the club's most ardent fans may be unaware of what happened. It was the night before the club's League Cup final clash with Southampton and within the ranks has gradually become known as one of THE nights when Clough and Taylor's man management skills were at their zenith. That night the pair of them took a gamble that, had it backfired, could have made them look idiots. As it happened, Forest went on to win the final 3-2 in front of 100,000 people. Yet members of that victorious side still recall with affection and disbelief, the Clough-Taylor masterplan. It borders on the astonishing. You could be forgiven for thinking it was made up. But when a number of players verify proceedings, you realise that truth is sometimes stranger than fiction. Garry Birtles scored twice that day and starts by giving his version of events on that famous Friday.

GARRY BIRTLES: I was the youngest member of the team at just 21 and had only really broken into the side that season. I'd been a carpet fitter not that long before so it really was all a bit of a whirlwind for me. My first three games for Forest had been Arsenal, Manchester United and a clash with Liverpool in the European Cup!

Now we were going to play at Wembley in a cup final and I wouldn't have been the only one whose nerves were a touch raw. We were spending the night at the West Park Lodge – a hotel where the England team met up before big matches. It was a lovely place and just a few years previous I would have dreamed of landing a carpet contract there, never mind staying the night.

We got there early evening and were told to dump our bags in the rooms and then report back down to reception. We all assumed that we'd be having a cup of tea and a sandwich, a bit of a team meeting where one or two things would be outlined and then off to bed. Wrong!

When we all got back downstairs the gaffer was waiting for us with Peter and one or two others and told us to order whatever we wanted to drink –

champagne, beer, the choice was ours. Some of us looked around to check we hadn't misheard. It turned out to be a right night. Cloughie and Taylor put on a double act which would have graced The Palladium, having us all rolling around with stories from their past. It's fair to say we had quite a few beers that night and ended up going to bed at around midnight. Archie Gemmill had got the hump because his idea of pre-match relaxation was to sleep and he made several pleas to leave the party.

'You'll go when the rest of us go,' the gaffer insisted, adamant that not one person would break this revolutionary stint of team bonding. It certainly took our minds off the match even though we were 1-0 down in the game. I do wonder what would have happened if we'd lost and anyone had found out about our pre-match routine. We'd have probably been slammed from pillar to post with the gaffer's preparation blasted as ridiculous and unprofessional. As it turned out, you can put it down to a stroke of pure genius and yet another incredible plan that the boss managed to get away with.

JOHN O'HARE RECALLS: I wasn't playing so I had no problem having a few beers. How can you begin to explain the pair of them pulling a stunt like that? They were a great double act. Peter was the funny guy without a doubt, but the pair of them together were dynamite. I do remember Archie being really brassed off because he'd gone to his bed and wasn't happy when he was fetched out of it. Relaxing and having a sleep was Archie's way of preparing for games and he didn't take too kindly to being kept up until late.

FRANK CLARK REVEALS: The boss was a revolutionary in things like that, but I have to say on this particular occasion, I wasn't sure about it being such a good idea. Everybody had gone off to bed when the call came for us all to go down into the lobby area. Archie refused, but the gaffer and Peter weren't having it. There was a crate of champagne down there but those who preferred a beer could have that. It has to be said that one or two of the lads were a little bit the worse for wear. I asked Brian a few years later just why he had done such a radical thing and he said that he sensed the players were tense because we were such overwhelming favourites to win the final. It was his way of taking our minds off things. He was a great believer that players could not play to their maximum if they were tense. To be fair, we didn't start off well in the match and it could have seriously backfired! Looking back, the whole episode was absolutely amazing. The one thing about the boss was that he was never afraid to try the unorthodox.

❛ At last . . . England have appointed someone who speaks better English than the players
- on Sven Goran Eriksson getting England job ❜

64

32

NEVER A DULL MOMENT

VINCE WILSON

Brian Clough was never over-whelmed by famous people or places, although he did feel important when he was invited to meet Prime Minister Tony Blair.

The moment came when he and his wife Barbara were seating themselves comfortably in a London taxi and his request to the cabbie rolled smoothly off his tongue . . .

'Ten Downing Street, please.' That did amuse him.

He received another surprise invitation – one which shocked our sporting nation – when he was asked to take charge of the faraway Iran Football Federation in 1974. He was contracted to Brighton at the time.

Brian, a vigorous 40-year-old, was also contracted to the Sunday Mirror, the newspaper which employed me for almost 30 years. I was their Chief Northern Sportswriter but, more importantly, I had shared a close friendship with him dating back to those happy days in our native North-East when he played for Middlesbrough and Sunderland.

Back to business, though. He confronted me one morning in his office at Brighton with: 'Fancy going to Iran next week? They want me to take charge of their country's football!'

Life was full or surprises during the years I'd known Brian, but that one knocked me sideways. He was still house-hunting in Brighton! How he'd reached agreement to speak to Iranian representatives I'll never know. He held a great respect for his new chairman Michael Bamber, who had told him, apparently: 'They don't have enough money to buy you.'

The story moves on . . . I met Brian by arrangement at Euston station. Our next stop was Heathrow Airport for the flight to Tehran. That was the plan anyway. Instead, we finished up at The House of Commons.

Brian had met Joe Ashton MP on his train journey from Derby and the next thing I knew we were being shown around that beautiful old building on the banks of the Thames. Time was slipping away, but an experienced cabbie steered us sharply to Heathrow. The final scamper between the check-in desk and the departure lounge was met with a sigh of relief. At last we were boarding for Iran. Never a dull moment with Cloughie!

It reminded me of another occasion when we had travelled from Derby to Brighton by train. He was scheduled to finalise his contract as manager. A courteous waiting director ushered us into his luxury car near the railway station and was soon heading towards the football ground.

'My colleagues are waiting at The Goldstone Ground for you,' the gentleman declared,' before Brian said:

'I don't want to see the Goldstone Ground just yet. I played there many times and I remember it well. I'd rather see the famous pier first and pick up some candy rock for my children.' The patient director agreed to both requests.

The arrival in Tehran wasn't as informal as that. We were secretly whisked away to our hotel in the black of night and were treated well. Nobody disclosed the name of the establishment where Brian was resident because Press people, naturally, wanted to know his whereabouts. Those foreign newspapermen caught up, however and were aware of the several meetings that were taking place.

The message was clear though – Iran wanted to qualify for the 1978 World Cup. Money and expensive travel posed no problems for them. Such incidentals were easily overcome. They saw Brian as their leader. He was barely 40, successful, forthright, bright and cheerful with an English First Division title behind him. He also visited the British Embassy and had long talks about housing and the education of his children Simon, Nigel and Elizabeth.

Then there was the night of the horses. They were big, beautiful, Persian thoroughbreds kept in stables and surrounded by armed guards. We were driven to a huge mansion nearby - home of a VIP - and were greeted by the butler. The massive residence was most impressive and the dining room elegant. Serving ladies wearing yashmaks hurried to the table whenever a knife or fork was merely placed on the table. They were highly efficient, pleasant and courteous. We dined well.

Goodness knows what the thoroughbreds were worth. They were sleeping, largely, when Brian followed dinner with a request to see ' the finest horses in the world.' The host obliged and didn't mind his guest filling his pockets with fruit from the biggest fruit bowl I had ever seen.

'I'd like to feed them,' he requested. It seemed the Iran Football Federation wanted him at any cost. So he did feed the famous horses. Some loved it, others kicked out loudly in protest.

The following day another gentleman showed us around an original Persian market where the people were very friendly. The streets were crammed with dusty cars and wagons while sheep seemed to be running around everywhere. The whole scene was chaotic, but the natives seemed to enjoy all the bartering and shouting.

Not long afterwards, we were taken to Tehran Airport, but not before an Iranian journalist offered me £500 to share the Clough decision – would he make the move or not? Would he say yes or no to Iran? He was wasting his breath. My newspaper, the Sunday Mirror, carried the story exclusively. After much thought, he was staying at Brighton.

Brian was a great character with a genius football brain and an uncanny, special, gift, for motivating others. His tongue was persuasive, to say the least. He was also a very kind man and nobody will ever know the amount of work he did happily for charities. He had the priceless gift of lifting young, talented players to very high levels. The late Ian Greaves, the former Manchester United player who did sterling work when manager at Bolton and Huddersfield, was an admirer.

'I would look at his team selections in a newspaper on the Friday night when Forest might have been playing Arsenal, Tottenham, West Ham or Chelsea and I would see virtually unknown youngsters' names there. And he would get great results in London with them in Forest's prime years.'

He did have the Midas touch but frequently said that his assistant Peter Taylor was the best talent spotter in the country.

The last time I saw him was in the manager's office at Nottingham Forest. He was sitting on the table-top, his preferred choice to a chair.

'I've been blessed with three gifts in my professional life,' he reflected.

'ONE . . . I scored 250 goals with those,' he proclaimed, pointing down to his dangling legs and feet.

'TWO . . . I was wanted regularly by newspapers, television and radio. They seemed to like my candid opinions and the way I expressed them.

'And THREE . . . I could manage a football club.'

‘He was head and shoulders above Clemence. Alternating the two was a massive insult to Shilton
- on policy to rotate Peter Shilton and Ray Clemence for England ’

A late night knock on the door changed the life of classy defender ROY McFARLAND. The Tranmere youngster was wanted by Clough who made it clear he wasn't prepared to take no for an answer.

33

DREAM MOVE

ROY McFARLAND

I might have the unique distinction of being the only player to sign for Brian Clough wearing his pyjamas! If it sounds bizarre then that's because it is. When Brian wanted a player there are no lengths he wouldn't go to to make sure he got his man.

And that's why he got me out of bed after calling at my parents' home after midnight and refusing to take no for an answer over a move from Tranmere to Derby.

It was a Friday night and I'd played for Tranmere in a win over Reading. I used to travel to matches by train from home in Liverpool. My cousin had come with me and we went for a couple of pints before taking a short bus ride back home. I then went to bed completely oblivious to the Morecambe and Wise routine that was just around the corner.

It must have been half-past-midnight when my mum woke me and told me to go downstairs because there were two gentlemen to see me accompanied by my Tranmere manager Dave Russell. What????

It was Clough and Taylor and they were here to get me to sign for them at Derby. Dave said a fee had been agreed and they had permission to talk to me.

'The financial side of it is all sorted. It's up to you. If you turn up for training on Monday, I'll see you there, if not then best of luck to you, son,' Dave said and left.

The thing was, I was in a decent job as an accountant at Ogden's Tobacco Company and wasn't really sure about making such a move. I'd only been there 12 months but I liked the job and the people I worked with. I thought my chance of being a big-time professional footballer had gone. I needed time to think this over.

'Take as long as you want,' they said, though they both took up my mum's offer of another cup of tea and seemed to make it last for ever. The pair of them never stopped talking. It was like being at a tennis match – one would pipe up with something and when he had finished, the other one would start. It was just a continual bombardment.

'Look, it's a big decision. I'm not sure. I need some time,' I told them.

My mum looked bewildered and

Clough, quite cleverly, took up her offer of yet another cup of tea. They must have had five or six cups, stretching things out, as they bombarded me with their plans for Derby.

I can remember it like it was yesterday. I turned to my dad for some respite. By now it was around 2am.

'I'm unsure. What do you think?'

'If they want you THAT badly son, I'd sign,' came the reply.

With that, Taylor whipped the relevant papers in front of me and was virtually signing my signature for me in his eagerness to get my name on the dotted line.

'This is the best thing you will ever do,' he assured me.

I was a big Liverpool fan at the time and the following day I went to Anfield with my cousin and watched them play Newcastle.

The game was around 30 minutes old when I turned to my cousin and said: 'I've made the biggest mistake of my life.'

I really felt that. I'd been bullied into making a decision I was far from sure about. It turned out to be the best decision I ever made.

Before too long I was a member of the Derby side that finished up champions and was in the England team. And all from that early-hours chat in my pyjamas and probably some of the soundest advice my dad Les ever gave me.

'If they want you THAT badly son, I'd sign,'

You know something, I can remember him saying that as if it was yesterday.

❛ Anyone who can do anything well in Leicester apart from making a jumper has just got to be a genius
- on Martin O'Neill's success at Leicester City ❜

BBC Radio Sports journalist DARREN FLETCHER became a friend of Clough and shared some magic moments with the master during his time working on local radio in Nottingham.

34

PIECE OF CAKE

DARREN FLETCHER

They say ignorance is bliss but not necessarily when it's your first week at work and the office mischievously send you to Nottingham Forest to get an interview with Brian Clough! Most people would have just cause to remember the first time they bumped into Old Big 'Ead, but I'll certainly never forget mine.

I was 18 and had been working putting up suspended ceilings when I somehow wangled a job with Radio Trent. I'd only been there a day or two when the gaffer told me to go down to Forest and get an interview. I naively presumed you could just go down and get the manager so I breezed into the front office and was introduced to Carole, his secretary.

'Hi, I'm Darren Fletcher from Radio Trent and I've come to interview Brian Clough,' I said.

Carole looked a little startled at my bullish manner and said: 'Okay, I'll see what I can do for you!'

She returned and said it wouldn't be a problem and he'd see me later. Piece of cake!

I waited in the corridor and the hours ticked by and though I was getting brassed off, I just assumed that was what you did. So I waited . . . and waited . . . and he knew I was there because he'd come through a couple of times. Del Boy the retriever was with him and at one point I was throwing the tennis ball for him down the corridor. The dog was barking, it was chaos all around with Cloughie bollocking the dog but eventually he called me in to his office.

By now I was shaking like a leaf. I was wet through with sweat and I could hardly talk let alone conduct an interview. I had my questions written down ready and put them in front of me as I was about to start. Cloughie screwed them up, tossed them on the floor and told me to start!

He proceeded to slaughter me in the interview answering each question of mine with a question but nonetheless I'd got plenty of words and I was quite pleased with myself. I'll never forget it – Cloughie said: 'Hey, you are a very handsome and pleasant young man – come and see me again.'

Well, I was made up and when I got back to the office I was to realise the magnitude of my good day's work.

'Who did you get?' my new boss asked.

'I got Cloughie.'

'You're joking.'

'No.'

'Hey that's fantastic. Fancy getting him like that. Well done. He must really like you.'

Well, I don't mind saying, I was well pleased with myself. I'd shown initiative and drive and I'd stuck it out when I could easily have gone home and not waited. I was in self-congratulatory mood. I admit it – I was very, very pleased with myself.

A few days later, Forest were at Plymouth in the League Cup and I drove down with my gaffer to the game. Cloughie was out by the dugout signing autographs for some kids and my boss said to me 'Why don't you go and have a word with him – he obviously likes you!'

I picked up my tape machine - a big cumbersome thing and hopped over the small perimeter wall and made my way towards Cloughie who was prob-ably about 50 yards away at this point.

He spotted me and warned: 'Hey, get away from me.'

It never actually occurred to me that I was the object of his attentions and so I carried on. I thought he must have been talking to someone else.

'Hey, shithouse . . . don't come near me,' he barked.

I just honestly assumed he was talking to someone else and so I carried on until I was no more than five yards away. Upon which, Cloughie walked towards me, right in front of all the Plymouth fans, and faked a stumble. I was startled, but even more taken aback as he caught me full in the chest with his shoulder and practically floored me. I staggered back and nearly went over on my backside as the fans behind me all started cheering and giving me almighty stick.

He just carried on signing autographs. God knows what my boss thought. But I know one thing. It was the first and last time I kidded myself that I was well in with him.

❛ I like my women to be feminine, not sliding into tackles and getting covered in mud
- on the rise in popularity of women's football ❜

*Former Wolves manager JOHN BARNWELL was one
step ahead of Cloughie as their two sides prepared
to meet in the 1980 League Cup final at Wembley.
But there was a price to be paid . . .*

35

A FAMILY AFFAIR

JOHN BARNWELL

I once tried to pull a couple of stunts across Brian – and found out that he'll always have the final say.

In 1980 I was manager of Wolves when we got through to the League Cup final at Wembley to play Cloughie's Forest side. During my playing career at Arsenal, I had lived in Winchmore Hill just on the edge of Southgate. In the area there was a lovely country-style type of hotel that was very well thought of and I reckoned it would be just perfect for our Wembley preparations. I knew that Arsenal and Tottenham had used it on many occasions in preparation for big matches so I reckoned on it being perfect for us. The very minute we knew we were at Wembley I said to our secretary Phil Shaw that he must try and get us in there. It was expensive but Wolves didn't get to Wembley every day and it's slightly out-of-the-way location meant it was perfect. The players could arrive at Wembley at the end of a proper coach ride – just like you'd always seen on telly for the FA Cup final.

As luck would have it, they could accommodate us and we were booked in which was even more pleasing a little later when I heard through a mutual friend that Brian had tried to get in there with his Forest team.

Anyway, it was perfect. The players could relax, have a sauna, stroll in the picturesque gardens and from my point of view it couldn't be better.

My assistant Richie Barker and myself were enjoying a coffee in the foyer one morning when a coach pulled up on the front and people started pouring out. I recognised one of the first off the bus to be Brian's assistant at Forest – Ronnie Fenton. I started to smell a rat – especially when he was followed by members of staff, women and a stack of children. Cloughie had booked them all in, presumably to make sure our peace was disturbed. Anyway, we got by, even if things weren't as quiet as we'd hoped!

On the day of the match, I wasn't really sure what to expect because this was all a bit new to me. But I had a very good relationship with the legendary Liverpool boss Bill Shankly who had been to more big finals than I could shake a stick at. I asked him to run me through it and also pass on any advice he felt would help me.

He was very helpful, but one thing he said was that when the officials come to knock the dressing room door to get you ready to go out, delay things.

'Keep 'em waiting son,' he cackled. It was the tip of a wise old owl and one that particularly appealed given what Clough had done over the hotel arrangements. I'd keep him waiting. I had some big players in my dressing room – players like Andy Gray and Emlyn Hughes. They didn't need to be wound up.

There was a knock on the door and a voice called out 'Five minutes please.'

I looked at the players and said: 'Sit down – we're going to make them wait. Let's make Cloughie wait!'

Well, the lads were clapping and hollering. They liked the sound of that. They really liked the sound of that . . .

Another knock on the door. 'Two minutes please fellas.'

'Hey, we'll be out there when we're ready lads. Let's make Cloughie wait for us!'

The roof came off the dressing room. The players clapped and whooped in delight and were laughing just at the very thought of vexing Brian.

The knocks got more frantic to the point where we had to come out and as we got into the tunnel feeling very full of ourselves, I noticed Brian wasn't at the head of his team. He'd sent out little Jimmy Gordon to lead Forest out and was making his way to the dugout on the far side, unaware of any commotion in the tunnel. When I eventually got over there, he shook my hand and said: 'Enjoy the day!'

I did – we won 1-0 thanks to an Andy Gray goal.

❛ That Seaman is a handsome young man but he spends too much time looking in his mirror rather than at the ball. You can't keep goal with hair like that
- on David Seaman's pony-tail ❜

Former Nottingham Forest skipper BRIAN LAWS followed in his old boss' shoes by going into management. But talking of shoes . . Laws reveals a behind-the-scenes secret from Cloughie's big FA Cup final trip to Wembley.

36

RED CARPET SLIPPERS

BRIAN LAWS

The one story that sticks out in my mind about Cloughie was our big day out at Wembley for the 1991 FA Cup final against Tottenham.

The gaffer hated the fact that he had to wear a suit, but the fact that we were being presented to none other than Princess Diana and Prince Charles, made any other form of attire unthinkable.

So, what he did was he arranged for his famous green top to be up near the dugout so he could change into that and got himself ready to meet royalty in his best suit. On it he had a big rosette, proudly declaring: 'World's Greatest Grandad.'

We were in the dressing room and he turned to our skipper Stuart Pearce and said: 'Hey, Pearcey, who's the fashion guru amongst this little lot then?'

Pearcey says: 'Lawsy's your man. He wears all the best gear!'

Nothing could have been further from the truth – in fact I was probably the worst person to ask.

However, it was enough of a recommendation for the gaffer, who turned to me for my approval.

'Brian, can you tell me son. Do I look smart?'

'Yes you do gaffer. Very smart,' I assured him.

'Thank you son.'

As we started to make our way down from the dressing rooms to the pitch, I couldn't resist one final observation. I tapped Cloughie on the shoulder.

'Hey gaffer! You know I said you looked smart?'

'Yes.'

'Well you do, but your slippers look a bit shit.'

'Oh, my God,' he exclaimed.

In the excitement and tension of it all, Cloughie was only going out to meet Lady Di in his comfy carpet slippers. He dashed in and put on his shiny new shoes and was finally ready to meet royalty.

❛I only ever hit Roy Keane once. He got up, so I couldn't have hit him very hard ❜

One man who saw the great man away from football was
PETER SMITH who tended his lawns. He and Cloughie
would often chat as he went about his chores at the
beautiful former family home in the village of Quarndon

37

ONE MAN MEANT TO MOW

PETER SMITH

It gets thatch out of the lawn,' I explained, looking down at the brand, spanking new machine.

'Hey, it's a pity it couldn't get Thatcher out of No10,' he replied with a broad grin.

So perhaps that's why someone had brought Cloughie this as a Christmas present after all. Imagine that . . . a machine which could have given him his dearest wish of all – a swift boot out of office for the woman he hated with a vengeance – Mrs T the Prime Minister. If I recall correctly, he'd been given the scarifier as a Christmas present by the then chairman of Nottingham Forest. He wasn't sure how it worked and was quizzing me about it as I set about my duties.

I recall Cloughie catching me off guard at our very first meeting as if he was firing a warning shot across my bows. He'd asked me to give him a quote for doing his lawns at the front of the house which involved cutting, scarifying, aerating, top dressing – the whole works and we agreed a price.

'What! You're joking aren't you?'

'No, I'm deadly serious. That's a really big lawn.'

'Well, you seem an honest enough sort of bloke,' he assured me.

'I am.'

'I'll tell you what, throw in the back lawn as well and it's a deal.'

'Done,' I said triumphantly, proud I'd stood my ground with such a feared and renowned negotiator.

Cloughie led me around the side of the house and gestured towards his 'small' back lawn. It was the size of two football pitches. Done? I had been.

Having assured him my honesty and integrity couldn't be brought into question. I stuck to the agreement. I came away feeling rather chuffed that I was to work in my greatest hero's garden for at least a fortnight, while he seemed happy enough to be one up on me with the 'game' barely having kicked-off.

❛ Football hooligans? Well, there are 92 football club chairmen for a start ❜

Former West Brom, Manchester United and Aston Villa boss RON ATKINSON was a close friend of Cloughie and did a TV interview with him in retirement. Here he reveals the old magic was just as powerful as ever.

38

KING OF THE HILL

RON ATKINSON

Yes, he was captivating. Yes, he was sublime. Yes, he had charisma in bundles. I didn't need to witness a quite extraordinary show of appreciation to realise just what a magnetic personality Brian was. But I did . . . and I just smiled and nodded and, to be honest, had a tear in my eye as I watched the great man take his acclaim.

Bear in mind, he'd been out of the game quite some time by this time. Take into account too that he had suffered with his health. Lesser people would have largely been forgotten. Forget Cloughie? Not a chance.

I'd always got on well with Brian. He and Peter Taylor seemed to take a shine to me in the early days at West Brom and I'd regularly get the call to pop in and have a drink with them. We shared a passion for football and Frank Sinatra. I swear to God, my Sinatra impression is the only thing I ever managed to do better than him. But copy Cloughie? Hey, many have tried and I'm not just talking about Mike Yarwood. I can think of one or two managers who have tried to model themselves on him and it just can't be

done. He was unique – a complete one-off. Yarwood did him brilliantly, but that was different. Funnily enough I sometimes used to see Brian as a caricature of himself.

Anyway, I had arranged to see him when he agreed to film a programme for a television series I was doing. I love the banter and I was really looking forward to chewing the fat with him again. When I was in charge at Albion, I once played four forwards against Forest and Cloughie remarked that I was either the most brilliant manager in the country or the daftest. Ironically, the match finished 0-0, so make of that what you will!

I started the programme with a clip of myself with my arm around the statue of Robin Hood in Nottingham and said something like: 'But now I'm off to meet another legend from around these parts . . .'

Obviously I knew Brian so I had an inkling of what he was like but the production crew hadn't a clue of what to expect.

'Hey, Big Head, you've got an hour,' was his opening line to me – four hours later we stopped and only then because we'd run out of tape!

He was absolutely superb – in his element. It was good, old-fashioned, typically vintage Clough – which meant we couldn't use half of it!

But boy, was he on his knock. I asked him a whole host of questions and, hardly surprisingly, he had an answer for every one. We seemed to cover every topic under the sun and he had an opinion on everything.

I remember asking him about David Beckham and saying something like: 'What do you think of the blond No7 for Manchester United?'

'I do know one thing. I don't care how brilliant he is, why the hell does he need four cars when you can only drive one?'

He had a line for everything and, as I said, many of them were extremely funny, but unusable. The fire in his belly was still there.

Production crews by nature tend not to be easily impressed. Because of the nature of the job, they can be a bit 'seen it, done it.' But this time they realised they had witnessed something rather special.

Completely unprovoked they rose to their feet and gave Brian a standing ovation. It was quite moving.

The programme actually got nominated for an award but we finished runner-up to Dale Winton's Supermarket Sweep! I can't begin to imagine what Cloughie would have said about that!

6 I think it might have been my next-door-neighbour because I think she felt that if I got something like that, I would have to move - *on guessing who had nominated him for a knighthood* **9**

77

*Radio broadcaster JOHN HELM was up close and personal
with Clough in the immediate aftermath of his sacking at
Leeds. In fact, he couldn't have been closer to one of the
biggest stories in football if he'd planned it that way.*

39

CHAMPAGNE FAREWELL

JOHN HELM

As I awoke on that September morning back in 1974 little could I have know that I was about to play a central role in one of the most talked about incidents in the history of English football. A massive story was about to unfold – and fate was to lock me in on it – quite literally. When I say massive . . . this one was huge. I was the Sports Editor on BBC Radio Leeds and was no stranger to big stories, big players and big personalities. Just 43 days previously I had been at Elland Road to cover the seemingly unbelievable story that Brian Clough had been appointed as Don Revie's successor at Leeds United. There was no way that as that new day started I could even have suspected this was to be one of the days of all days.

I took a call from one of my really good contacts saying that something was going off. There had been talk of a players' revolt and even a sit-in but the magnitude of what was about to unfold was unimaginable. I went racing down to Elland Road to make sure I was right there if anything happened. One or two people were coming and going and gradually the whispers became stronger that Clough was on his way. It hardly seemed credible. Even now looking back I can recall the sense of disbelief. For sure, things hadn't gone well for him . . . but Clough on his way? Bizarre things had been happening from the very second he'd set foot through the door, but this? It just didn't seem possible.

Clough came out and issued a statement and then went back in with me in hot pursuit. I'd been interviewing him a couple of times a week at this point so while I couldn't say I was close to him, I think we had developed a reasonable relationship. We went into his office – THE office. This was the place that Don Revie had called his own. This was the office Clough had breezed into not six weeks ago. This was the office that he would soon be clearing out on the day that helped change the face of football. Clough's finest hours were yet to come. But there was a strange feeling about it all at the time.

It wasn't to be a straightforward parting as I was soon to discover. The two of us sat and talked and he rang The Dragonara Hotel where he'd been staying and asked them to send down some champagne. We sat there, talking and having a drink, only to discover that the offices had all been locked up and we couldn't get out! Brian tried ringing reception but everyone had gone. And so there we were, just him and me, drinking champagne and blissfully unaware that this would later be seen as one of the defining moments in football. If the rage of having his prolific goalscoring career cruelly cut short by injury was to light a fire within him, then this would follow a close second.

Looking back, if I had to describe his state of mind in one word, I'd say he was shocked. He wasn't bitter. More disappointed – but that would be putting it mildly. He was convinced he could have turned things around given time. I think he knew he'd made a mistake not having Peter Taylor there at his side. He thought the Leeds board were a bunch of old duffers.

We must have been in there three or four hours just talking things over. Years later, he told me that he had never forgotten it – and, interestingly, never got over it. Eventually someone with a key let us out and as we appeared, Keith Macklin was waiting outside. Keith was the Yorkshire Television football commentator at the time and had been sent down to try and persuade Cloughie to go into the studios that night to do a live TV interview. In the studio was Revie and the two argued their case in front of millions of astonished viewers. It turned out to be one of the most historic TV interviews ever as the two of them

slugged it out. Clough remained adamant that he could have done things better than the legendary Revie and that he was a better manager.

Even then, no one could have envisaged the fallout from Clough's humbling.

* * *

It didn't seem like five minutes that I'd interviewed him on his very first day at the club – well, it hadn't been that long ago! Part and parcel of a radio journalist's job is to get a good 'out.' An 'out' is where an interview ends – hopefully on an interesting or funny note. Some subjects haven't a clue, some naturally speak in such a way that you can edit the interview accordingly to finish on a particularly pertinent note. Some are brilliant and Cloughie was one of those. He had an instinctive feel for when an interview should finish and didn't mind telling you! Clough almost thought like a radio man.

As the Sports Editor of Radio Leeds, I'd been going to the ground every Friday to get the latest team news from Don Revie who had always been fantastically co-operative. All of a sudden it was Clough and I don't mind admitting that his reputation for being, at best, awkward on occasions, had me on edge. I'd got a one-on-one interview with him after the written Press boys had finished with him – or he'd finished with them! As it came nearer the time for me to get ready, I couldn't help thinking 'Oh, my God!'

Clough's first day had been bizarre

enough up to this point. He'd come with his very young son Nigel who had been kicking the ball about on the training pitch with seasoned internationals like Allan Clarke and Norman Hunter. It was all rather extraordinary to say the least. Clough had conducted his interview brandishing a coat hangar with which he played imaginary cricket shots from time to time.

The appointment had already gone down like a ton of bricks in some quarters because of his openly hostile condemnation of Revie's championship side. Clough had already said at a dinner in Leeds that he felt they should be relegated for cheating!

And now here he was at his very first Press conference saying that if Leeds' Scottish international Eddie Gray had been a racehorse he'd have been put down referring to the much-loved winger's record of injuries.

I was waiting my turn when Terry Yorath stormed in with a face like thunder because someone had smashed into his car on the car park. It was getting more bizarre by the minute.

Now my turn was here and I was left in no doubt that it wasn't going to be on my terms.

'I will give you two minutes and no more – and remember that,' declared Clough.

'Right,' I said and began to ask my questions. Things were going fine, when suddenly it was brought to an abrupt halt after what, I guess, was about two minutes!

Clough jabbed his finger at the 'off' button on my tape recorder and said: "That's it. Hey, and that was a good 'out' young man.'

I don't mind admitting there was a fear element about interviewing him because you never knew quite how he was going to be and, in stark contrast, I recall a time when he INSISTED on being interviewed just 10 minutes before a match started!

I was working for Radio Two with the well-known football correspondent Bryon Butler. It was a Saturday afternoon at Nottingham Forest and we were getting on with our business when Cloughie appeared over our shoulders.

To say we were surprised would be an understatement. Given that his side kicked-off in around 10 minutes, we were gobsmacked!

'Do you want to do an interview?' he said with a grin.

'Well yes, but don't you want to be with your team Brian?' I said politely.

'Why would I want to be with them?' came the reply.

'Err well . . .'

'Well, do you want an interview or not?' he continued.

We had to get on to the studio, tell them what was happening and, naturally, agreed that we'd love to do one. So we interviewed Cloughie with his team running out onto the pitch.

❝ . . . Sacking me was a very bad day for Leeds United and a very bad day for football ❞

Sports reporter IAN EDWARDS covered Forest for the Nottingham Evening Post for four years and witnessed many sides of the club's charismatic boss. Here he gives an intriguing glimpse of how the man ticked.

40

BOOZE CONTROL

IAN EDWARDS

Sometimes Cloughie would make a point in such a witheringly funny way that it was as much as you could do to stop yourself laughing. But if he was determined to get his message over, which he inevitably was, then lo and behold anyone caught smirking or tittering.

I remember one day being down at the City Ground just hanging around to see if Cloughie was in or would see me when I bumped into Forest player Terry Wilson who I got on pretty well with. 'Wilse' was a smashing lad who liked going out and about on the town and enjoyed having a bevvy with his mates – nowt wrong with that for a healthy young footballer earning a few quid. The trouble was it hadn't escaped Cloughie's attention. Little did. It seemed his days at Forest could be numbered because although he was in the team and playing quite well, the manager had allowed him to go and talk to Norwich City.

Wilse had been down to Carrow Road and held talks and was a bit in limbo as to exactly where his future lay.

I was in an equally precarious state, wondering whether I would get a story this particular day. As per usual I asked Carole, Cloughie's secretary, if he was in and, more to the point, could he spare me five minutes.

Carole would normally pop in and make the request but she came back to inform me that he wasn't in his office. I started to worry that I would have to head back to my office without the notebook full of stuff you inevitably got when the master held court.

Wondering where my next story was coming from, he suddenly appeared, wearing the hallmark green rugby top. Cloughie was marching up the corridor with Wilse and about to give me the back page lead story I'd virtually abandoned hope of getting just a couple of minutes earlier.

'Hey, shithouse. This young man isn't going anywhere and you can put that in your paper!'

'Oh really? Is there any particular reason why . . .' I didn't get chance to finish the question.

'The reason this young man is staying here with me in Nottingham is that since news leaked out he might be off, I've had every licensed victualler, pub landlord and nightclub owner on the phone begging me not to let him leave!'

Wilse looked sheepishly at me, I had to stifle a chuckle and Clough just carried on making his point in his inimitable way.

'Oh yes, they reckon their profits would be down 50 per cent if he left. Hey and you can use that in the paper as well!'

Poor Wilse didn't know what to say or do and I had to wait until I'd got well out of sight before having a real chuckle to myself. He'd made his point.

❛ Who the hell wants to take 14 pairs of shoes on holiday? I haven't had 14 pairs in my life
- on the revelation of just what was in Victoria Beckham's missing luggage ❜

*As Notts County boss, NEIL WARNOCK plied his
trade just across the Trent. But, as he reveals here,
it was his young son James who got closer to
Clough on one memorable occasion.*

41

CALL ME BRIAN!

NEIL WARNOCK

My son James has good reason to remember Cloughie – even if he did give me a minor heart attack at the time. We were up at Forest for a game. I'm guessing it would have been a reserve match or something similar because I remember things about the place being a little more casual.

I'd taken James, who was then about four or five, to the game and had asked him to stand outside in the tunnel at half-time for just a couple of minutes. I had one or two choice words to say and most of them weren't meant for his delicate ears!

Anyway, I gave the lads a quick blast before opening the door to let James back in. He'd disappeared! Oh, my God, where could he have gone?

I raced down the tunnel towards the pitch to look there. No trace. I raced back up to the other end of the tunnel desperately asking anyone in the vicinity if they had a seen a little boy wandering about the place.

I was starting to panic. The second half was about to start, but that could wait – where the hell was James? As I got to the end of the corridor by Cloughie's office, my son has walked out looking like a contestant in Crackerjack. I kid you not, he's got about six Easter eggs in his arms, built up in a pile up to his chin.

'Where the hell have you been?' I asked

'I've been with Brian'

'Brian? Don't you mean Mr Clough,' I replied, mindful of just where I was.

'He said I can call him Brian,' insisted James.

'Oh did he? He doesn't even let me call him Brian,' I said, a huge grin cracking my face.

Talk about making an impression. My lad has grown up now but he has never ever forgotten that meeting.

❝ **When I got the sack at Leeds it hurt,
but I was financially sound for life and
that's a beautiful feeling** ❞

As one of Clough's truly great players VIV ANDERSON could never have imagined that one day he'd have to escape across back gardens and over open countryside to get away from his Forest boss.

42

THE LATE ESCAPE

VIV ANDERSON

I was at home recovering from a dislocated knee cap one afternoon when the phone went and I was informed that the manager wanted to see me at the ground.

'What for?' I asked.

'No idea,' came the reply, leaving me to stew on what I could have possibly done wrong.

When I got there my Forest team mate Mark Proctor was hanging around as well and, after a brief conversation, we were both at a loss as to why we'd been summoned to see the great man. Eventually we were called in and the gaffer outlined his plan.

'I want you two to go to Derby on loan and help Pete out there. He'd love you to go.'

I immediately had reservations. I got on well with Peter Taylor who was now in charge at Derby, but crossing the massive divide to Forest's archrivals wasn't something I really fancied at all.

'It's not for me, boss,' I said and Proc said that he'd rather fight for his place at Forest too.

'Right! Well you're going to have to tell him yourselves,' Cloughie

insisted before virtually bundling us into a waiting car. It was quite unbelievable.

Ronnie Fenton drove and we eventually got out to Pete's house which was in the middle of nowhere. To cut a long story short, Pete tried his best to sell the idea to us and said that we would be perfect to bring on some of his younger players. And he understood when we explained that, with no disrespect, it wasn't something either of us fancied.

It was all slightly embarrassing but after we were left hanging around in another room we asked the boss if we could get back now.

'You can find your own way home, the pair of yer,' Cloughie said, prompting us to ask Mrs Taylor if she could get us a cab. We were there another hour – no cab. Bear in mind that we had been 'kidnapped' at around 4pm and it was now a good five hours later. We'd had enough. Proc and myself agreed to make a run for it, said our goodbyes to Mrs Taylor and made our bid for freedom out across the garden.

It was absolutely pitch black by this time and there was us two clambering over fences and through prickles without a clue where we were going. Remember, I was just in the final throes of recovering from injury.

We carried on over the fields and eventually got to a village we had spotted in the distance. I'm guessing we walked four or five miles. We got to the village pub and decided to have a couple of beers and ring for a cab from there.

It also seemed like a good idea to ring home and explain where we were.

'Where the hell have you been until now?' came the understandable question.

'You really don't want to know. You wouldn't believe it,' was our just as understandable response!

And you know something, for all the escapades like that, he was revered by everyone who played for him. Clough and Taylor worked superbly together. They were the proverbial 'good cop, bad cop,' and life at Forest was never dull when those two were around.

Cloughie had a quite brilliant mind and a lot of his methods were totally revolutionary – that even includes his habit of demanding a kiss!

I was captain of Sheffield Wednesday when we played Forest at Hillsborough. I came off before the end of the pre-match warm up and noticed Cloughie sitting on his own in the dug-out. There was a group of fans congregating around the place. I was about to walk down the tunnel when he shouted at me.

'Oi! Come here.'

'Oh hello, Mr Clough. How are you?'

'Come here and give us a kiss,' he exclaimed.

I said I wasn't sure it was such a good idea with so many people around but he refused to take 'no' for an answer, so I had to walk over and give him a kiss on the cheek. Then I quickly scampered down the tunnel to get back to the business of preparing for a big football match. It could only happen with him . . .

' Players lose you games - not tactics. There's so much crap talked about tactics by people who couldn't win a game of dominoes '

*By his own admission LARRY LLOYD enjoyed a love-hate
relationship with his boss and it proved a costly business
at times as he squared up to the man, who scared the
living daylights out of most people.*

43

BLAZER-ING ROW

LARRY LLOYD

My most famous spat with Cloughie really hit the headlines and became known as 'The Great Blazer Row.' Two headstrong bastards locked horns head-on in Greece and it all ended up with me handing in a transfer request.

Half the trouble was that Cloughie simply had to have the last word – and that was something I wanted.

The whole business blew up the morning after we'd beaten AEK Athens in the 1978-79 European Cup campaign. Let me state here and now, that to this day I remain adamant I received no instruction to wear the club uniform that day. But when I got to the coach that was taking us to the airport all the lads, bar me, were wearing the blue blazer and grey slacks. Good old Lloydie is standing there in jeans and an open necked shirt. The thing was there was no one prouder than me in wearing the club uniform and I wouldn't have had a single problem with that – but I wasn't told. I even thought it was a wind-up, but Cloughie didn't see the funny side if it was.

'How come you're the odd one out?' said the gaffer with a scowl. 'Go and get changed.'

I couldn't because my clothes were in my case which had already been loaded onto the coach. Nothing more was said but it didn't take a genius to work out that the boss was far from happy.

Next day he handed me a 'Red Tree.' Club envelopes had Forest's red tree crest on them and whenever players were given one it was always referred to as getting a 'Red Tree.'

'What's this?'

Clough told me to open it when I got home but I just tore it open to discover I'd been fined £100 for breach of club discipline.

'I'm not paying it. I wasn't told.'

'That, Lloydie, has cost you another £100'

'Stick it.'

'Lloydie, every time you answer me back, your fine goes up a hundred.'

'Well let's call it a grand then because I've got plenty left to say,' I hissed.

Neither of us would give way and then he spitefully crossed my name off the team sheet. I sat on the bench and stewed over my future and then went in the next day determined to ask for a transfer.

But he'd gone away on one of his many Spanish holidays and so I ended up venting my spleen on Peter Taylor and the then chairman Stuart Dryden.

They calmed me down and it wasn't long before a compromise was reached – I would forget all talk of a transfer and all the other stuff, but I would pay the original fine. So there you go . . . I won, but it cost me a hundred quid! Work that one out . . .

I learned to handle things better after that. Yet, years later with hindsight, I think I desperately wanted him to be warmer with me rather than at loggerheads all the time.

Cloughie knew all players needed a pat on the back, yet he so rarely did that to me. He never said 'Well done, big fella' and that's something I craved. I ended up playing every week, but it's as if he felt he had to keep me at arm's length to get the very best out of me.

Occasionally he'd look at me and wink and that was about as good as it got. I felt ten feet tall if I just got an acknowledgement like that. It's odd really, because us two were at loggerheads virtually from the word go. The rows we had became legendary. But I find myself talking about him with increasing regard and it's not surprising really. He took me from being an out-of-favour player at Coventry to

being a king of Europe. For that, I'll be eternally grateful.

Strangely enough, I sensed from the word go that we might struggle to get on. I knew nothing about him really – he was just some mouthy git off TV and I thought 'I don't know if I fancy this guy,' when it became clear that he wanted to sign me.

But, you know. He was a clever bastard from the very first time we met and it sticks in my mind all these years later.

Bear in mind Forest were mid-table in the Second Division and a move to them didn't appeal to me a great deal. He sensed that, so turned it around to make out like I was in control!

He told me that what he would really like was to take me on loan for a month saying: 'It's not about us having a look at you, it's about you having a look at us.'

And that's how it all started. Clough took me from a downward spiral of being surplus to requirements at Coventry to become one of the most fined players in Nottingham Forest history! But, boy oh boy, there was some fun and no little success around the corner.

Coventry boss Gordon Milne reckoned big raw-boned centre halves were going out of fashion. Really!

Clough believed he could do something with a gobby, hot-headed rebel who was in great danger of becoming a has-been. For that I am thankful.

❛ Don't send me flowers when I'm dead. If you like me, send me some when I'm alive ❜

*Not doing things the Clough-way was never advisable,
especially if you were out on the pitch. KENNY BURNS
found out to his cost when he dared defy the
principles everyone was expected to stick by.*

44

PASS THE CASH

KENNY BURNS

I was once fined £50 for making a square pass across the face of my own box – can you honestly imagine any of the modern day pros putting up with that!

The gaffer based everything he preached on simplicity and when I did something he considered to be totally at odds with that philosophy, he came down heavily on me.

Only Cloughie could do it and get away with it. We were playing Manchester City when I received the ball on the edge of our box. Peter Shilton had come so far out that it shocked me and so I attempted to hit the ball right across the box to Frank Clark. I didn't get quite enough height on it and City striker Dennis Tueart intercepted it. Fortunately it went out for a goal kick. We were in the dressing room at half-time and nothing was said about it. The boss turns to Liam O'Kane and says 'Go and get that done.'

He came back and handed me a fine of £50 with Cloughie barking at me. It was so that I'd learn never to do it again. I just accepted it and that was it.

No player, no matter how big a name, was exempt from pouring the tea – we'd all get our turn at it and never questioned it.

And the boss was just incredible for giving the players time to rest. Quite often we'd play on the Saturday and then he would tell us not to come in until the Thursday.

'If I find anyone has been training, I'll fine him!' he'd shout. That was the beauty of Clough. Some top coaches think they have to run the arse off you every day, but he could see absolutely no sense in that at all.

**❛ I don't want any epitaphs of profound history
and all that type of nonsense. I would just
hope they'd say I contributed and
that somebody liked me ❜**

Sometimes there's just no shaking off Old Big 'Ead as former Derby and Forest player BARRY BUTLIN discovered. But here he reveals how it took Clough years to win over his missus.

45

TROUBLE AND STRIFE

BARRY BUTLIN

Cloughie honestly believed his charm and charisma could win anyone over – but he hadn't counted on my missus! True to form, he did win her over, but it took him a fair few years and a bunch of flowers that came hurtling back at him.

Jackie and I had only been married a couple of weeks when I was injured in a training ground accident following a collision with my Derby team-mate Steve Powell. We clashed heads and I ended up in hospital with a depressed fracture of the cheek.

'Leave him alone, there's nowt wrong with him,' Clough shouted as I lay on the floor. Three hours later . . . I woke up in hospital.

Jackie was expecting me home, so had become a bit worried. Bear in mind, mobile phones were a thing of the future and so, growing increasingly concerned, she walked to the Baseball Ground. In those days we got changed at the ground and took a bus up to the training pitch at Sinfin Lane.

Gordon Guthrie, the kitman, informed her: 'He's had a bit of an accident.'

'Accident? Where is he?'

'He's up at the hospital . . .'

'Hospital?' My wife can be fiery and she was in no mood for any more of this nonsense. She marched towards the dressing room to get my clothes that were still hanging there when she bumped into . . . Cloughie.

'Hey young lady, where do you think you're going?'

'I'm picking my husband's clothes up – he's had an accident,' she said, clearly not happy.

'Hey, I'll tell you when he's had an accident!' Cloughie replied. Big mistake – and he knew it. I guess it played on his mind because he sent a big bunch of flowers – which my missus sent back because of his attitude.

Anyway, years later we were at Jimmy Sirrell's 80th birthday party when Brian came in, clearly not well, and took his seat. He was on sticks and struggling with ill health.

We went over to say hello and he made such a fuss and gave Jackie a kiss. My wife just melted because she appreciated what a massive effort he'd made to get there when he was visibly suffering quite badly health-wise. The old bugger had done it – but it had taken him a bit longer than usual!

*   *   *

How ironic that I should end up scoring the goal which proved to be the final straw in Cloughie's ill-fated 44-day spell at Leeds. I played under Brian for eight years and he ended up selling me twice. Our paths always seemed to cross. But they positively collided that day – September 7, 1974.

I was playing for Luton who had just been promoted to the top flight and we were playing Leeds at Elland Road. Cloughie's controversial reign there hadn't got off to the best of starts. This was his sixth match in charge and so far he'd managed just one win. Mighty Leeds were near the bottom of the table and the pressure was well and truly on.

The crowd, who had been used to nothing but success in recent years, were baying for blood and the newspapers were having a field day with Brian's struggle to turn things around and win over the Leeds faithful.

Allan Clarke put them ahead to ease the jitters temporarily but I, of all peo-ple, helped myself to the equaliser and the game finished up 1-1.

I remember being one of the last out of the dressing room because I was trying to avoid him. It could have been a bit embarrassing.

When I eventually emerged, Cloughie was surrounded by reporters quizzing him on his position at the club.

I tripped out gingerly, kind of hoping I wouldn't be spotted, but Brian clocked me. Suddenly he breezed through this bunch of reporters and headed towards me.

'Hey, what a great goal,' he says, turning back to face the press boys.

'You lot should pack up talking about my position and give a mention to this lad's great goal!'

Much as I might have liked that, there wasn't really much chance. This was Leeds' worst start in 15 years and Clough was only days from being out of a job.

Pretty quickly I changed clubs – Allan Brown signing me to join Nottingham Forest. Brown wouldn't be in charge that much longer . . . in comes BRIAN CLOUGH!

❛ We used to go the pictures every Saturday night but we had to leave a little bit early and get home to watch Match of the Day. To this day my missus complains that she's missed the last five minutes of every film we saw ❜

*When Clough was pestered by two scruffy kids at a
North East hotel he took matters into his own hands
and here ex-Forest defender JIM McINALLY
recounts a remarkable story.*

46

CHIPS A LA CARTE

JIM McINALLY

Two scruffy little kids got more than they bargained for when they were pestering the players for autographs one day. The team was playing up in Newcastle and after tea at our hotel we all went out for a walk - a favourite exercise of Cloughie's. There were these two filthy, dirty kids running in and out of the foyer and generally being a bit of a nuisance to the hotel manager. They were probably about nine or ten and were really grubby little scallywags who looked like they hadn't been near water in years. To say they could have done with a good scrub would be something of an understatement.

Anyway, they were dashing in and out of reception, making a racket as kids do and generally making themselves very unpopular with the hotel boss.

He was basically telling them to bugger off when Cloughie intervened. You can say what you like about the gaffer, he loved kids and he'd always stick up for the underdog and he felt the hotel manager perhaps wasn't being as understanding as he might be.

'Get off home the pair of yer,' he said, before Cloughie came up with one of his own inimitable solutions.

'Hey, you two, listen. If you come back in the morning, I'll sort it for you to get all the autographs you want and some photos with the players alright?'

'Ta Brian,' came the reply.

'I'll give you Brian, it's Mr Clough to you,'

'Ta, Mr Clough,' said the two urchins agreeing to run along and return in the morning. The hotel manager smiled and nodded, seemingly happy that the problem of the unruly little scruffs had been sorted . . . for now.

In the morning they were back, as if there was ever a doubt they wouldn't be, and as dirty as ever. They were in exactly the same clothes as they'd been in the previous day and they were just as grubby. They must have slept in the stuff they had on, but that didn't deter Cloughie from his next mischievous suggestion. The players were just about to go in for our lunchtime meal and the gaffer made the two lads an offer which must have had the hotel boss tearing his hair out.

'Hey, come and eat with us. The

pair of you look like you could do with a good meal!'

The gaffer guided them in to where we were all eating and tossed them an a la carte menu telling them they could have whatever they wanted.

'Just chips, Brian,' they both insisted. Bless 'em, I don't think they'd probably had much other than chips in their entire lives.

It was just so funny seeing these two poor little kids, sitting with the entire team and the one and only Brian Clough with menus in their hands. I could imagine them going to school and telling the teacher what had happened and getting a clip around the ear for telling lies!

Cloughie saw that they were given a day to remember after asking me to phone their mother and tell them that they were being looked after.

'We haven't got a phone,' one of them insisted, which wasn't that sur-prising. I ended up ringing an auntie, trying to explain that they were with the Nottingham Forest football team, being treated royally and were last seen ordering chips off the a la carte menu!

Incredible, but there's an even more bizarre twist to the tale.

Years later I was in a newsagent's shop owned by the Clough family when the young man serving behind the counter looked at me and smiled as if he knew me. I nodded back so as not to appear rude.

'You don't remember me do you?'

'Your face looks familiar,' I tried, vying for time.

'I met you a few years ago. Remember the two young lads . . . I was one of them.'

How bizarre. Cloughie, you can only presume, had kept in touch with the families and helped the youngsters out financially over all those years.

❛ Me, walk on water? There's one or two people out there saying instead of walking on it I should take more of it with my drinks. Hey, and they're absolutely right ❜

Life at Leeds proved tortuous for Cloughie and, as his first Elland Road signing DUNCAN McKENZIE explains, finding a friend was something he had found increasingly hard to do.

47

IN THE WEE SMALL HOURS

DUNCAN McKENZIE

It was a late night phone call in my hotel room which rammed home to me just how badly Clough needed an ally at Leeds. Things were going badly wrong and just how isolated he was becoming was apparent that night in the Dragonara Hotel.

Clough and I were both staying there and had returned late one night having just flown back from a testimonial game for Ted Bates in Southampton. God knows what time we had got in to Leeds-Bradford airport but needless to say it was the early hours and I couldn't wait to hit the sack.

I was knackered and had just dropped off when the phone in my room started to ring. Who the hell could it be?

'It's Cloughie here. I want you down here in reception in five minutes.'

I couldn't believe my ears, but was not really in a position to argue no matter how unorthodox the request. I threw some water on my face, chucked some clothes on and made my way down to see the gaffer. His opening statement was stunning . . .

'Don't you ever get off the plane in that condition again young man.'

'What do you mean?'

'You were drunk.'

'Drunk? I was sober – I don't even drink,' I exclaimed.

'Well you do now. Tea or coffee?' Cloughie continued.

And, despite what some people might think, it was tea and the pair of us sat in a deserted lounge chatting.

He wanted someone to talk to. A good manager can't afford to have too many friends among the players, but Clough could count his on one hand and still cut a few fingers off.

He wanted me to give him an insight into what was being said about the place. I suppose you could say he wanted me to divulge some of the private conversations and that was something that I wasn't prepared to do.

'I'd like you to mark me card,' was the expression he used. 'At lunchtime you were sitting with those lovely people like Paul Reaney and Terry Cooper. What were they saying?'

I told him most of the conversations were just the usual small talk. Just everyday stuff. I also told him that I wouldn't have told him if he had been the main subject of conversation.

I understood why he was asking and with me being his signing it wasn't unreasonable to assume I was on his side to some extent.

But I would never tell tales and made him have no doubts about that. The truth was that he was virtually the sole topic of conversation. His unorthodox methods were the total opposite from what the players had been used to under Don Revie. Dossiers on the opposition were the order of the day, now they had a man who didn't mention the opposition or give team talks. Some of them thought he was barmy.

Clough was different, possibly too different at the time and there were some serious issues bubbling under.

The Leeds players just weren't ready for the whirlwind which had been unleashed on them in Clough. The mutiny was under way and there was no way I wanted to get involved in any of it, not least passing information back to the gaffer.

Things were bad – very bad. Clough's ability – and suitability – was being called into question. The tension got so bad that the coach Syd Owen, who had been Revie's right-hand man, was even heckling Clough from the back of the room during an address to the players. Every time Clough said anything like he wasn't going to tell them where to stand for corners, he would sigh and mumble 'What a load of rubbish!' Cloughie could hear every word. He was siding with the players and clearly undermining the manager's authority.

You didn't have to be a genius to work out that there were those at the club who just didn't want him there at any price.

Things had to come to a head, but no one could have expected that it would all happen quite so soon . . .

6 A foreman was almost certainly on the shop floor; a bus inspector once drove a bus, but how many FA officials have ever been footballers? 9

*The principles of coaching were easy to Cloughie
and, as right-hand man ALAN HILL recalls, he
couldn't understand why everyone else
seemed to complicate matters.*

48

SIMPLE AS ABC

ALAN HILL

When he first asked me to work for him, I was working at Derby. We agreed everything and he said to me: 'Now young man, watch, listen, learn and ask questions.'

I don't mind admitting he half-scared me to death. He just had that way about him which was quite intimidating. After about four weeks, I plucked up the courage to ask him a question.

'Gaffer . . . what are your thoughts on coaching?'

'Don't fucking talk to me about coaching,' came the reply.

'You told me to ask questions,' I said.

'Right then, I'm only going to say this once, so make sure you get it.'

I nodded and waited for the great man to pass on parts of the coaching masterplan that he used. And he did.

'Right, well the goalkeeper is there to stop the ball going in the net. Then you have full backs to defend. Centre halves head the ball, preferably in the opposite direction to your goal. Midfield players pass it and if you can possibly get yourself a centre-forward who comes up with a few goals, then that's as much as you need to know about coaching. Got it?'

And you know what? For all the simplicity of that answer it was his philosophy. Coaches who went on for hours with chalkboards and detailed graphs drove him bonkers. He believed that you just got players to do jobs and the rest, with his own unique style of man management, would hopefully fall into place.

* * *

The gaffer's madcap sense of humour had us rolling around in stitches one day when we were invited to pop into his office. Well, actually, we were told, but couldn't have imagined the sight waiting for us when the office door swung open.

I was having a chat with coach Liam O'Kane when the gaffer shouted out: 'Come and get your arses over here!'

As we approached the door of the gaffer's office, it gently swung open and there was a surprise occupant of the manager's chair.

It was Del Boy, Cloughie's faithful golden retriever, sitting upright behind the desk with the gaffer's cloth cap perched on his head. Cloughie was laughing and we just burst into fits as well.

'There, see, told ya. Anybody could manage this club!' he said.

He loved that dog. The ironic thing was that Del Boy was the only one who could take not a blind bit of notice and get away with it.

Del Boy ended up going everywhere with him. He was his constant companion and would often be beside him at training or sitting by his desk looking suitably unimpressed.

Like I said, the gaffer had this air about him that could frighten people to death, but he was a softie with Del Boy because the dog didn't give a hoot who he was. He would shout at him, but he took barely any notice at all. Perhaps that was the key to it. Del Boy the dog discovered the formula and got closer than most to discovering just what made Brian Clough tick. And he could keep a secret . . .

6 I adore roast beef and Yorkshire pudding but you don't want it every night and twice on a Sunday do you?
- on too much football on television 9

Picture: Derby Evening Telegraph

Stark contrast . . . Chairman Sam Longson welcomes Clough and Taylor to the Baseball Ground.

It ends in tears . . . protestors make their feelings known after the pair's shock resignation.

Clough meets Derby's players for the first time while (left) it's arrival time for new signing Roy McFarland as his new boss shows him around the Baseball Ground

At his Baseball Ground desk in 1968.

All mine . . . Clough admires the League Championship trophy

The kids are all right . . . Clough with sons Nigel and Simon in 1968
and (below) larking around with a local cub pack.

*Stars in his eyes. Sock it man . . . Clough shakes hands with Muhammad Ali.
Rocket Man . . . pop superstar Elton John seems wary while legendary
Dutch superstar Johan Cruyff sees the funny side of it all.*

The beautiful game . . . Cloughie shows he has an eye for talent as he acts as a judge at a local beauty contest.

The last bus . . . Nottingham Evening Post photographer Steve Mitchell captured this magical shot of a clearly choked Clough giving, and getting, the thumbs up from fans as he boards the team bus for the very last time at Ipswich.

Master chef Cloughie tries to cook up some cash for charity

Champs . . . Forest's players parade the League Championship trophy and the League Cup.

You beauty . . . Trevor Bartlett's stunning picture of Forest keeper Peter Shilton with the European Cup.

Kings of Europe . . . Forest players celebrate after winning the 1979 European Cup in Munich.

Pictures: Nottingham Evening Post

Like father, like son . . . Scot Gemmill signs on for Cloughie just like dad Archie(left) had done years previously. Nigel Clough looks on to complete the family double act.

Forest players can't help but smile as Cloughie shows the easiest way to get the ball under control.

The board room is that way young man . . .
Cloughie shows Robin Hood the way to do it.

That's my boy . . . Trevor Bartlett's lovely picture of Del and Cloughie.

*Nottingham Evening Post journalist TREVOR FRECKNALL
had something of a bumpy start to his relationship
with Clough. The Forest boss banned him
from the ground on his very first day!*

49

HELLO – YOU'RE BARRED!

TREVOR FRECKNALL

Having Brian Clough literally kicking your backside and yelling 'You're banned,' is hardly an ideal start to your first day covering a football club for the local paper. Not the best of introductions, as you can imagine, though I must say it was all remarkably civil!

My newspaper – the Nottingham Evening Post – had become the focal point of the National Union of Journalists' strike back in 1979. To cut a long story short, there had been a national pay dispute the outcome of which was that 28 Post journalists had lost their jobs. Among them was John Lawson who had become close to Cloughie covering Forest for the newspaper.

The strike had made national headlines and the fact it was happening right on staunch socialist Clough's doorstep, put the whole business all the more in the spotlight.

So, my introduction to him was always going to be interesting. The meeting was set up by the chairman Stuart Dryden. I was ushered into his office to await the manager.

I explained to Brian that I was the new sports editor and, to his credit, he listened to everything I had to say.

Then he explained that being a very close friend of John's and a staunch supporter of the Labour Party, he couldn't work with me. So he promptly escorted me to the door and said: 'Don't take this personally, Trevor, because I think under any other circumstances me and you could have got on just fine. Hey, just remember, all life's a game.'

I probably gave him a slightly perplexed look. I don't know . . . what was I supposed to say?

'Hey, and you just remember that I'm playing the game to win as well,' I replied.

'Good lad,' he said. 'Now, fuck off!'

And then he promptly stuck his boot into my backside and barked: 'You're banned! Tara.'

So, it's little surprise really that all these years later, I have a pretty good recall of our very first meeting.

I was supposed to be banned from the entire ground but the Forest committee realised that being at loggerheads with the city's evening newspaper wasn't a prospect they were entirely happy with. Although some football clubs would have you believe that they don't need the local paper, it's always interesting if ever that gets put to the test. How do they tell fans where to get tickets for certain matches? Bear in mind these were pre-internet days. People tended to look to the local paper for club news and information and so keeping myself and the Post entirely in the cold wasn't really an option.

An unspoken compromise was reached. I took up a seat in the committee's box with the stipulation that I stayed in there and out of sight until His Lordship, as they called him, had left the ground.

One Saturday, I thought the coast was clear and started to make my way out of the ground. There was a small gathering of national newspaper reporters, known as the Midlands Mafia, in a huddle clearly discussing a line to a story they had picked up. What I didn't realise was that John Wragg of the Daily Express was inadvertently shielding Cloughie. Wraggy must be six feet four and I didn't have a clue that Clough was there. Suddenly a voice boomed out of the group.

'Oi, you're fucking banned,' on which Clough grabbed a pen off one of the reporters and hurled it at me. It quite literally exploded as it hit the wall behind me and shattered. I made a less than dignified exit with Clough pointing me towards the exit doors.

But, you know, we went on to strike up a good relationship and I was extremely blessed to be the sports editor of a paper in a city where so much was happening.

These were the real glory years as far as Forest were concerned, just across the river Notts County were going well and over the road we had Nottinghamshire County Cricket, Richard Hadlee and all, plus Test matches. It was sporting heaven in many ways.

And one of my all time great memories was being on the team bus as it pulled out of the big gates at Wembley holding the Littlewoods Cup aloft.

Forest had beaten Luton and Cloughie had presented the cup to me and urged me to show it to the fans waiting outside. I gave it a quick shake and I'll bet the supporters were wondering who the hell I was.

Not bad for a guy who who'd had his arse kicked the first time we'd met 10 years earlier!

❛ People said you could drop off the end of the world there. Sometimes I wished I had
- on going to Hartlepool ❜

*Former Tottenham and England boss TERRY VENABLES
gives the inside track on just why he and Cloughie
came out holding hands for their epic
1991 FA Cup final clash at Wembley.*

50

HELPING HAND

TERRY VENABLES

The pictures of Brian and me holding hands as we led our teams out for the FA Cup final at Wembley have gone down in the competition's folklore. Because of everything that happened subsequently – not least Paul Gascoigne being stretchered off – our hand-in-hand entrance from the tunnel has never really been fully explained. Well, here goes . . .

I'd always had a lot of time for Brian, mainly because he always made me laugh. He was a very funny, warm guy and I found his whole demeanour very engaging.

Fate threw us together on that warm afternoon in 1991 and a lot of the media build-up to the game had been based around the fact that the FA Cup was the one trophy to have eluded Brian in all his trophy-laden years in the game.

We were waiting to get the nod to go out of the tunnel on that famous walk in front of our teams and it's an exhilarating feeling because you know once you step out into view, the eyes of zillions of people all over the world are going to be on you.

You could hear the crowd waiting out there in the stadium and Cloughie leans towards me and says: 'Terry, how are you?'

'Fine, Brian, how are you?'

'You've got to hold my hand – I'm feeling nervous.'

'YOU nervous? You're kidding me!'

'No, I'm not actually.'

I thought he was winding me up, but as we started to make the walk, and unbeknown to me, Cloughie grabbed me with a vice-like grip and wouldn't let go.

I tried to free my hand a couple of times but in the end just carried on with it. I wondered what people would think, the pair of us waltzing out to meet Lady Di holding hands.

But as it turned out, it proved to be a nice touch that a lot of people seem to have remembered.

❛ I'm dealing with my drinking problem and I have a reputation for getting things done ❜

51

WIMBLE-DONE

JOHN McGOVERN

A day out at Wimbledon for the tennis will stick with me forever as underlining just how unpredictable Cloughie was.

I loved tennis and was desperate to go to Wimbledon when I got wind of the fact that the gaffer had tickets. I went to see him and asked him if there was any chance of going along. Imagine my delight when he said I could join him.

'Hey, but I want you turned out immaculately.'

Not a problem . . . so I duly turned up having put a smart shirt on and making sure that, as requested, I was suitably dressed for a lovely day down in SW19.

Imagine my horror when the boss turned up in a shabby blue England tracksuit top with the badge half hanging off and baggy white shorts.

Just for good measure he had his socks rolled down over a pair of scruffy, scuffed trainers and he was carrying a squash racquet.

I didn't know which way to look as he breezed around the public galleries swinging his squash racquet and generally seeming oblivious to the dress code he'd imposed on me.

I've got to say despite all that, it was an absolute honour and education to play for the man. Cloughie was like a comet blazing a trail through the sky. He just burned so brightly and maybe, just maybe, he burnt himself out at the end.

You find that can happen to a genius. George Best and Hurricane Higgins were supremely gifted in their own field and yet they burned out too quickly.

Clough was a genius. Let no one tell you any differently. His like will never be seen again.

❛ If God had wanted us to play football in the clouds he'd have put grass up there
- on the importance of passing to feet ❜

Former Forest star PAUL HART recalls how a magnificent Clough gesture helped ease the pain as he lay in hospital wondering if his career was over after breaking his leg.

52

KIND HART-ED

PAUL HART

I once witnessed Brian Clough's unbelievable thoughtfulness first hand as I was lying in a hospital bed wondering whether my career as a professional footballer was over.

I'd spent two years under the gaffer – I still call him that – at Forest but had moved on to pastures new. I'd had a brief spell at Sheffield Wednesday and then moved on to Birmingham City.

On the day in question I'd shattered my leg just 38 minutes into my debut for Birmingham and things weren't looking good. It was New Year's Day and it's fair to say I was feeling pretty depressed.

New Year's Day or not, suddenly I found myself surrounded by loads of my former Forest team-mates. Clough had heard the news that I'd been taken to hospital with a badly broken leg on the radio and diverted the team to come and see me.

There I was lying on my back, not knowing whether my career was over having suffered a double compound fracture and in strolled a bunch of lads I'd not seen for a while.

How magnificent a gesture was that? I'll never forget it and that is the measure of the man for me. I only had two years with him, but I wish it had been a lot more.

Don't get me wrong – he destroyed me at times and you just had to learn to take it. But he was the genuine article – a genius.

PS: The gaffer didn't come in to see me that day. He had this thing about injured players, hospitals, crutches etc and you can only speculate that he couldn't bear to be reminded of how his own career was cut short by injury.

❛ When I signed Peter Shilton, Stoke's chairman said he was brilliant but he would get me the sack. I told him straight 'He's not that fucking brilliant!' ❜

*Legendary keeper PETER SHILTON discovered
early on that when it came to negotiating with
Clough, nothing was ever as straightforward
as it might appear.*

53

FINANCIAL RACQUET

PETER SHILTON

Clough had little or no time for agents, financial advisers and their kind. I was left in no doubt about his take on them the day I went to see him in his office at the City Ground just prior to signing in September, 1977.

I was one of the first players to have advisors representing me and Clough made a point of letting them know in no uncertain terms that he couldn't be doing with them. I had two guys there to look after my side of the transfer after Forest had made an official approach to Stoke City. My two advisers had smart pinstripe suits on and when Cloughie turned up he was decked out in scruffy trainers and a rugby top. We hung about outside his offices for what must have been well over an hour until we were summoned.

I motioned them to go in first and that I would follow, which was probably just as well given what happened next. Clough burst out laughing as the pair of them were sent sprawling across the floor, their briefcases flying everywhere.

I couldn't believe what I was seeing and just stood there with my jaw hang-ing down. Clough had been hiding to one side of the door and as my two friends walked in he had angled a squash racquet across their path and tripped the pair of them. I have no idea if he'd done it to try and gain some psychological advantage right from the word go or whether it was just a prank. It certainly threw them out of their stride – quite literally.

When we eventually sat down to discuss my personal terms it turned into a bit of a disaster. Clough seemed totally disinterested to the point of appearing to ignore a lot of what was being said.

As my advisors outlined a particular point, Clough would stare at the ceiling while beating the squash racquet against the side of his leg.

Things just went from bad to worse until Clough brought the meeting to a close saying something to the effect of it was all a waste of time and he was going to go for a meal!

I left the meeting totally bewildered and it crossed my mind that perhaps the move wouldn't go through even though Stoke and Forest had agreed a fee of £250,000.

A few days later the phone went and it was Clough who said he wanted to see me – on my own – at a local hotel. I was desperate for the move to happen and when I got there, Clough and Peter Taylor were waiting for me with a bottle of champagne.

The deal was as good as done after all the shenanigans with the squash racquet. I ended up having the best five years of my career at Forest.

The most common thing you will hear people say about Brian Clough is that he was a bully. It's perhaps significant that you never hear that said by anyone who played for him. If he had bullied the players at Forest we would never have gone out and given him our all on the pitch. Without exception we gave him 100 per cent.

Yes, he could be awkward, confrontational and controversial but he could also be very understanding and compassionate.

He had this image, which everyone picked up on but he was a quite incredible man-manager.

He had a knack of keeping things uncomplicated. His philosophy was that football was a simple game and he asked that his team play it that way.

You never saw Clough with complicated dossiers outlining opponents' strengths and weaknesses. Clough and Taylor concentrated on their own players and if they wanted to make a point they never seemed to have too many problems getting it over!

❛ It should be a rule that if a chairman sacks a manager he appointed in the first place, then he should bloody well go as well ❜

Ex Forest, Manchester United and England striker
PETER DAVENPORT recounts a long-distance taxi ride
that revealed how fear of the gaffer went way
beyond the confines of the City Ground.

54

HE'S BEHIND YOU!

PETER DAVENPORT

If ever anyone needed an illustration into just how Cloughie instinctively struck fear into anyone, then this story really takes some beating.

I was in talks about a new contract. My mum and dad had been to watch the game one Saturday and after the match the gaffer invited us all up to his lovely house in Quarndon for a bite to eat. The gaffer loved my mum and dad and always made a huge fuss and they were quite impressed getting the invite up to his family home. The only problem was that they had come down from Liverpool on the train and as the chatting went on and on, they were getting increasingly anxious that they needed to make their way to Derby railway station.

I remember Dad insisting they were going to have to get on their way otherwise they would miss their last connection – but Cloughie was having none of it!

By this time, dad was starting to panic until in the end Cloughie came up with the solution – a cab – all the way back to Liverpool. Mum and dad kept saying it wasn't necessary but the gaffer was having none of it. He'd get a cab sorted and the problem was solved. Meanwhile . . . my contract.

But the fun and games really started when Cloughie clocked the poor cabbie who had pulled up on the drive to take us home! The fella had a fag in his mouth which was a huge mistake. The boss zoomed in.

'Hey scruffy bugger, get that out of your mouth for a start off. These nice people here are Mr and Mrs Davenport and they don't smoke.'

I can still see the stunned look on the driver's face as he abandoned any attempt to answer and just nodded.

'This young man here is Peter Davenport. He's one of my footballers at Nottingham Forest and he certainly doesn't smoke. So for the purposes of this journey, scruffy bugger, you don't smoke either. Got it!'

The poor cabbie nodded and Cloughie waved us off on our way back to Merseyside having done another brilliant job on mum and dad in his efforts to keep me at the club.

Once we had gone a little way, my dad said to the cabbie that if he wanted to have a smoke, just wind the window down a little and feel free to have a fag.

'I'd better not – he'll find out,' insisted the cabbie.

'Ah, you're okay. There's only us in here and we won't say anything,' dad assured him.

'He'll still find out,' said the petrified driver. I think then mum and dad really saw first hand the daunting presence of Clough.

❛ Some stupid people questioned me spending all that money on Peter Shilton. But I'll tell you one thing - a team with only an OK goalkeeper is always looking over its shoulder ❜

*During Clough's Forest years no one got closer than
freelance journalist JOHN LAWSON. The two became
close friends all through the great trophy-laden
years and remained so after his retirement.*

55

LET'S WORK

JOHN LAWSON

First impressions, they say, can often be misleading. And sometimes they can provide a rich insight into what the future holds.

The latter certainly applied in January 1975 when Brian Clough ceased to be a mere television and newspaper figure in my fledgling journalistic career.

Working as Forest's correspondent for the Nottingham Evening Post, I'd started with Matt Gillies, had some very pleasant times with Dave Mackay and some often bewildering ones with Allan Brown. None of them were very taxing but then along came Brian Howard Clough.

Bearing in mind Nottingham Forest's parlous Second Division state, I have never before seen so many media representatives assembled at the City Ground on the day he arrived on Trentside.

Wisely or not, I felt I had to make an impact in the Press conference that followed and hit the new manager with a barrage of questions.

After about the third or fourth he stopped me in my tracks for the first of many times and rather pointedly inquired as to whether I was from the local paper.

At least I had got my instant recognition – I also got my first bollocking. "Keep your mouth shut and I'll see you in my office later when this rabble have left," he bellowed. Can't argue with that, I thought.

You might think that was mission accomplished but the first week of our relationship was something of the roller-coaster ride that was about to hit the rails for the following 18 years.

His first order was to get back to my office and tell (not ask, you might note) the Sports Editor I was going away with him and the team to Bisham Abbey in Berkshire on a 'getting to know you' few days.

It would be accurate to use the words lead and balloon to describe how that request went down. But the Sports Editor relented and I was on my way to Bisham Abbey and the small matter of an FA Cup third round replay at Tottenham for his first match and a game the following Saturday against Fulham at Craven Cottage.

It's history now that Scotland striker Neil Martin craned his neck to score the goal that gave the great man an unexpected lift-off at White Hart Lane and on the way to Bisham Abbey and in the hours that followed I lay in wait for the opportunity to get the exclusive copy that would keep my twitchy bosses happy.

Vince Wilson, who has made what I am sure will be a knowledgable and informed contribution elsewhere (chapter 32) was Clough's 'ghost writer' at the time and was the only other journalist around.

Vince's paper, the Sunday Mirror, was paying Brian handsomely for his words and I rapidly began to wonder where the hell the Evening Post copy would fit into the equation.

The hours and the drinks passed and it was around 2am that I plucked up courage to break into their conversation and ask: 'Is there any chance of me having a quick word yet, Brian?'

'Can you hear him, Vince... I think he's got an empty back page.'

That was only part of the story. The reality was that there was a sizeable space on the front page as well as the back and, if you're interested, there was a gaping hole on the remainder of the sports coverage as Nottingham waited to feast on his incomparable words.

I cannot remember what time it was when his embargo ended – I think it was well after three o'clock. But eventually he turned to me and said: 'Young man (which I was in those days), let's work.'

We only 'worked' for about ten minutes on that occasion but I got enough copy to last me most of the week, which is just as well because he spent the remainder of it trying to knock centre-half John Cottam into shape by playing non-stop tennis with him.

But the week ended well when Barry Butlin scored the goal that gave him a second successive victory over Fulham. Happy days.

I worked closely with him for the following 18 years and in the years between him leaving Forest and his sad passing in 2004 but, unlike some of my contemporaries, I never felt the need to burst into print and abuse our relationship or friendship.

I could probably recount more stories about him than any other journalist – but I'm much happier that they stay as wonderful memories. I'm a lot richer for that.

6 Most directors are shithouses and backstabbers who would have given Julius Caesar a good going over 9

The day might have started normally but little did Derby Evening Telegraph sports writer GERALD MORTIMER know that he was about to play a key role in footballing history.

56

TYPING DUTIES

GERALD MORTIMER

A Monday morning in October had not given any indication that I would end up playing my own small part in football history. Who would have thought that some hours later I would be typing out the resignation letters of both Brian Clough and Peter Taylor?

I had made my way to the Baseball Ground that day with the main priority being to get a preview for England's World Cup qualifying game against Poland. It was becoming increasingly obvious that the relationship between Clough and Taylor on one hand, and the Derby County board on the other, was becoming more and more strained.

Quite how bad it had become did not emerge until I was actually at the ground. Once there, you could sense something was seriously wrong, but even then no one could have predicted how the events of the day would unfold.

Spending hours of your day waiting for Cloughie was nothing new to me or anyone who knew him. Usually it was worth it and, quite often, it was fun.

I must admit with hindsight, the lot of a journalist covering the town's team seemed a lot more fun in those days. Being an 'insider' back then really meant that. There was little or no distance between the management, the players and yourself.

This was to be one of those days when you breezed into the ground before lunch and emerged nine or ten hours later to discover there was a real world out there. But by any standards this was to be an astonishing day.

The situation was hard to credit. In 1971-72 the Rams had won the League Championship for the first time in their history and had then gone on to reach the semi-finals of the European Cup before they were beaten – and cheated – by Juventus.

Now, 18 months after the title and six months after the European Cup campaign had ended, the board wanted the most successful management team in the club's history out.

If the reasoning was difficult to understand then, time has done nothing to make the board's thinking appear more rational.

There were two directors digging in. One was the chairman Sam Longson and the other was Jack Kirkland. Longson, who ran a haulage business in Chapel-en-le-Frith, liked to think of himself as the club's great benefactor and had been instrumental in appointing Clough.

For four years Longson could not do enough for Clough and treated him like a son.

But he became increasingly irritated by the stir which followed Clough's outspoken and controversial comments to the press and television.

Clough, articulate and potentially explosive, had become the darling of the media. He enjoyed the publicity and the fuss he created by attacking administrators, chairmen and other clubs.

Longson fancied a place on the League management committee and believed Clough's outspoken views were jeopardising his chances. Other chairmen had begun questioning him on why he could not control Clough, but it never dawned on Longson that very few had heard of him until he appointed his talented and successful management duo. Suddenly two very stubborn people were locking horns.

To say I was close to what was happening might be an understatement! Clough got me to listen in to his conversation with Longson on an extension down the way. Can you honestly imagine that kind of thing happening today with the likes of Sir Alex Ferguson or Arsene Wenger?

'Pick that one up,' Clough urged me. 'Just listen to this – it's incredible.'

Longson was installed at his home and was insisting he wouldn't be coming back to the ground. I couldn't help thinking it didn't seem that important to him.

The upshot was that Clough and Taylor decided to quit and because all the secretaries had gone home by this time, I was judged to be the most proficient at getting my way around a typewriter keyboard.

And so it happened that me, the local newspaper journalist, who should endeavour to be as close to a story as possible, ended up typing out Clough and Taylor's letters of resignation!

The rest is history. Clough, more than Taylor, believed the swell of public support would lead to reinstatement – but that was a miscalculation that he would regret to his dying day.

Supporters were outraged and the players devastated. Players came close to breaking their contracts with threats of training on their own and even strike action.

For two or three weeks, reporters from all over were camped outside the Baseball Ground. A Keep Clough movement was formed and the players were on the brink of rebellion. But the upshot was that Cloughie never got back.

❛ On occasions I have been big-headed. I think most people are when they get in the limelight ❜

Journalist JOHN SADLER tells of how he watched on in awe as Clough addressed an assembly of high-flying businessmen and left them in no doubt as to his powers of man-management.

57

MY WAY

JOHN SADLER

I've heard a lot of people described as charismatic who couldn't hold a torch to Cloughie. You've either got it or you haven't and Brian had it in bucketloads.

I once had the privilege of watching him in action at a conference of really top businessmen at the Midland Hotel in Derby. These were really top management people and it was going to take a big man to step onto a big stage before a big audience. For the briefest second, you just worry that he might struggle to carry it off. These were top, top big-wig business people – chief execs, managing directors, the lot. These guys worked at, or near, the top for huge firms like Rolls Royce. These guys weren't going to be easily impressed.

I watched on as Brian took the stage and I admit I was nervous for him. I needn't have bothered. The first thing he did was whip off his jacket. Then he loosened his tie and then with a sense of drama that would have done Sir Alec Guinness proud, undid his cuffs and rolled up his sleeves.

'Right gentlemen,' he boomed. 'If you did that from time to time, you might just find you'd be a lot more effective!'

He then went on to talk about management, man-management, how and when to kick somebody's backside, talking to parents, etc, etc. He had them mesmerised. He was absolutely sensational. When he'd finished, the entire audience stood up and applauded for at least five minutes. He was that good.

I'd have loved to have seen him in parliament. My God, would he have made things interesting. He would have asked the questions other MPs would have been too frightened to ask. It would have been wonderful.

What Cloughie had was the secret of man-management and how to get the best out of people.

I recall sitting in his office at the Baseball Ground one day and briefly mentioned coaching and the 'modern day' coaches around at that time.

'Fucking coaches?' he said with a quizzical look on his face. He paused briefly . . . then continued.

'I don't believe in a lot of this coaching nonsense. Dossiers, Don Howe and all that stuff. These people talk about getting a 16,17,18-year-old joining the club and coaching them morning, noon and night. It's bollocks most of it.'

I probably smiled.

'Hey, I'm not kidding. If a lad of 18 comes to me and he can't trap a football or head it or kick it then I don't want him – EVER!' he said, finishing with that inimitable growl at the end.

'I'll tell you what coaching is – I've had that smart arse Roy McFarland in and told him to get his hair cut. That's coaching.'

The elegant McFarland was a classic example of a player licked into shape by Cloughie. He went to Tranmere and virtually camped out to sign the young centre half. It wasn't too long under Clough and Taylor's magical guidance that McFarland got into the England team and became, arguably, the best footballing centre half England has ever had.

Oh, and by the way he looked smart!

❛ David Beckham? I do know a couple of things about that young man - his wife can't sing and his barber can't cut hair ❜

*For the first time, Clough's loyal secretary
CAROLE WASHINGTON talks of her 11 years
working with the Forest boss and reveals a
scam which had remained a secret . . . until now*

58

SPOT OF DECEPTION

CAROLE WASHINGTON

If the boss wanted a relaxing moment or two he'd often pop in a favourite tape of his and just listen to the music. People at the club would know better than to disturb him if the strains of the Ink Spots or Frank Sinatra could be heard coming from his office.

Very few people would risk bothering him at the best of times but when there was a bit of music on in his office then there was no need to put a 'Do not disturb' notice on the door.

I have to confess it led to the occasional bit of deception only myself and the boss knew about. He was like a father figure to me and that's why we kept in touch after he'd retired. But I still smile when I recall the scam we used to pull to convince people that he was in the office.

Sometimes he'd call me in on a Friday and just let me know that he was going to go home early. He'd tell me roughly how long the tape was and say: 'I'm putting this on now. Sneak back in when it's near the end and put it back on for me. No one will even know I'm not here!'

The chairman or someone would come in occasionally, stroll past his office and half-whisper to me:' I won't bother him now – I'll pop back in a bit.'

In between times I'd sneak in and either turn the tape over or change it and no one was any the wiser.

Eventually the music would finish and someone – possibly even the chairman - would come to me on the pretext of trying to have a word with him before he made his way home.

I'd just say something like: 'Well, you can try him, but he did say to me just a minute ago that he wasn't going to be hanging around. You might find he's gone!'

❛ I'm not saying Arsenal have got a lot of French players but their dressing room smells more of garlic than liniment ❜

*When Central TV's BOB HALL told his cameramen
to see what Cloughie did at the end of the game,
he got more than he bargained for. A real scoop
as the Forest boss was caught hitting fans.*

59

CAUGHT IN THE ACT

BOB HALL

I was doing the game for Midweek Sports Special and I had to leave early to go back to the studio and start editing because the programme was due to go out at 10.30. Forest were playing QPR and Trevor Francis, the man who Cloughie made the first £1m footballer, was in charge of Rangers.

My last words to the cameraman were: 'Listen, at the end, look for the green sleeve and the pointy finger. Cloughie is bound to go over to Trevor and say something to him. That's the shot I'd like to go out on.'

At around ten past ten the cameraman walked in with the tape and said as matter-of-factly as you like that Clough hadn't shaken hands with Francis.

'What happened then?'

'He started hitting people,' he adds.

'What?'

'Honestly, he started hitting some fans who had come on the pitch.'

So we put the tape in and the whole dramatic but somewhat bizarre episode unfolded in front of our eyes.

The thing I remember most about it was that there was a policeman looking at him who then just turned away as if it was not happening. It was most odd.

I rang through to ITV Head of Sport Trevor East at around 10.25 and heard him ask someone at his end what the lead story was.

'Ditch it, we've got a new one,' I heard him say. 'Let it run.'

I recall Elton Welsby saying something to the effect of 'And tonight we have got the pictures which are going to be all over tomorrow's newspapers.'

He was right in a way, but the twist in all this was that the newspaper snappers had missed it all. No one had got it. The photographers must have packed their gear up because the pictures that appeared in the paper were grainy snatched shots taken off a TV screen.

It had all gone brilliantly and I had a phone call to say 'Well done,' although to be fair we were just in the right place at the right time.

All hell let loose and on the Friday, Clough was embarking on some serious PR damage limitation. He'd invited the fans he'd clipped over to the ground. All the media were invited – except ITV. He was no one's fool and didn't need it pointing out that had we not got exclusive footage of the bizarre incident, he'd have got away with it.

The front page of The Sun, a paper Cloughie did columns for, gave it a massive show. Their front page exclusive was 'I offered to quit – by Brian Clough.'

On the Saturday, I was at Forest for the Star Soccer programme. I parked my car and then saw some kids milling around and noticed Cloughie.

I thought I'd give him a wide berth just for that day, because I knew he'd not be best pleased to see me on this occasion. But he spotted me. 'Hey, Robert,' he said using my full name as he was prone to do.

'Come over here. You've got me into a lot of trouble.'

'Now, come on Brian, you've got yourself into a lot of trouble,' I replied.

'Don't split hairs with me,' he continued. 'I wouldn't dream of it Brian, but . . .'

'It's cost me a lot of money,' he said, referring to the £5,000 fine imposed on him by the FA.

'Well, by my reckoning it's a good job you did that big exclusive in The Sun then. I hear you got ten grand for that, so you're in pocket.'

'Good answer,' he said grinning. 'I like you Robert – come and have a drink with me!'

It was absolute classic Cloughie.

Unless I'm mistaken, it's the only time he ever had a fall-out with me.

* * *

Cloughie at his mischievous best was a sight to behold. I'd been lucky enough to witness it on a number of occasions, but the one that absolutely sticks out in my memory is the time he did a 'live' studio discussion programme with us.

John Bond, the former Norwich City and Birmingham manager, was with us, along with the then Aston Villa chairman Doug Ellis.

Cloughie was holding court, as ever, and naturally Doug, nicknamed 'Deadly' was lapping it up. Eventually, as Doug made his way to leave, Cloughie shouted to him.

'Hey . . . chairman. Anytime you want me to manage your team, just say the word.'

Doug looked gobsmacked, but you could tell what was going through his mind.

'I'd walk bare-footed to your door to manage a club like yours,' said Cloughie.

Doug almost keeled over and smiled in acknowledgement, nodding at the thought of it before making his way.

'Fucking serves him right,' said Cloughie. 'I'd tell all the papers and then turn him down!'

❛ . . . I call myself Big 'Ead to remind myself not to be one ❜

Teenager PAUL RICHARDSON started his day at school and finished it on News at Ten. He recalls how he got a clip around the ear from Cloughie and then apologised!

60

SORRY MR CLOUGH

PAUL RICHARDSON

I'd taken my earring out because the great man's secretary Carole had told me he couldn't tolerate them. I waited for him to enter, so that I could apologise to him! There was something slightly surreal about it all.

I was here to say sorry to my hero Brian Clough because he'd chosen to whack me in front of millions of TV viewers! But the thing is . . . I idolised the man and getting him into trouble was the last thing I wanted to do.

I'd had my 15 minutes of fame and I wasn't sure I cared for it that much. Just a few days earlier I'd been a 16-year-old kid going about my life – the next thing I knew I was on News at Ten and my picture was in newspapers all over the place. How bizarre was that? And all because fate had put me quite literally within swinging distance of an angry Cloughie who was taking umbrage with supporters for running on the pitch.

Before I go any further, there's something I would like to get straight – I wasn't a hooligan hell bent on trouble. I was just a Forest fan who had ventured onto the pitch like hundreds of others following the 5-2 League Cup win over QPR.

The events that followed are still hard to believe over 20 years on. What basically happened was that loads of fans spilled onto the pitch, but it was more of a celebration than anything sinister.

Forest striker Lee Chapman had scored four goals and was just making his way down the tunnel. I was just patting him on the back when I felt this real clap around my ear.

I turned instinctively thinking it must have been a QPR supporter when, to my astonishment, I saw Cloughie. I thought I was dreaming.

'Get off my pitch young man,' he barked and I dutifully followed his instructions and made my out of the ground. It was nothing more than that, though my ear was throbbing after a hefty clout from the back of his hand.

I caught the bus home and saw a few friends. I told them that they'd never guess what had just happened to me.

'You're not going to believe this but Cloughie just belted me for being on the pitch.'

They looked at me and kind of said: 'Oh yeah, okay,' but I could tell that they weren't convinced. To be honest, I thought that was the end of it. It was merely the start.

I got home just before 10 pm and my mum Sandy had got the TV on. We caught the end of Central News and it showed the incident. Mum quizzed me on just what I was doing on the pitch.

A mate of mine got in touch with Central and said he knew who the supporters were and the next thing I knew was that a TV crew came around and was interviewing us. I then said something that I still regret to this day.

'Brian Clough said he was trying to get hooligans off the pitch but the only hooligan was Cloughie!'

I really wish I hadn't said that. It was broadcast all over the Six O'clock News and the whole business had been front page news in the local paper. I thought that might just be the end of it . . . Wrong!

News at Ten featured it at the start of the bulletin. Alistair Burnett was reading the news and at the start with the 'bongs' it said that Clough had lashed out at supporters.

To cut a long story short, we took a phone call from Carole, Mr Clough's secretary, asking us if we would like to go and see him.

By this time we'd had to go to the police station to see if we wanted to press charges, which we declined.

I also turned down a large sum of money from a national newspaper to give Cloughie both barrels because it was the last thing I wanted to do. This guy was my hero! Anyway, myself and Mark were invited to the City Ground

on the Saturday to see Mr Clough.

'I'd take that out if I was you. He, doesn't like them,' Carole advised me, pointing to my earring. I put it in my pocket!

We went into his office and the only way to describe it was feeling like a naughty schoolboy, waiting for the head to come in. Eventually he came into the room. There was an aura about him.

We chatted for a bit and I told him I'd like to apologise for running on the pitch. He just said something like 'You're not going to do it again, are you?'

We assured him we wouldn't. It was about the time Neil Webb was set to leave the club and I asked him to do his best to try and keep him.

'I'll try my best,' he assured us.

He gave us a couple of tickets to the League Cup final against Luton at Wembley and we thanked him and went on our way.

I was chuffed to have met him but regretted the circumstances really. He shouldn't have done what he did but I shouldn't have been on the pitch. He'll always be a hero of mine. When I heard the news that he'd died, I was in bits. My wife said: 'He's only a football manager!'

I just said: 'No, he was much more than that.'

* * *

The funny thing was that a mate of mine went to a book signing where Cloughie was signing copies of his autobiography. When he got to the front of the queue he asked Cloughie if he'd sign it 'To Paul' and informed him that 'Paul' was one of the lads he'd hit on the pitch that night.

'Was he now? Well, you can tell Paul he cost me five grand!' came the reply.

❛ He was a horrible man. I can't libel him now because he's been dead 20-odd years. I just wish it had been 120
- on Hartlepool chairman Ernie Ord ❜

*Former Manchester United and England star NEIL WEBB
wanted time to think over a move from QPR
because Aston Villa were interested. But he
wasn't going to get away that easily.*

61

GOING NOWHERE

NEIL WEBB

I actually signed a blank contract when I joined Nottingham Forest. I was so wrapped up with Brian Clough's legendary persuasive powers that I could quite easily have ended up committing myself to playing for Forest for 10 years at the rate of just a pound a week.

How many players these days would negotiate a big move by just signing a blank contract and letting the boss fill in the figures? Let me say that when I returned to wrap things up, Cloughie had filled in the blanks to the letter and everything that we had agreed was in place. So how did it happen? Well, it's like this . . .

Aston Villa were keen to sign me as well and I'd been there the day before I went to Forest. I went down with my dad Dougie and I think he was more in awe of the gaffer than I was!

Dad and the boss got on like a house on fire and we all had a good chat about everything. He knew of Villa's interest and I told him that I'd liked what he said, but I was going to go home to think about it.

'No you're not,' he insisted.

'Pardon?'

'I'll tell you what you're going to do. You're going to go and have a walk around the pitch and then come back and give me your answer.'

So I did as I was told, as you'd expect, then came back and said I'd join! Job done.

Cloughie opened a bottle of champagne and we had some of that then went over to an Italian restaurant on Trent Bridge and had some food and a few more glasses of wine.

When we left, the gaffer said that it was no time to go over the figures again.

'Just sign that and I'll fill it in tomorrow,' he said matter-of-factly. And I did!

❝ How come we can't get everybody with talent in work? We've got enough shithouses in work without talent ❞

*Not many people can render Cloughie speechless but
former Forest coach LIAM O'KANE recalls
the day on a club trip to Rome when even
Old Big 'Ead was struck dumb.*

62

STRUCK DUMB

LIAM O'KANE

In all the years I worked with the gaffer I can't recall too many occasions when I've seen him dumbstruck. The joke was that Cloughie could walk on water but his face was a picture when we were privileged enough to meet Pope John Paul II in Rome. I'm a Catholic so I know that I'll never experience anything like that again if I lived to be 500. It was a truly magical experience for me and I'm sure the gaffer actually took a step back to let me get closest.

We were in Rome with Forest's youth team who had been playing in a tournament there. A few of us took a bus trip to the Vatican to see some of the sights there. There was myself, the boss and his wife Barbara in a small party who made our way to St Peter's Square.

I know the old Sinatra classic Three Coins in a Fountain was one of the gaffer's favourites so he was probably more interested in looking at the water features than getting even the briefest glimpse of the Holy Father.

We'd been there about an hour and nothing much was happening. Cloughie was getting a bit impatient – surprise, surprise – when, totally out of the blue, the Pope came down to a spot right where we were standing. We were so lucky because there were thousands of people there.

He was walking around, shaking hands and when he got to us, I just stretched my hand out that bit further and he put his hands on my shoulder. Brian insisted that he backed off and let me go in front of him. Just as well really, because it was well known that Pope John Paul was keen on football and was a goalkeeper as a youngster. Imagine the boss trying his level best to try and persuade him to come out of retirement!

Brian admitted to me later that he was just awestruck and felt totally humble. Now, let me tell you, that was something that didn't happen very often.

❝... Rome wasn't built in a day, but I wasn't on that particular job ❞

When Brian Moore came to the Clough family home to do a TV interview in the garden PETER SMITH was ordered to keep out of the way. But he still came close to getting his baggy shorts on the box.

63

SHORTS SHRIFT

PETER THE GARDENER

My khaki shorts were never designed for a big TV audience. Cloughie would often take the piss out of them, but they were just the job on hot summer afternoons.

I turned up to do some garden work one day when Brian explained that his good friend Brian Moore the ITV commentator was coming and the filmed interview was to be shot informally in the garden.

Cloughie explained that while he was more than happy for me to carry on doing tasks around the place, I'd be in danger of my life if I were to suddenly start up the petrol mower or make a racket with a chain saw or any other noisy piece of equipment. I was also to keep out of the way. No problem.

Cloughie had a great deal of time for Brian Moore and later that morning the television crew arrived and started to set up the equipment. They placed one bench with a wonderful panoramic view of the garden and half of Derbyshire as the backdrop. As the two of them enjoyed a general chit-chat. I got the distinct impression that it was time for me to take a break while the interview took place.

I grabbed my sandwiches and sat behind a hedge where I could hear the interview but was well out of sight.

The interview was a very informal affair and was going beautifully as the two Brians exchanged views on all manner of subjects, but mainly football. I was spellbound to be enjoying my 'ringside' seat.

Everything was going great when a soundman interrupted proceedings to say he could hear a vehicle passing.

'It's a bus. Don't you have bloody buses where you come from?' Cloughie bellowed.

The interview went on for another 20 minutes and was so good that when the two of them wound it up, all the crew burst into spontaneous applause. That was my cue to walk over to the shed and get a large grass rake for my next job. Surely it was safe to go there now . . .

But things hadn't finished and Cloughie had sprung a surprise on Mr Moore by presenting him with a signed picture of many of the footballing greats from his commentary era.

Just as the touching moment was being caught on film, Cloughie spotted me and my khaki shorts on the horizon.

'Oi! Lord Baden Powell . . . get out of the fucking way!'

He scared me to death and the TV crew could sense it. They seemed highly amused at my impromptu appearance – or was it the shorts?

❛ Brian Moore was the best. He knew that silence could sometimes be as important as a whole string of sentences ❜

A routine car journey took a bizarre twist with an unscheduled stop-off outside a church. Local journalist GEORGE EDWARDS reveals he could hardly believe what he was seeing.

64

ALTAR EGO

GEORGE EDWARDS

Having been lucky enough to strike up a close relationship with Brian, I have to say that nothing he ever did really surprised me. The word unpredictable might well have been made just for him alone.

Living close to each other, we would often share a car into town. On one particular occasion we passed a church just at the time a wedding was about to take place.

Brian pulled up, dashed across to the church and I wondered what the hell he was going to do. He just stood there at a suitable vantage point, applauding for all he was worth as the bride emerged nervously from the car clutching her father's arm. I watched him mouthing 'you look lovely,' or whatever.

Bear in mind that he was a famous face at this time. He was incredibly well known and there must have been countless people who, to this day, recall Brian turning up at a wedding and just clapping his heart out.

Somewhere, I am sure there is a woman telling the tale of how Brian Clough clapped her into church, not knowing quite how or why he had got there.

He strolled back to the car beaming broadly and you could tell that it just gave him genuine pleasure to do that even though it was quite an extraordinary thing to do.

But the most bizarre thing about it all was that, when he got back into the car, you could have been forgiven for thinking nothing had happened.

He just got back in, got behind the wheel and started talking football again as if nothing had happened in between. It was the sort of thing you got used to and in the end I got to think nothing of it.

❛ Peter Shilton was absolutely brilliant that season. He won us the title, but I didn't dare tell him. One big head at our club was quite enough ❜

122

With a bottle of beer in his hand, GARY MILLS looked like any other 18-year-old. Except this teenager had just been told he was playing in the European Cup final in a few hours time.

65

DREAM FACTORY

GARY MILLS

I was just 18 and standing there with a bottle of beer in my hand. Nothing unusual in that you might think – but in around three hours time I was going to be playing in the European Cup final against the crack West German side Hamburg.

In a few short hours I'd be out there going for glory in Real Madrid's magnificent Bernabeu Stadium. This really was the stuff of dreams.

I'd had an idea that I'd be in the team because I had been playing regularly but it wasn't until the lunchtime of the game that the gaffer had confirmed the side for the match that May night in 1980.

He didn't pull me to one side or anything. I'd been part of the set-up for a couple of years anyway, having made my debut against Arsenal when I was just 16. The gaffer probably did not want to make a fuss.

We went to our beds in the afternoon and at around 5pm we met up and were handed a bottle of beer, just to keep things calm. Peter Taylor was telling jokes, which he was brilliant at, and then we were basically told to just go out and win a football match. Some

match!

People make a big deal about that fact that I was so young, but I'd been on the receiving end of Cloughie bollockings since I was 14 and playing in Forest's reserve side.

I might have still been a kid at school but I was treated exactly the same as anybody else. I did see quite a few young players wilt under the pressure of the gaffer's unique style of management. By and large, he knew how much you could take, but I think he also took the view that professional football was no place for shrinking violets. To some extent it was sink or swim and he must have been satisfied in his own mind that I was more than capable of handling it.

I'd played against AEK Athens in the European Cup at just 16 which was absolutely incredible looking back and taking time to think about it. Now my time had come and we went on to win it 1-0 thanks to a goal from John Robertson. I was 18 with a European Cup winners' medal in my hand.

The ironic thing is it could quite easily have been my second. The previous year, when Forest had beaten

Malmo in the final, I had originally been named as the sub.

Cloughie had named the side at lunchtime and then packed us off to bed to rest. When we stirred, we came down for some tea and toast and he told me that he was taking me off the bench.

'Your career has only just started and your time will come again,' he assured me.

I was really disappointed because there were no guarantees that the chance would ever come around again. There are great, great players who have never even had the opportunity to play in a final. This was a big chance for me and I had just been told that I would miss out.

'Your turn will come,' Clough assured me.

He was right. Twelve months later I would be out there helping Forest retain their crown and create my own little bit of history.

It was a very special time and I was privileged to be part of it. Having missed out the first time, how sweet it felt to help Forest become Kings of Europe for a second time.

❝ Football is like a golfer's swing. The more complicated you make it, the more likely it is to go wrong ❞

Forest legend IAN BOWYER has seen some imaginative training sessions in his time, but here he reveals how the unpredictable boss managed to come up with one to just about cap them all.

66

DIGGING FOR VICTORY

IAN BOWYER

Nothing Cloughie did should have come as a surprise but the day he had the entire first team squad planting conifers did raise one or two eyebrows. Not only that, but he got us all to put our hands in our pockets and pay for them!

I'll never forget it. We all reported for training one day when the gaffer informed us he'd come up with a solution to the problem caused by the wind. The training pitch was very open which meant it was prone to blustery weather and wasn't very private.

'Hey lads, we're not training today. I've got something else for you to do,' said the boss with a broad grin and pointing at, I'm guessing, around 100 conifers. 'We're going to plant these!'

'Right, they cost me two pounds apiece so you lot owe me four quid each!' And, make no mistake, he made us cough up. So not only did we man the spades and plant them, but we forked out for them as well. No one else could have got away with it. Bear in mind, this wasn't even the apprentices he was talking to but several of the European Cup winners including myself and John Robertson.

He had a bloody thing about trees. Often when we went on foreign trips he'd come back with trees and make the junior players bring them through customs. They all ended up in his beautiful garden.

Now, when I take a walk past the old training ground, I always think to myself just how well spent my four quid was.

The conifers are all 25-30 feet now and I think of Cloughie whenever I see them. It probably costs the club a fortune to keep them all trimmed and if the gaffer is looking down, I'm sure he'd afford himself a little smile about that.

❛ I'm thinking of opening the Brian Clough Academy of Management. It couldn't fail - they'd be queueing overnight ❜

As the Daily Express's Midlands football writer for over 30 years JOHN WRAGG was one of the fixtures of the press pack that followed Clough and his Forest side around Europe.

67

PLAY YOUR CARDS RIGHT

JOHN WRAGG

The thing was I had to get to know Brian Clough. . . . He was the biggest name in football, two European Cups, League Championship, there was no-one bigger than him in football and I was going to have him on my new patch.

I was moving to the Midlands after some very enjoyable years in Manchester covering United and City. Malcolm Allison was manager at City and I'd got to know him well.

'Do you know Cloughie, Mal?'

'Course I do, son.'

'Couldn't put a word in for me, could you?'

Two weeks later I'm at the City Ground. I'd just done my first Forest game and my plan was that when Cloughie came out to do his post-match press conference I'd introduce myself and hand him my business card. That way at least he'd remember my name. Good start. Good planning. I even put the business card in the top pocket of my jacket ready to whip it out.

'Aye, I'm going now, I've spent long enough with people from your profession,' said Clough after holding court in the corridor. He was about to go back inside and once he was through that door with its security number lock I'd had it.

'Mr Clough? I'm John Wragg. I'm going to be covering the Midlands for the Daily Express. I think Malcolm Allison's mentioned me to you. Here's my card.'

Cloughie looked at me. The rest of the press had stayed just to see what happened to the keen new guy

'Eh, Malcolm did ring me. I'm very pleased you've got a business card. But I don't want it.'

And he'd gone.

I'm 6ft 4 inches but he'd slashed me down to about four feet. The lesson was that you don't impress Brian Clough. You don't get through the door on the say-so of somebody else. You do it the hard way. You prove yourself.

The next attempt was a few weeks later. The Daily Express ran an exclusive Brian Clough column at the time and my job was to ghost it.

I'd got to be there on Monday morning to do my first one.

I checked in at the ground with Janice, his then secretary. 'He's still training. He's over the back, just walk up by the side of the Trent, you'll see them," she said.

So I did. It was an early autumn day. About 9.30, ten, in the morning. Still a bit misty.

I was going to see how Brian Clough, maker of footballing miracles, worked his magic. What an insight, what a privilege. This is what football reporting was all about, getting to see something you'll remember all your life. Seeing how genius works.

The shouting of players playing football was loud enough for me to head for it and find the training pitch. But where were Clough and Peter Taylor? Ah, there they were in the far corner. Both of them. Walking near the touchline they were, obviously planning, going through the theory, for Saturday. Both of them were carrying something. White in Cloughie's hand; brown in Peter's. And they kept squatting down. Walk a few paces, maybe a dozen or more, sometimes less, haphazard, then bend or squat.

What's this? A new fitness routine, maybe? I've only been here five minutes and already I'm learning something new. The two of them came closer and closer. The mist had gone.

Cloughie came up to me. 'Shithouse, do you want one? Want some to take home to your mam? Lovely they are.' I'd been watching them pick mushrooms.

I was young and very fit. Played a lot of squash, trained for it, had coaching. Did you ever see those photos of Cloughie in his green top, blue tracksuit bottoms, swinging a squash rac-

quet in his hand?

He was always at it. The racquet was even with him when he had his feet up on his desk in his office. He'd twirl it as he launched into an attack on someone. For instance, the then chairman of Manchester United, Louis Edwards, a man who had made his millions as a butcher, had dared to say Clough would never manage United.

'John, get this down, please. Do you do shorthand? Louis Edwards . . . I know he knows a lot about pork chops, but what does he know about football? That do ya? Got your intro? Got your headline? Tara then.'

Clough hit the fan the next morning as he lambasted United, Louis and his son Martin, destined to be the next chairman, exclusively in the Express.

But there was still that racquet. Did Cloughie play? Was he any good?

Time to find out. 'Fancy a game one day, Brian?'

'Hey, I'd love to, shithouse. Tomorrow?'

We played on the courts at nearby Notts County. Ronnie Fenton, Cloughie's No 2, was referee up in the balcony. Advantage Clough!

Cloughie was useful, but I could beat him. Except that whenever he played a drop shot from the front of the court he'd never, ever, move out the bloody way, making it impossible for me to get past his big arse and get the ball.

It should be a let ball. Every time. But appealing to the ref was pointless. Which way was Ronnie going to call it?

And Cloughie beat me. And the next

time we played. And the third . . .

But what was I going to do? How could I row with him? It'd be like shutting the door on a gold mine. So I bottled it and kept my gob shut. Then, as we were walking back after his third victory, he said with a grin:

'Hey, John . . . you know I cheat, don't ya?'

People said he should have managed England. On ability, on his record, he should have. Why didn't he? Because he wouldn't have lasted five minutes. Diplomacy was not in his DNA.

Here's an example. Forest were away to an Austrian team. 'Lads, I don't want to talk at the airport, I don't want to do it on that noisy aeroplane, can we do it at the airport when we get there? Have a chat? Promise ya, I'll do it, I won't bugger off.'

And he was as good as his word. We sat down, about five of us from Her Majesty's press, around a table in the upstairs cafeteria, teas all round, and he was in great form.

Word got round. Austrian journalists turned up and there they were, three and four deep, behind us listening as he gave us a line.

Cloughie clocked them. He singled out one Austrian wearing a long, white coat.

'Who are you, please?'

'I'm so-and-so from the Austrian paper Derwotsitcalled.'

'Are you Austrian?'

'Yes.'

'Hey, it was you lot that said to Hitler 'Come on through, come on . . .'

There was a dumbstruck silence. Then it was: 'Vot did he say? He said that?'

And all hell broke lose. HM Press bundled Cloughie out and on the team coach and away.

Imagine all that with an FA badge on it.

PS: When he'd retired I went to interview him at his home. It lasted from morning till late tea time, Cloughie's lovely wife, and very strong lady, Barbara, serving us lunch and tea as we talked and talked.

At the end he walked with me to his front door. As he said goodbye, tears streamed down his face. He'd loved talking and laughing. He thanked me for coming.

❛ What pleased me most about winning two European Cups was that when you win something once there's always someone who can say it was down to luck. Win summat twice and it shuts them up ❜

There's nothing like a kiss to boost TV ratings, but GARY NEWBON reveals that when the smacker came from Cloughie . . . all hell broke loose.

68

PANSY PLOTTER

GARY NEWBON

When Cloughie kissed me live on television one Wednesday night, it was an instant passport onto the back pages of the nation's tabloid newspapers the following morning. If the hard-bitten Fleet Street editors were shocked, then spare a thought for me. It was Clough at his unpredictable best and if that little smacker on the cheek was meant to deflect the attention from his side's 4-0 hammering at home against Everton, then you could say it worked!

The game had been shown live on TV and had a little bit of extra-significance in that Nottingham Forest had an impending date in the 1990 League Cup final against Oldham. I'd been down to the tunnel area beforehand and Brian had taken me into the dressing room before asking me what I wanted.

I told him that we were live and needed to do an interview with him after the game and he promised me win, lose or draw, that he'd do it.

'You're on,' he said in that inimitable way. 'Now get out of here because we've got work to do.'

In fairness to Brian, the one thing you could say about him was that he would always keep his word. I knew he'd keep it because I'd never known him let anyone down if he said he'd do it. I was getting one or two anxious looks from our lot and I could tell there was a growing feeling he wouldn't appear – when he did. I told him I only wanted 30 seconds. As you would, I tried to soften the initial approach to him given that they'd just been stuffed and said something like.

'Do you think it's because you have the League Cup final on the horizon?'

'Only Albert is sure of his place on the coach to Wembley,' Clough growled.

I looked at him . . . Forest hadn't got a player called Albert.

'He's the coach driver. My lot did not want to know. They weren't professional and they just didn't want to know," he said.

'Why do you think your players weren't professional and didn't want to know?' I asked.

'Because they're just like you and me, Gary – they're a bunch of pansies!' he exclaimed and, no more to do, he grabbed me and planted a huge kiss on my cheek.

I was all over the shop. I'd learned to expect the unexpected whenever Cloughie was holding court but this was something out of the ordinary. He's kissed me in front of nearly 10 million people, live on TV and just before the evening news.

The tabloids lapped it up and Brian's ability to make the news was evident yet again. He was a master at it.

Mind you, I have to say, he was the best. I have been lucky enough to interview some of the very top sports people of our time and Brian was the master. That's not a bad compliment coming from someone who was fortunate enough to interview Muhammad Ali three times.

Brian had the ability to just silence a room by his presence. It could be packed but the minute he held court, people wanted to hear what he'd say. Ali could do that too. But Brian was the undisputed No 1 and I'm in absolutely no doubt about that.

Sir Alex Ferguson is excellent and Chris Eubank was superb too. Ali was a master, but right there at the top was Brian Clough. There was never a dull moment when he was around.

❛ The cooker the club had was knackered. I nearly picked it for the bloody team because it was better than most of the squad
- on buying a cooker on joining Nottingham Forest ❜

*Award-winning sports journalist and author
JAMES LAWTON was a relative babe-in-arms
when a phone call to Clough provided
him with a cracker of a tale.*

69

GOT A PEN?

JAMES LAWTON

Have you got the tools of your trade?' Clough said.

'Sorry?' I replied, instantly taken aback.

'Have you got a notebook and pen?'

'Oh . . . yes,' I assured him.

'Right then . . . take this down.'

This was the first time I'd ever spoken to Brian Clough, now manager of Derby County, and I was never to forget it. He was about to give me a cracking exclusive – and he knew it! I was working in the Manchester office of the Daily Express and one of the more onerous tasks I had was to ring around a number of clubs and contacts trying to drum up a back page 'lead' story for every edition.

There were the obvious stronghold editions such as the North East, Lancashire, Merseyside and Yorkshire and then what, in newspaper terms, could be classed as a sort of intermediate area covering the likes of Stoke and Derby etc.

These were the days when you actually could ring a club, get through to the manager's secretary and hopefully be put through to the man himself. It seems almost bizarre now! I'd never met Clough, but I was put through and explained, politely, that I was sorry to bother him, but had he got any team news such as injuries.

He virtually dismissed me and asked me if I'd got the tools of my trade and, if so, to take what he said down. I was about to land a story that would solve all my problems, because it was about to be the main back page story in every edition.

Clough had recently signed Dave Mackay from Spurs. The legendary Scottish international was a terrific player and a colossus of a man. He continued.

'I've just had Dave Mackay in my office and told him he's an absolute disgrace to the game and if he turns in another performance like that, I will kick his arse out of here. He's let me down, he's let his team mates down and he's let the supporters down.'

'Are we on the record, Mr Clough?' I gasped, hardly needing to be told the enormity of what I'd just heard.

'Absolutely,' he confirmed and promptly dropped the phone down on me.

I could hardly believe what had just

happened and when I rang my boss in London he enquired as to how I was progressing with getting the required stories.

'I think we're all right,' I said. And we were. Clough's outspoken attack went through every edition and caused quite a ripple. That was almost 40 years ago . . . and I've never forgotten it.

❛ Team talks? Quite often I'll just stick a ball there and tell 'em that's the tool of their trade and the thing you have to work with. I tell 'em treat it kindly, get hold of it and caress it and you'll be okay ❜

*Former Daily Star journalist KEN LAWRENCE reveals
how he would quite happily have taken the stairs when
Cloughie decided a German in the lift should
be told exactly why they had lost the war!*

70

TERROR AT 30,000 FEET

KEN LAWRENCE

I reckon the only reason Cloughie found out he could walk on water was because he hated flying so much. He really wasn't good on a plane at all and one flight to Bilbao for a pre-season friendly became memorable for a number of hair-raising reasons – not least because all the reporters suddenly found ourselves with a front-page story on our hands.

Forest had just won the European Cup for the first time and there was a fair contingency of press guys out on the trip because the club had become more newsworthy than ever. As a journalist, the biggest problem justifying the expense of an overseas trip – particularly for a friendly – is whether the copy you provide makes it worthwhile. In fairness to Cloughie, he appreciated that better than anyone and, even when he was in one of his more awkward moods, would invariably take time to give the lads a decent line to keep them happy. In that regard, he was absolutely first class. Cloughie appreciated we had a job to do and that sending copy back was our No 1 priority. Invariably, he made sure the cupboard was never bare.

I was lucky enough to work closely with Cloughie for some years – he used to have his young son Nigel go and get fish and chips for us as we chatted in his office. There's this theory that he couldn't stand the press – it's rubbish. He couldn't stand some members of it, but overall he liked all that interacting with them. I'm absolutely positive about that. He was a bit of a drama queen if the truth be known – always on stage. When he was holding court, there was no one better. He lapped it up – loved it.

Well, he certainly got his opportunity on this particular trip to Spain. Bilbao was a hazardous enough airport anyway. It was on a hill and considered to be one of the trickiest to land at.

Eventually we got to the hotel where we were all staying to be met by a member of the British Consulate who informed us that there had been a terrorist attack by the Basque separatists and that we should not go out alone and preferably all together as a group.

The press lads checked in and then made our way to the foyer where

Cloughie was holding court. We needed to get a story of some kind because it was now quite late in the afternoon and our desks back in London and Manchester wouldn't wait forever to find out if we had got 'a line.'

'Go on, tell 'em,' Peter Taylor prodded Clough.

Cloughie looked a little coy despite Taylor's goading.

'Go on, Brian, tell 'em what you've been told!'

Clough explained he had been told by British Embassy staff that because of his high profile he was a No 1 terrorist target. What a story!

*   *   *

Diplomatic incidents? They were nothing to Cloughie. I could have been mistaken for thinking I was in Fawlty Towers the day he launched an astonishing tirade on the Germans. It was in a hotel too - but not in Torquay. Oh, no. This was Munich!

Forest had reached the final of the European Cup for the first time and prior to the game with Swedish outfit Malmo, Clough had an obligatory press conference to attend in a rather swish rooftop restaurant overlooking the city.

I remember it being quite a sophisticated place and I also remember hanging around for ages for Clough to grace us with his presence. It was a Tuesday lunchtime and the conference was due to get under way at 1pm. Of course, nothing happened. Over an hour later, Cloughie breezed in swinging a squash racket to do his press conference.

Everything seemed okay and, purely by chance, I got in the lift with him and a poor goafer from the German Football Association who, at this point, wasn't aware that he was about to get both barrels.

Cloughie starts going bonkers about the reasons for him being late, saying that he'd been waiting for ages for his car to pick him up. He wasn't a happy bunny.

'No wonder you lost the bloody war,' he says to this poor guy in a grey suit, as I try and avert my eyes.

'Hey, your cars don't work. Your tanks don't work. It took me longer to get across this city than it took your lot to get halfway across Europe!'

The German FA guy is absolutely crestfallen – and he's still got another eight floors to go. It must be the longest elevator ride he's ever experienced.

I felt like getting out and walking a few flights of stairs but at the same time it was the kind of bizarre entertainment only Clough could provide.

❛ . . . Bugger me, it's no wonder you lot lost the war! *on being delayed and consequently late for pre-1979 European Cup final Press Conference* ❜

From the pyjama meeting to coming close to conquering Europe with Derby, ROY McFARLAND says people have forgotten just how close Clough came to an even more astonishing record.

71

BACKING IT UP

ROY McFARLAND

Brian Clough and Peter Taylor HAD to win things. Not only was it their destiny, but the gaffer continually shooting his mouth off and upsetting all and sundry meant they had to back it up.

Peter once said to me: 'Listen, with all the things Brian comes out with, if we don't win things we'd be out on our ears and cast aside as idiots. We don't have any choice in the matter!'

He was absolutely right and what they went on to win was nothing short of incredible – and yet it could have been even better. Because of the double European Cup wins and the title successes at Derby and Forest, one thing gets forgotten. The pair of them came within a whisker of winning the European Cup with Derby – now how would that have looked in the record books? Their achievements are impressive enough already – but to win the European Cup with two provincial clubs?

No one mentions that an outstanding Derby side reached the semi-finals of the European Cup and were cheated out of it by Juventus. History has revealed that there were all sorts of shady goings-on surrounding that match. We were robbed of a place in the final and now it's all a case of what might have been.

I know he regretted that whole episode with a vengeance. When Brian and Peter resigned from Derby and there was all the fuss and threats of strikes form the players, it wasn't merely because we didn't want anybody else in charge. The major reason was that the players knew just what a great side we had and that success was ours for the taking.

Brain said years later that walking out was one of the biggest regrets of his life. He went on to conquer Europe anyway – twice. Few people realise just how close he came to making that three.

❝ Hartlepool weren't just stuck at the bottom when I went - they were cemented there ❞

135

*Former Yorkshire and England off-spinner Geoff
Cope tells how a surprise visit to Forest's
ground led to an even bigger surprise
for him and his cricketing pals.*

72

IN SAFE HANDS

GEOFF COPE

Cloughie loved his cricket and it wasn't unusual to see him around largely because of his big friendship with Geoffrey Boycott. He'd been in our dressing room at Headingly a few times and, like I said, cricket was an escape for him that seemed to give him an awful lot of pleasure.

Anyway, a few of us Yorkshire lads witnessed a real piece of Brian's legendary man-management at work one day, when we called in to see him at Forest.

We were down at Trent Bridge for a match with Nottingham and there was no play due to rain. So a group of about four of us decided it would be a nice idea to take the short stroll to Forest's ground and see if Cloughie would help us break the boredom and maybe even treat us to a cuppa.

Anyway, we walked the five minutes between Trent Bridge and the City Ground and introduced ourselves to someone in reception who went in to pass on the message.

Brian's secretary came out and said that, yes, he would be delighted to see us.

'I can't believe you've come here just to see me – I suppose you want a cup of tea do you?' Cloughie said with a grin.

I think he was genuinely pleased we'd made the effort of popping over and it probably made a little break in the day from the routine of football management. Footballers were the big stars and the guys who got paid a lot in our eyes, but I'll always remember from that day that there was no one at Forest who got the star treatment.

'Did I just see Shilton out there?' Cloughie called to his secretary.

'Yes.'

'Hey, tell him we need four cups of tea in here, please.'

A little while later in walked England's top goalkeeper with a tray of tea as requested. We looked at each other in disbelief. I think it's fair to say we were absolutely stunned if the truth be known.

'Thanks,' we all said.

'No problem at all,' said Shilton.

'If ever they think they might be top of the tree, they've got a lot to learn,' said Cloughie.

'Anything else, boss?' asked Shilton.

136

'No that's all thank you, Peter.'

It was just fascinating to see his ways so close up. He wasn't trying to show anyone up or anything like that, it was just his way of saying no one was treated any differently at his club.

Having seen him close up you were aware that there was an aura about him. He used to sit and watch games from our dressing room balcony and you can't help but wonder if his values and beliefs would have crossed over to cricket.

To my mind, his man-management skills didn't have boundaries. He believed people were better people if they had and showed discipline. He wouldn't allow anyone the star treatment.

He was a genius and as for motivational skills and all that, he was the king.

❛ . . . He was standing there with his back to me. It had a big No1 on it and I told him there and then 'There's only one No1 at this club and it isn't you!' - *on Peter Shilton* ❜

Top boss MARTIN O'NEILL admits it's taken years as a manager for him to see things with fresh eyes and get a totally different perspective on the most disappointing night of his life.

73

PURE GENIUS

MARTIN O'NEILL

People often ask if things you might have picked up from your days under someone like Brian Clough have stood you in good stead as a manager. Listen, if you are in the presence of someone that special it would have been difficult NOT to learn things from him.

When he arrived at Nottingham Forest on that January morning back in 1975, I was just 21 years of age, just wanting to play football. I wasn't even thinking about management or a career beyond playing football.

The man was a genius. Out of work for a few months following his controversial 44-days in charge at Leeds United, Clough was ready to weave his magic again.

Let me make it absolutely clear – there was no feeling that he'd somehow failed at Leeds. Even we knew it would have been hard work for him at Elland Road because not only had he despised them, he had ridiculed them and that was the most surprising thing about him ever going there in the first place.

I think that with hindsight, even he realised it probably wasn't the brightest thing to do. That Leeds team was a phenomenal side, but they and Clough were oil and water.

The day he walked through the door there was a feeling that we were now on an upward path. You just knew it – it was just a question of whether you were still going to be there or not!

I'm quite pleased – and proud – that I was there that morning he arrived and I was still there when we lifted the European Cup for the second time.

I missed the 1979 final despite playing an important role on us getting there. I was devastated.

Who is to say that had the final been played the night after we played Cologne in the semi-final he wouldn't have gone with the same team?

Now, as a manager, I can see the game in a different light to that of just being a player. It hurt like hell because not only does the disappointment of being told you are going to miss out shatter you, you never think you will get another chance.

But I'd picked up an injury, along with Archie Gemmill and Frank Clark, and was struggling.

If he'd been able to say to me 'Oh,

by the way, you'll miss this one but you will play against Hamburg in 12 months time so don't worry', that might have been okay.

But even with the great man in charge, this was Nottingham Forest and what were the chances of the club playing in two successive European Cup finals?

Having done a lot to get the team there, it was incredibly difficult to take. He left me out - and Archie too. He would have had a phenomenal allegiance to Archie. He was appreciative of people who had helped create great moments. I think Archie, like myself, can appreciate his reasons more now.

I'd scored a really important goal in the quarter-finals against the Swiss side Grasshoppers. We had won the first game 4-1 but in the second game they were leading 1-0 when I grabbed the equaliser that knocked the stuffing out of them. Words can't convey my disappointment at being told of his decision.

My problem was that I'd taken a bang on the thigh from Dave Watson of Manchester City, three weeks to the day before the final. I had a large haemotoma and I just couldn't shift it. So Archie and myself missed out and it was very sad.

It goes without saying that we were delighted when the lads won the Cup and I remember the bus ride into the city centre on our triumphant return.

We were laughing at the start because the place where we started off was deserted. There was absolutely nobody there and so I got off the bus and ran after it waving wildly behind it as if I was a supporter.

But as we progressed there were more and more people and by the time we arrived into the city centre, the place was packed with thousands upon thousands of well-wishers.

It was fantastic. I was part of it and yet there was still that burning disappointment of missing out in the final. Little could I have known then, that exactly 12 months later we would do it again.

I had what I now consider to be the peerless privilege of working with the most charismatic manager of the twentieth century.

He changed my outlook on football, possibly on life, and for that I remain eternally grateful.

He walked through the door with an unbelievable aura about him – and retained it for 18 years.

❝ I've dropped off to sleep long before Sven Goran Eriksson has finished droning on. There's more emotion in a dead reindeer ❞

No one knows Derby County better than GORDON GUTHRIE. He's seen it all as a player, coach, physio and is now the club's kit manager in over 40 years devoted service with The Rams.

74

FIRST IMPRESSIONS

GORDON GUTHRIE

It's over 40 years ago and yet I can still hear the sound of his heels clicking when he walked into Derby County for the very first time. The passageway at the old Baseball Ground was concrete. The players were waiting in the dressing room for him to come and address them. What you have to bear in mind, to put this in real perspective, was the man we could hear down the corridor was not the Brian Clough that everyone came to know. This was a 32-year-old, relatively inexperienced young manager who was stepping up from Hartlepools. It was May, 1967 and yet the distinctive sound of the metal tips on the heels of his shoes remains with me.

Brian walked like a sergeant-major – very quick, crisply and with authority. Though we heard him in the distance, he was standing in the dressing room in no time. Peter Taylor stood at the back.

'Morning gentleman,' he said. 'How are you?'

The players nodded and mumbled their greetings as players do and waited for him to speak. We didn't have to wait long.

'Right gentlemen, I've taken time to have a look at all your contracts and I personally think some of you are being paid far too much for your contribution on the field.'

There was a stunned silence. This sounded pretty serious and none of us dared think what he might say next.

'I won't name any names, but what I will do is give you all ONE month and then I will review it. You've got a month and then I will decide whether I'm not paying you enough, or whether I'm paying you too much!'

He looked at Reg Matthews, our England goalkeeper, who was the most experienced player in our side and said: 'Oh, by the way, I know you like a fag so if you want one at half-time you can. If anyone says you can't, send them to see me. You might be the only player worth me paying as it happens. See you all tomorrow!'

And he was gone, quickly followed by Taylor. Reg must have felt 40 feet tall, the rest of us didn't know quite where we stood. That's what he was good at. You never quite knew where you were with him. And so from that very first meeting he'd got people on edge.

After the month's deadline, he sorted one or two out and yet pretty quickly most of us realised that he was a very fair man.

You can speak to anybody who has played for him, whether they liked him or not, and mostly all of them will say he was fair. If someone had a bad game, he'd just say: 'Son, we've all had bad games – just don't let it happen too often.'

He kept things really simple. At the training ground there is a shield with the club's Ram mascot on it and the inscription reads: 'The biggest crime in football is to give the ball to the opposition.'

Quite often, Brian would stand underneath it and say to the players 'Just read this above me.'

From that very first day, his footballing philosophies shone from him and never, ever changed. He felt people over-complicated things and he firmly believed that certain players should do certain jobs and anyone else should leave well alone. One day at the training ground Jeff Bourne, our centre-forward, placed the ball down and was about to take a corner when Brian started bellowing at him.

'Hey, young man! Put that bloody ball down and get away from it. You're a centre-forward who I employ to score goals so get in there.

'Also, what do you think I employ Alan Hinton to do? Hey . . . and he does it a darned sight better than you as well!'

I can't remember anyone attempting to take a corner kick after that. He only said it once, but the message got through loud and clear.

And the strangest thing of all was that 42 years later his son Nigel, who we often saw around the place as a youngster, strode into the place as the new manager of Derby County. No clicking of metal tips but sometimes when he does certain things I swear to God, there's more than a little bit of his dad about him.

When he tries to get a point across, he sometimes wags his finger just like Brian. He stands like his dad too. But Nigel is very much his own man as you'd expect. There really was only one Brian Clough. . .

❛ If a player had said to Bill Shankly 'I've got to speak to my agent,' Bill would have hit him. And I would have held him while he hit him! ❜

*Maths wasn't always Clough's best subject - unless
he wanted it to be. ALAN HILL recounts the day
when one youngster got a bit too cocky
and was left counting the cost.*

75

CAP IN HAND

ALAN HILL

The gaffer wasn't the easiest of men to negotiate with, particularly when it came to money, so I instinctively sensed danger when one of our young players came back after playing for the England Under-18 team.

The youngster came to me as first port of call and said that while away on international duty he'd discovered that his money didn't compare with what some of the lads at other clubs were on.

'Do you think I can see the gaffer?' he asked me.

'If I was you I wouldn't even think about it,' I advised him, trying to give him the benefit of my not inconsiderable experience of watching people try to get more money out of Cloughie. His tender years were also hardly in his favour. He couldn't be deterred, so I watched him light the blue touchpaper and stood well back! So, in he went, to go head-to-head with one of the shrewdest negotiators you'll ever come across.

'Boss. As you know I've just come back from playing for England and talking to quite a few of the lads, I've noticed they're on a lot more money than I am here.'

'And . . .' Cloughie said deliberately trying to draw him in.

'Well, is there any chance of a rise, boss?'

'Young man, how many appearances have you made for England?'

'One, boss.'

'No, actually young man, you've made two.'

'No, boss, it's one.'

'TWO . . . your first and your last. Please close the door on your way out. Tara.'

> **6** Our mam . . . what a lady. What an example and source of inspiration she was to the entire family. She's up there with my greatest heroes - just below Len Hutton! **9**

142

Former assistant boss RON FENTON was there at Clough's side and was at the very heart of the Forest inner sanctum. He explains why there has never been the great man's like before or since.

76

A HEAD START

RON FENTON

When I first joined up with Brian I'd obviously been warned by people about what a big head he was.

After I'd been with him a while and got to know him better – I realised all the warnings had been absolutely spot-on!

We were having a laugh about something one day and by this time I was close enough to dare say to him: 'You know, you are a bit of a big head, you.'

'Ron, you're right. I am. But you know what, the massive difference is that I know I'm a big-headed bugger.' I must have looked surprised at his brutal honesty.

'The thing is you see, it's the people who don't know they are big heads who are the ones you have to worry about. And I'll tell you something else – there's so many of them waltzing around, it's untrue. Big heads, who don't know they are.'

And he was absolutely right. Where Brian was different was that he spouted off about something, but backed it up. If he had gone on the way he did on TV and in the papers and in all manner of ways and won nothing he'd have looked a fool.

But that's why he holds a unique place in the British public's affection because he would shout his mouth off and say things others just dare not say.

He thought he was right. But lots of other people did too – and he backed it all up with results.

He was a unique character. I worked with him for 17 years in all and there was no one like him.

I see people being interviewed on TV today and they can't hold a candle to him and, bear in mind, he was doing this over 30 years ago.

He was different class and football is a poorer place for him not being in it.

❛ The England thing hurt me a great deal, but the main trouble was the FA knew I thought they were all as weak as pisswater ❜

143

Match of the Day and Grandstand presenter RAY STUBBS
found a little bit of politeness often went a long way
with 'Mr Clough' and ended up getting him
an interview at an important time.

77

DOUBLE FIRST

RAY STUBBS

Mr Clough (I still struggle to call him anything else!) once really helped me out as a fledgling reporter and I'll never forget his kindness for that.

I was working on the commercial staff at Tranmere Rovers Football Club and we had a celebrity dinner. Mr Clough turned up and it was his birthday, so we got him a cake and thanked him for keeping the engagement on such a special day etc.

Anyway, at an opportune moment I said to him: 'Mr Clough, I hope you don't mind, but I do a little bit of free-lance work for Radio Merseyside and I wondered if you'd mind me doing a quick interview with you?' If my memory serves me correctly, it was the League Cup final that weekend.

'Certainly young man,' he said. I remember that's exactly what he said because his use of that phrase has kind of gone down in folklore, but that was precisely what he said. Anyway I did the interview with him and was obviously well pleased to have got such a big name.

Years passed . . . and I was at Selhurst Park for a Crystal Palace v Nottingham Forest FA Cup game. It was my first game for BBC TV Sport and, as you can imagine, I was pretty nervous. Cloughie wasn't talking to the BBC at the time for some reason. Before the game he was walking down the corridor and I spotted the opportunity to say: 'Mr Clough, you won't remember me but my name is Ray Stubbs. I once interviewed you at Tranmere Rovers Football Club - it was your birthday. In fact . . . it was my first ever interview for local radio. Thank you very much for that and all the best for the game today!'

He came out at the end of the game and there didn't seem much chance of us BBC lads getting him because, like I said, he'd fallen out with us for some reason. Anyway, our floor manager Dave Bowden, who is one of the most experienced guys around and a legend in stage-managing at football matches, spotted Cloughie and said:

'Excuse me Mr Clough, would you have a quick word with the BBC?'

'No I won't,' he snapped. 'But I will have a quick word with that young man over there,' he said, pointing in my direction.

He came over and did a very quick interview in which I called him Mr Clough and got a bollocking for being far too reverential to a football manager. It wasn't the best of interviews, partly because he still scared me to death, but nonetheless at least I'd got him. I was nervous, but he'd done me a big favour.

I thanked him at the end and smiled and he said: 'There you go, I did your first interview on the radio and now I've done your first on the telly. Well done. Tara.'

6 Everything that I've achieved or that has directed or affected my life - apart from the drink - stemmed from my childhood. Maybe it was the constant sight of mam, with eight children to look after, working from morning till night and working harder than you or I have ever worked 9

Forest legend JOHN ROBERTSON could get away with having a crafty cigarette most of the time, but he admits he really should have smelled a rat when his hotel room door was knocked after striking up a bet with Cloughie

78

WHIFF OF SUSPICION

JOHN ROBERTSON

We had played at Liverpool and got turned over late on. We had been 3-2 up with probably seven or eight minutes to go and ended up losing 4-3. After the game, the gaffer said I looked a bit tired and said: 'I'll have a bet with you. You stop smoking and I won't have a drink.'

So I took the bet on even though, if I'm honest, I had no real intention of stopping. I couldn't imagine for one minute that he wouldn't have the odd drink here and there, so it just became a case of not getting caught.

The first time it was really put to the test was when we were going away somewhere and stopped overnight at a Heathrow hotel.

After dinner I went up to my room pretty sharpish. I lit a cigarette up, but had the window open because I was sharing with one of the other lads, plus you never knew who might give you a surprise visit!

I just had this feeling that he might check on me and the next thing I know there's a knock at the door.

I dropped my fag in the loo before opening the door. It was Ronnie Fenton informing me he'd brought my boots up because I'd left them downstairs!

'Right. Thanks very much,' I said before clicking the door shut. I thought it was a wee tester and I'd passed with flying colours.

I lit up again and within minutes there's a knock. I assumed it had to be my room mate. I opened the door and there was Cloughie.

'I've caught you, so we'll call the bet off for tonight!' he informed me which was his way of saying that he could now enjoy a sociable drink in the bar without worrying about me lurking around a corner finding him out.

6 When I'm gone I want to be remembered as somebody who contributed good things to that great English game of ours 9

146

*Former Nottingham Forest and England midfield star
STEVE STONE says that days doing chores in Clough's
garden revealed a side to the football legend that very
few outsiders could ever even imagine existed.*

79

NO STONE UNTURNED

STEVE STONE

Brian Clough had one of the loveliest gardens you are ever likely to see – hardly surprising considering he had his own special task force to call on. One of the 'joys' of being a Forest apprentice was the times when you would be called in for gardening duties at the manager's beautiful family home in the rural village of Quarndon just outside Derby.

Actually, while one or two young lads would probably have seen it as a diabolical cheek, I have to say I quite enjoyed it. I certainly learned a lot about life, talking to Cloughie as I raked leaves or moved rubbish about the place.

Looking back I do feel quite privileged to have seen the great man in a very different kind of light. I saw a side to him that many people would probably be surprised even existed.

Yes, he could be the ranting maniac roaring at people and pointing that famous finger menacingly. The general perception of him is of someone who would fly off the handle at any given moment. But when he was at home he was calmness personified and you could tell just what a real family man he was.

I think he used the gardening duties for a number of purposes. First, it was free labour, I'm under no illusions about that. But, secondly, there was always a purpose behind things he did and I'm pretty sure he got to know the young players at the club and maybe what made them tick while they were pottering about in the garden. The thing that might surprise people is that he was really knowledgeable about the various things in the garden. He'd know what the name of a particular rose was, how long it had been there etc. He knew the names of all the tress and shrubs and was generally pretty knowledgeable about all that kind of stuff.

As 17-year-olds you would often think: 'What's he going on about?' but now I can appreciate how much I took in about the knowledge he was passing on. I have vegetables and all manner of things in my garden at home now though, like Cloughie, I get someone else to do it – the missus!

The other thing that would surprise people is his cooking prowess. He was brilliant. Cloughie loved his cooking.

He had a massive AGA in the kitchen and when me and my apprentice pal Craig Boardman had just worked up a hunger, out would come the most fantastic meals. The gaffer thought nothing of bringing out big joints of roast beef - the works.

Was this really the man who had people scarpering down corridors at the City Ground, desperately trying to get out of his way? He put the fear of God into people most of the time. And yet here he was, dishing out hot roast beef sandwiches and taking time with the apprentices, trying to work out what sort of characters they were. He was always interested in your mam and dad and what they did.

I remember one hot day, we thought he was testing us by offering us a small glass of beer. We were probably 16 or 17 and starting to go out and stuff away from the club. But when someone like Cloughie asks you if you'd like a beer, you wonder if he's sussing you out. He wasn't. I think he just wanted you to see the fruits of success and the wonderful family life he had. It was like his way of saying that this kind of future could be yours if you buckled down and worked hard. He

liked his players to be settled down.

I learned an awful lot as a person during those days. I'd like to think he taught me a lot about how to be a proper person. He gave his players a good education in football and in life. The things he instilled in you are there for life. He taught me the importance of time keeping – astonishing really considering he turned being late into an Olympic sport. And he was a stickler for manners – again, quite incredible, given that he could be the rudest man on earth at times!

But they were great days. Having a sandwich and sipping a beer in Cloughie's garden after a bit of graft hold such happy memories. Let me tell you, it's not just coincidence that Cloughie's players had a reputation for not falling foul of referees. He instilled things into players that went far further than the 90 minutes on a pitch. Some of Cloughie's ways stuck with me for life.

I had some success as a player, I've got a lovely garden and on a hot summer's day if I have a glass of beer, I think back to those days. It was the gaffer's idea of heaven – and, as usual, he might have been right.

❛ They humiliated McGovern at Leeds but he had the last laugh when he lifted the European Cup twice ❜

Be careful what you wish for was the advice to midfield star
NEIL WEBB. The former Forest, Manchester United
and England star volunteered to go in goal one
day and wished he'd kept his mouth shut.

80

GLOVE MUPPET

NEIL WEBB

I once found out to my cost that when it comes to making decisions – you're best off leaving that to Cloughie. In fact, I'd go as far as to say, don't even think about volunteering to help out if a crisis crops up because it's just not worth it.

I'd not been at Forest that long when an away game at West Ham suddenly took a bizarre twist. Our keeper Hans Segers was injured and those were the days of only one substitute. When it was clear we needed an outfield player to go in, I quickly volunteered to pick up the gloves.

It appeared to make sense to me. Colin Walsh was our substitute and so, seeing as I was playing wide left of a midfield four, it seemed the best option.

Anyway, I'd played in goal as a kid on the local park and had quite fancied myself between the sticks. Yeah, when I was seven or eight, I used to watch The Big Match on telly and then go out onto the local field and quite fancy myself as Peter Shilton. Cloughie did struggle to see it that way.

I swapped tops and went in, putting on gloves that made my hands look four times bigger than they actually were. At half-time, the gaffer had a right go. We were 3-0 down, although I'd only let in the one, but that didn't save me.

'We've got someone who can't even play in midfield who wants to play in goal,' he moaned, giving me a right dressing down for having the nerve to take the keeper's jersey.

We ended up losing 4-2 and the boss dropped me for the next game at home to Ipswich. I was out of the team for trying to help and they won that match 3-1. Fortunately for me I was back in for the next game, but had certainly learned my lesson to keep my mouth shut!

❛ Sinatra sang 'Let's take it nice and easy' and he's right you know. But we don't. We dash around like mad buggers and it kills you in the end ❜

*Award-winning sports writer JAMES MOSSOP has covered
10 World Cups and eight Olympic Games. He first
interviewed Clough when he was recovering
from injury at Sunderland in 1963.*

81

WORTH WAITING FOR

JAMES MOSSOP

Late in 1982 Nottingham Forest had been drawn away to Derby County in the third round of the FA Cup. It was not long after Brian Clough's acrimonious split with his long-time partner at Forest, Peter Taylor.

Taylor was now managing Derby with Cloughie going solo at Forest. I thought it would be a good time to interview Taylor ahead of their tie, which Derby eventually won 2-0.

I could not reach Taylor by phone so I drove from London to the Baseball Ground. Taylor was very polite, offered me a cup of tea but firmly declined the interview opportunity.

I left with an empty notebook but decided I would drop in on Forest in the full knowledge that Cloughie simply did not give one-on-one interviews unless there was a strict, prior arrangement.

At the little inquiry window I asked if I could see Mr. Clough. As I waited to be turned away, the receptionist returned to say that I should proceed to the Jubilee Club, order myself a drink and he would come and get me.

After 40 minutes there was no sign of the great man and I decided to make my way home. I knew he liked 'playing games' and I deduced this was one of them. I was halfway across the car park when the receptionist came dashing out.

'Mr Clough says he is very busy and he has to go somewhere with the chairman,' she said. 'But he says if you can come back around 5.30 he will see you before the reserve team match.'

It was now around 1.30pm. It was looking as though I would be granted my interview. Always worth waiting for, of course, so I bought a paper, had something to eat and whiled away the time looking at the River Trent.

He was ready for me when I returned with the old, familiar greeting: 'Hey, young man, come in.' Everybody was 'young man.' He would have greeted a centurion in the same way.

'We'll go into the chairman's room,' he said, and offered a drink. 'Now then, we are not working are we?' he asked. 'We'll talk about old times because you know you can't just drop in here for an interview. Fix it up ahead of time and I will give you the best interview you have ever had.'

I timidly suggested that I might ask a couple of questions.

'Right, ok, fire away. You've got two questions.' he said. Needless to say he rubbished the first one and the second question fared no better, but he began talking and talking and talking and I was listening and listening and listening.

I had my notebook out and began scribbling notes. I heard the studs of the reserves on their way out and at that point I suggested that I should leave as he would want to watch the match. He dismissed the notion with some uncomplimentary remarks about the players and the opposition and kept talking.

It is true that we were enjoying the chairman's cognac but an important punctuation occurred when the groundsman, or whoever was responsible for locking up the ground for the night, appeared at the door jangling his keys.

We left and I drove home to London. Early next morning I looked at my notes and realised I had a great feature. I could hardly wait to get to the Sunday Express office to write my piece.

I was just getting to the point where he had said he liked his team to play with the rhythm of the Ink Spots (a 40's close harmony group) when the phone rang.

A woman's voice said: 'Mr Mossop, this is Nottingham Forest. Mr. Clough would like a word with you.'

I probably went white as the blood drained. I waited for him to come on the line insisting that I use not a word of the previous night's profound opinions.

He simply said: 'Good morning, young man. I hope you got home all right. I felt I wasn't very helpful last night. Was there anything else you would like to know?'

The whole episode was another warming hint of the gentle eccentricity and jesting mischievousness of a very generous man.

*   *   *

If Brian Clough ever had a favourite journalist it might well have been his namesake, but no relation, Frank Clough of The Sun, a trustworthy old-timer who was a gifted raconteur and very much on Brian's wavelength.

Forest were on a European trip and due to play in London at the weekend. He invited Frank and me, as Northerners based in London, to pop into the Hendon Hall hotel on the Friday night.

We arrived at the hotel reception and asked for Mr. Clough and the Nottingham Forest group. We were told quite firmly that they were in a private room and Mr. Clough had issued instructions that absolutely no one was to disturb them.

But, we said, we had been invited by Mr. Brian Clough himself. The man behind the desk removed to budge from his stance saying that even a phone call to the room would be against Mr. Clough's wishes.

We prevailed, looked hurt and disappointed and eventually the man made the internal phone call.

Eventually he came back to us with a bemused look on his face. He said: 'Mr. Clough says he will be pleased to see you but that there is an entrance fee. It is a bottle of vintage port.'

We chipped in together and were escorted to the room where we yarned the night away and he made sure we drank most of the port.

Vintage port, vintage occasion. As usual he talked complete sense about everything from the state of the game, his love for his family and politics about which he had the most committed views.

Any time spent in his company sent you away feeling the better for the experience even if his sharp tongue carried a lacerating edge for those who could not keep up with him.

‘ It's no wonder Jim Smith has no hair - he has to start writing the team sheet out on Monday just so he can have all the foreigners names spelt right by the time Saturday comes around ’

The Derby Evening Telegraph's GERALD MORTIMER was privileged enough to be invited to Christmas lunch at the Clough home and saw a young future England player getting his first tackle in.

82

PUT THE BOOT IN

GERALD MORTIMER

Brian kindly offered me over to his house for Christmas lunch one year. It would have been very early in seventies –around 70-71 I would imagine - and it was there that I was to see the emerging football talent of the next generation Clough.

Nigel, who of course went on to play for Liverpool and England, was only a very small boy at the time and had been given a new pair of football boots in his stocking. Nigel had put them on and was parading around the house showing them off, but no one was taking quite enough notice of him. So he showed six studs to family friend and Derby director Mike Keeling, with a firm kick on the shins. As Mike winced, Brian moved in to reprimand the youngster who promptly took the wind out of his sails somewhat.

'Good, aren't they?' asked Nigel, looking rather pleased with himself.

Looking back, I regard memories such as that with a mixture of warmth and incredulity. Can you honestly imagine a local reporter having Christmas lunch with Arsene Wenger or Sir Alex Ferguson? They really were the fabled good old days in so many respects.

Brian could be difficult at times – no one in their right mind would say anything to the contrary - but he also had an incredibly warm and sociable side to him. We would regularly go for Chinese meals in Derby with him.

My mother Win thought he was absolutely marvellous. He always made such a fuss of her to the extent that she got terribly cross when he resigned.

After games, you could sometimes wander down to the Midland Hotel bar, which was virtually their HQ, and half the side would be in there with Cloughie. How times have changed!

Don't forget, these were the days when Derby were the top side in the country – the champions of England.

Golden days indeed. . .

❛ Most injuries these days are caused by players' money belts slipping ❜

83

HEAVEN AND DEL

CAROLE WASHINGTON

It goes without saying that the boss wasn't used to having instructions ignored.

Enter Del Boy. The golden retriever that became such a loved figure around the place was the only thing that ever dared not take a blind bit of notice of him. What's more, he became the staff's secret alarm that the boss was around the place! Whenever the boss pulled up in the car, Del would start barking, alerting everyone in the offices that he was back.

Del Boy would run around the place with one of the boss's trainers or socks in his mouth. Yes, the introduction of his faithful pal brought out a previously unseen side of him.

Up to that point he'd hated dogs. 'Dirty, filthy, smelly creatures,' he'd say. But his daughter Elizabeth was desperate for one and he eventually decided to relent.

No one could believe it when he actually decided to get one. But even then the dog had the last laugh.

We'd asked him what it was going to be called, but that was obviously to be Elizabeth's choice. He joked that if it messed around the house he might just call it 'Shithouse'.

The following day he came in and raised his eyebrows to the sky, revealing that the dog had kept him up half the night. It was very clear from that point that this dog wasn't short on courage.

'So what's he called then?' came the question.

'Del Boy,' he said.

'Why Del Boy?'

'Because his mum thinks his dad's a plonker!' said the boss with a resigned chuckle.

❛ Taylor always said: 'When you get shot of me there won't be as much laughter in your life' and he was spot-on. He did make me laugh a lot - *on former partner Peter Taylor* **❜**

*Deadly Leeds United and England striker ALLAN CLARKE
was at Elland Road when Clough breezed in. The man
known as 'Sniffer' for his predatory goal instincts
went on to become manager of the club.*

84

RIGHT MAN, WRONG TIME

ALLAN CLARKE

By the way, how many goals did you get last year Allan?' a tanned Clough asked, shaking my hand.

'Twenty-six, boss,' I replied.

'Well, I want twenty-seven from you this season,' he said. I could tell he was really nervous. Here he was meeting this team of internationals for the very first time – the team he'd slagged off at every single opportunity. Despite all the bluster, I could sense he was as nervous as hell. Make no mistake, he knew what he had walked into. He was tanned because he'd been sunning himself in Spain and missed the start of pre-season training. It was never going to be easy for any of us. But I would like to put the record straight over those famous 44 days of football history – Leeds players did not get Clough the sack. I think Brian was the right man at the wrong time and I think he tried to change things too quickly. But directors hire and fire managers and it was the board who pulled the trigger, not the players.

Thinking back it was all quite bizarre. The gaffer used to have his team talks at 1pm on a Saturday, allowing all of us to watch Football Focus on the TV which was a half-hour slot from 12.30 – 1pm. It was essential viewing back in those days. That programme was THE football show before the day's action got into full swing.

Picture this . . . the Leeds squad used to sit around the TV wherever we were and watch that show where Clough always seemed to be on having a right go at something or other – and quite often us! On occasions he would slaughter the gaffer, Don Revie, our players and the tactics he felt we employed. I remember thinking: 'Christ, I couldn't play for him,' but I also learned to listen from an early age. Clough called a spade a spade and in that respect we were similar. Perhaps it could be misinterpreted as being too honest, but it's a quality that can quickly ruffle feathers.

What you have to remember is that apart from myself, Mick Jones and Johnny Giles, the bulk of that great side had come through the youth development scheme at the club. The gaffer was the only boss they had known and his presence was all around the place. That and his repeated digs at Leeds was always going to make it very difficult for Brian.

Leeds fans to this day still ask me if I think Brian would have brought success to Elland Road. It's one of those things we will never know, but his record will ensure he goes down as one of the greatest managers of all time. His record is second to none and what he achieved at Nottingham Forest was just unbelievable.

I do look back on it all with a touch of sadness because I honestly believe Leeds were ready and equipped to conquer Europe. Brian showed that he could do that a few years later, so there's no reason why he couldn't have done it at Leeds.

Like I said, right man wrong time, but I liked him and would like to think a few of the things I took into management came from the likes of him and the gaffer. That's why I was never a 'yes' man. I was like Brian in that respect.

When I took over at Barnsley, I took them to promotion in my first season. It was in my second season that I felt I had inherited one or two cheats in the squad. They needed to be sorted out along with a few others who just seemed to take for granted how privileged footballers are.

Obviously, Barnsley is a huge mining area and a lot of the supporters who pay good money to watch the team earn their living in one of the toughest environments in the world.

Our physio Norman Rimmington was the proverbial Mr Barnsley. He's been a player, first team coach, physio, groundsman, you name it.

He arranged through a relative to take the players down to the pit face.

We reported to Oakwell at 6am and took the players all the way down to the faces. We spoke to one guy who was a father who worked down there with his two sons, eight-hour shifts, starting at six. Coal faces? You should have seen the players' faces! I don't think I had a bad performance out of them after that.

That was very much Cloughie. I think he'd have given that tactic his full approval.

6 **There wasn't a clash of personalities because half of the people we were clashing with didn't have personalities**
- on behalf the scenes wranglings at Derby 9

156

When IAN EDWARDS described a Forest win in the local paper as 'flattering' he could hardly have imagined the ear-bashing he was about to get from someone who was less than impressed.

85

FAINT PRAISE

IAN EDWARDS

I consider myself fortunate to have worked with Clough and seen him up close for four years. As a young reporter with the Nottingham Evening Post, a relatively brief spell with the undisputed master was like a lifetime's journalistic education. But the thing with him was – which anyone whoever met him properly will vouch for – is that if you were ever lulled into a false sense of security that you had been accepted, he would send you crashing back down to earth in an instant.

The phrase 'build 'em up, then knock 'em back down' could have been his creation. He was a maverick, a magician and a stickler for manners, despite the fact that he could be so astonishingly rude at times.

It was typical Cloughie to show you some affection and then jab you in the solar plexus. It kept everyone on their toes – and that's just how he wanted it.

I recall once dishing out faint criticism on the premise that it was fair comment and merely being constructive, following a disappointing League Cup match against Burnley. Forest ended up winning 4-1 but courtesy of three late goals and I described it as a 'flattering' scoreline. I certainly never thought such a description would be sailing too close to the wind, but Cloughie was on the warpath.

I was standing in the entrance of Forest's Jubilee Club, talking to John Robertson. We used to chat for ages and Robbo was always good value. Now he was a big favourite with Cloughie, but not so much so that he didn't get it in the neck at times.

Cloughie came bounding over bouncing a tennis ball with his faithful golden retriever Del Boy close by.

"Hey, shithouse. How dare you call that win flattering. I've won two European Cups, you know! Who are you to tell me it was bloody flattering?'

Robbo was directly behind me and it was like schoolboy stuff because he was grinning at me and clearly enjoying me getting a dressing down. But not for very long. Quick as a flash, Cloughie turned his attention to Robbo and barked: 'And you can put that fag out for a start off!'

Robbo quickly stubbed it out and when Clough had gone, said to me: "Fucking hell . . . I'm 37, married with kids and I'm still frightened to death of him! What is it with him?'

It was a surreal, beautiful moment. And I still don't know the answer.

I went for a job at the Yorkshire Post and was invited back for a second interview where I met the editor of the paper. Howard Wilkinson was manager of Leeds United at the time and had a reputation for being somewhat prickly. So, the editor tested me out by commenting what a big job covering Leeds was and said something like: 'You do realise that if you got the position it would mean you having to deal with Mr Wilkinson on a day-to-day basis which has proved to be difficult on occasions.'

This was clearly my big test question. I stifled a chuckle. 'Howard Wilkinson? I've just had four years dealing with Brian Clough . . .'

He looked at me and smiled as if to say 'fair comment.'

❛ Someone's been putting it around Nottingham that I'm barmy! - *to local journalist* **❜**

And so just who was the man flouting the dress code when Frank Sinatra came to town? ALAN HILL recalls high jinks when Old Big 'Ead went to the Albert Hall to see his hero Old Blue Eyes.

86

THIS IS THE LIFE

ALAN HILL

Cloughie's admiration for Frank Sinatra is well known. Old Blue Eyes could do no wrong in the gaffer's eyes. You'd often catch him singing a few lines of one of his classics. I wish I'd had a pound for every time I'd heard him down the corridor singing Fly Me to the Moon or You Make Me Feel So Young. There were plenty of people around the club who welcomed his singing if only because it acted as a warning signal that he wasn't far away!

But I was lucky enough to be in a party that went with him to see Sinatra at the Royal Albert Hall and it's one of those occasions I'll remember forever.

There was a party of about 10 of us going and it was a proper dickie-bow affair. We were lucky enough to have fantastic tickets up in a box and so everyone was bristling with excitement at going to see such a legendary performer. None more so than the gaffer. There wasn't much that impressed him, but he was like a kid waiting for Christmas.

We didn't even have to arrange transport for the evening. We took the team coach down to watch the concert - how's that for doing it in style! But the one thing that stood out for me was something that just summed the gaffer up.

The way it worked out was that I was on the front row of seats in the box and the gaffer was at the back. Half way through he called me.

'Hey, Hilly,' he said, urging me to turn round.

I turned to see Brian there, very smartly dressed in his dinner suit, but he'd put his grubby flat cap on and had a broad almost child-like grin.

'Hey, Hilly . . . this is the life isn't it?'

That memory of how chuffed he looked will never leave me.

❛ I'd rather be with the strongest than the weakest. Give me a choice between a gun that fires a single shot and one that keeps firing and I'll take the machine gun every time ❜

Celebrity gardeners are a relatively new thing but not in a certain household. PETER SMITH reveals how he was the shock recipient of the OBE for his services to Clough's lawns.

87

ORDER OF THE BRIAN EMPIRE

PETER THE GARDENER

How many humble gardeners can say they've been presented with an OBE and then handed it back? Didn't The Beatles do something like that? Well, the only beetles I mix with are the ones in the garden and that's about as glamorous as it gets in my line of business.

Cloughie was very proud of the award he'd been given by the Queen for his services to football. Quite a while after he'd received it, I was having a coffee break with him and we were talking about achievements. It goes without saying that mine finished a distant second to his, but that's to be expected. Anyway, he took me by surprise saying: "You've achieved more than a lot of people.'

I must have looked a shade puzzled as he continued: 'Well, you won my friendship for a start and not a lot of people can say that.'

It was praise enough considering he'd been in the company of Lady Di, Muhammad Ali and Frank Sinatra to name but a few. As I finished off the day's gardening, Brian came out with a common-or-garden carrier bag and handed it to me, saying: 'Take this present from me as a good friend and don't open it until you get home.'

When I got home, I opened up the bag, only to find it contained Brian's OBE in its presentation case. To say I was stunned is an understatement. All of my family gathered around to see what I was gawping at.

I spoke to him on the phone and informed him I would bring it back. He said it was a present. We agreed a compromise – I would keep it for a week, then return it to its rightful home.

It was a very long week – I never let it out of my sight, even putting it under my pillow at night for fear of it being nicked!

❛ I took my son Nigel and Roy Keane to visit some handicapped kids. We lit the place up, but they lit us up. When we came out I felt a million dollars ❜

Clough might have had a shocking time at Leeds but loyal servant JOHN McGOVERN had an absolute nightmare too. There was only one answer - go and win the league title and two European Cups.

88

CRAP PLAYER EH?

JOHN McGOVERN

When I lifted the European Cup, the dark days I'd endured at Leeds suddenly seemed light years away. I had an absolute nightmare at Elland Road. I was slaughtered by the fans and there was no shortage of people who thought I couldn't play. Now, here I was – a European Cup winner.

I was pilloried at Leeds. I couldn't do a thing right. Cloughie had brought me to the club and when he got sacked after 44 days in charge I was in no man's land.

It was a big enough problem from the start that I was understandably seen as a Clough man. In fairness the players were fine, but the fans saw me as a complete waste of time. What didn't help was the fact that legendary skipper Billy Bremner had been sent off in the gaffer's first match in charge – the infamous Charity Shield clash with Liverpool. Bremner and Kevin Keegan had a ding-dong and threw their shirts off in disgust. Unbelievably, by today's standards, Bremner was hammered with an 11-match suspension and I was suddenly in – and wearing the No 4 shirt he'd made his own over the years.

Nothing went right. The Leeds fans hated me and with the way things were going, there was no way I was ever going to win them over. Then Cloughie got the bullet and I was really in limbo. He said he'd come back for me, but where would he turn up next?

I joined him at Forest and the trip he took us on from that point on was the stuff of fairytales. We won promotion, then went on to take the First Division championship and then on to two European Cup successes. I wonder if there were any of those Leeds fans who had bad-mouthed me, who were man enough to admit that they might just have got it wrong?

6 Derby should have gone on to be every bit as big as Liverpool - possibly even bigger. And there's only one man to blame for them not doing that - me! 9

Caller on line one . . . and two . . . and three.
DARREN FLETCHER reveals that when the
master was in full flow there was no one
around with such pulling power.

89

LIGHTING UP THE AIRWAVES

DARREN FLETCHER

In all my years in radio, I know of no one who could get a switchboard lit up with calls like the incomparable Brian Clough. I was lucky enough to be inside the studio watching him close up and having a cup of tea with him and I marvelled at it, Lord knows what the punters were thinking. Cloughie was electric and bear in mind that I'm talking about a time when his management career had come to an end.

I was working for Century Radio in Nottingham and when Cloughie did a piece to help us with the launch of the station, he enjoyed it and gave the impression that he was a bit annoyed people weren't doing things with him. When Garry Birtles became involved with the station he suggested we try and persuade his old gaffer to do a bit. Cloughie agreed to do a monthly phone-in. He loved it and to say there was a buzz in the air every time he came in would be an understatement. He would stick around for an hour or two after the show and drink tea and tell stories. It was fabulous.

'I only come across because you are my friends,' he'd say and you could tell he genuinely had a good time reminiscing and giving his forthright views on things.

You cannot believe the volume of calls we took the nights he was in. We would get the amount of calls you'd normally expect for an entire week whenever he was in. He was absolutely awesome and I know other people have said it, but he did have an instinctive knack of knowing what needed to be said, how to say it and when, which just made for fantastic radio.

I feel privileged to have spent so much time with him later on in his life and have to say that no one has captivated me more before or since. He was like no other. I was lucky that we did some live commentaries with him and he took to that like a duck to water – just as you'd expect.

We did the infamous England game where about eight players captained the team because of substitutions and they were tossing the armband around everywhere. Cloughie went berserk and it made fantastic radio as he slaughtered Sven-Goran Eriksson.

I've never been in a situation with him when he wasn't in total control.

He would enter a room, no matter how big or how full and it was like in the cowboy films when the guy in black walks in and even the piano player stops.

The room would just go quiet, people would be nudging each other and pointing and he had their total attention without having said a word. It was phenomenal to see him close up. I think it's commonly referred to as charisma. Not many people have it. Whatever it was, Cloughie had it in bucketfuls.

❛ On one memorable occasion I met Sinatra. He said: 'Are you all right?' They were the historic words. They are the words, the only words he uttered to me. I said 'Yes, thanks for coming over' ❜

When a story knocks the Arab-Israeli war off the front pages
of a national newspaper you know you've arrived.
JEFF FARMER recalls getting the big exclusive
on a story that shocked the football world.

90

HOLD THE FRONT PAGE

JEFF FARMER

Get your arse over here and I will give you the biggest story of your career!' It was Clough – and, as usual, he was absolutely spot on. Exclusive stories like the one I was about to break don't come much bigger. They were those once-in-a-lifetime occasions that you can still savour all these years later. I'd had big stories before and many since. But this was high-octane explosive. I guess I'm biased, but you don't have to take my word for it. This was October, 1973 and this particular exclusive was about to blow the Arab-Israeli war off the front page and Sir Alf Ramsey's England off the back. This was a 24-carat cracker and looking back now it's almost like being some part of football history. I suppose it is, but it's always a bit harder to look at it objectively when you are slap bang in the middle of it.

When I took a phone call at home at around 5pm that October day, little could I have known the bizarre events which would unfold in the next few hours.

'Hello, Jeff Farmer.'

'Hey, I know who it is you soft bugger. What ya doing?'

'Well . . ..'

'How quick can you get over here?' he asked.

'About 45 minutes.'

'Get your arse over here and I'll give you the biggest story of your career,' boomed Cloughie.

I've never known a man outside of journalism with a more acute sense of a story's value. If Clough said this was a big one, it must be. As I drove along the A38 towards Derby's Baseball Ground, I mulled over the permutations. Cloughie and Peter Taylor had a love-hate relationship with the Derby chairman Sam Longson so it was a powder-keg waiting to go off, but I couldn't imagine what was waiting for me on my arrival.

Local journalists Gerald Mortimer and George Edwards were in the office with Brian and Peter.

'We've just resigned,' declared Cloughie, never one to beat about the bush. I was gobsmacked.

I rang my Fleet Street office and told them. You can imagine the reaction. But it was getting late in the day and they needed the copy as quickly as possible.

I had around half-an-hour with Cloughie, Peter chipping in occasionally, and set about getting my copy across. I had this one all to myself because my paper would be out in the morning before local journalists could beat me to it and these were the days long before mobile phones, web sites, Sky TV, 24 hour news. This was a good old-fashioned, proper exclusive and there was no one to touch me.

I wrote my 'Brian Clough has sensationally quit . . .' intro long-hand and the first two or three paragraphs and then ad-libbed the rest to a copytaker in London, who took it down through headphones.

When I eventually left Cloughie's office at around 9.30pm, rumours had started seeping out and I was met outside on the car park by a few of my Midlands-based newspaper colleagues, who had gathered there was something afoot.

'I can't say anything lads,' I said, but tried to give them a steer that whatever they had heard might just be right. It was enough to make sure they covered themselves to a certain extent but they were hours behind me and, given the access I'd just had, there was no chance of them catching me up.

The story caused a right stir when it broke the next morning and I walked around like the cat who'd nicked the cream for quite a while. Exclusives like that are what newspapers are all about and there's no feeling in the world quite like coming across one.

Clough was hot news. He did things differently. He was a maverick. A genius. Cloughie was a complete one-off.

There's been no one like him before or since. I have met a number of charismatic figures like Tommy Docherty and Big Ron Atkinson. But I have to say I've never met anyone so complexly charismatic as Clough. He stands alone.

❛ Some people think you can take your football boots off, put a suit on and become a manager. Then they find out there's a bit more to it than that ❜

When Cloughie shattered the British transfer record to sign elegant defender COLIN TODD, there was one man he forgot to tell just how much he'd paid - not to worry, it was only the chairman.

91

DON'T TELL THE CHAIRMAN

COLIN TODD

It seems hard to believe now that when I moved from Sunderland to join Brian at Derby the fee of £175,000 smashed the British transfer record. But this was 1971 - a time of political unrest and manoeuvrings and not just out there on the streets. From the minute I signed it was clear Cloughie was causing headaches for his chairman Sam Longson.

There was a quite emotive backdrop to splashing out that kind of money for a footballer – like a miners' strike for one thing. Plus there was the little matter of keeping Mr Longson informed of everything that was going on.

'Listen Colin, I've signed you. It's gone through in my eyes but when the chairman finds out I don't know what he's going to say because I haven't told him yet!'

Not telling the chairman seemed a fairly extraordinary thing to do, but not telling him that he'd just splashed out a new British transfer record in the process was even more remarkable.

The story from the other side looks something like this:

Derby chairman Longson had agreed in principle to let Clough get on with things before jetting off to the Caribbean. He received a cable from his brash, young manager, saying: 'Signed you another player. Todd. Running short of cash.'

Apparently, Longson was sitting down enjoying a meal in Antigua when Derrick Robbins, the chairman of Coventry City, bumped into him in the restaurant.

'I see you've been spending again, Sam,' said Robbins.

'So I believe Derrick.'

'What do you mean 'believe'?

'To be truthful Derrick, I don't know the price.'

'Well I do. But I should finish your meal and I'll tell you.'

Longson almost choked on hearing the price, retired to the gentlemen's bar and lit a Havana cigar.

❛ It doesn't take me long to spot if they can play - usually about a minute ❜

166

*Bristling to make a point . . . striker GARRY BIRTLES
explains exactly why his team mates were held up
for the biggest game of their lives while
he was ordered to have a shave.*

92

IN A LATHER

GARRY BIRTLES

The gaffer's acute sense of how to handle players came home to me on the day of the European Cup final against Malmo in Munich.

It was a red-hot afternoon and the Forest party was congregating in the foyer of the hotel when the boss stopped me in my tracks.

I always used to have stubble on my face – it was a kind of superstition and I'd always got away with it.

Not this time, it seemed. Cloughie, was clearly up to something as he pointed me out and said: 'What's that on your face?'

'Oh it's a superstition thing,' I assured him.

'Get that stuff off,' Cloughie insisted.

I told him that I couldn't. For a start off, all of my shaving stuff was in my bag which was already on the coach and I couldn't get it out.

'Anyone got any shaving stuff?'

Cloughie asked. Our keeper Chris Woods rather sheepishly said he had and he was instantly made shaving monitor!

'Go up to my room with Gaz, watch him and make sure he gets that shaved off.'

This was bizarre and I didn't know what to make of it until I twigged. Clough had seen that I was a bit nervous and fretful which was hardly surprising really. I'd been fitting carpets less than three years earlier. Now I was about to play in the European Cup final!

The reason he was so bothered about me getting a shave wasn't to humiliate me, it was just to take my mind off things. I'd become so involved with the shaving episode that I'd taken my mind off the match and that's exactly what he wanted.

That 20-minute distraction had done the trick.

❛ I always tell directors and chairmen that they only have one decision to make - to pick someone to do the job they can't do ❜

Clough's aversion to flying was legendary, but PAUL HART reveals the straw that broke the camel's back when the team were on the runway ready to fly out to the Middle East.

93

RUNWAY RUNAWAY

PAUL HART

The gaffer had this aura about him which made you feel he could just about do anything – even walk an entire party off an aeroplane while it was actually on the runway!

I'll never forget it to the day I die. We'd been knocked out of the FA Cup by Arsenal on the Saturday and the next day we were flying out to the Middle East for an exhibition match which was arranged to bring in some much-needed revenue.

We had set off really early – like 6am or something like that – and the gaffer was already in a stinking mood after having a row with Garry Birtles on the bus before we'd even got out of Notttingham.

Gaz had been turfed off the bus because he'd been moaning which was hardly the best start to the trip and by the time we arrived at Heathrow, you could feel the tension in the air.

Our party was right at the back of the jumbo which was jam packed with what appeared to be mainly families. There were lots of kids and there was a baby screaming. The gaffer and his assistant Ronnie Fenton came and sat in the next seats to me and as this baby kept yelling I could almost see the top coming off Cloughie's head. He was ready to explode and we hadn't even taken off yet! He hated flying anyway and what with the Arsenal defeat and the antics with Gaz, things weren't looking good. What a nightmare this trip promised to be.

We were taxiing down the runway for take-off when suddenly the pilot slammed the brakes on. The pilot came over the intercom and informed us that there was a slight problem that needed sorting and we might be forced to sit on the plane for quite some time while the matter was investigated. That was it.

'Not for us, Harty!' exclaimed the gaffer.

'What?'

'We're off here pal.'

I hadn't a clue what was going on or what was about to happen, but that wasn't particularly unusual when you were in the presence of a certain Brian Clough. The unexpected was often just around the corner.

'We're getting off, love,' he said to a startled stewardess.

'You can't do that,' she replied.

'Hey, you watch me. Get your captain to get me a bus. We're off this plane.'

I really honestly don't know how he arranged to get an entire party of footballers off that plane, but he managed it. The stewardess insisted it couldn't be done, but it was.

As we walked right down the plane and through first class, Cloughie spotted the agent who had set up the trip.

'Goodbye!' he said in a raised voice as the startled agent looked on.

I don't know what his cut of the deal was but he'd just seen it fly out the window. Well, not fly . . .

That was Cloughie for you. Never a dull moment. But, you know, I thought he was absolutely brilliant. I learned so much from him and possibly the biggest thing I picked up was to keep things simple.

He was an absolute master at stripping things down to the basics. He wouldn't entertain complicated graphs and detailed breakdown of this, that or the other.

And when you analysed what he said it all made so much sense. There was nothing complicated about it and, invariably he was right. If he wasn't, you'd still leave thinking he was!

❛ I was worried early on for Trevor because of the size of the fee. But I quickly saw he was the type to carry it off - in fact, he seemed to thrive on it. If it had been me as a player, I'd have worried about it
- on paying £1m for Trevor Francis ❜

Striker DUNCAN McKENZIE outlines the compassionate side of the manager and just why he was spared penalty duty in the infamous 1974 Charity Shield final at Wembley.

94

PAYING THE PENALTY

DUNCAN McKENZIE

In all the furore about the Kevin Keegan and Billy Bremner sendings-off, one fact about the 1974 Charity Shield match has virtually been forgotten. A little bit of history was written that day, but it's the story behind that which not many people know.

The images of Bremner and Keegan tossing down their shirts after their infamous scrap is one of the abiding memories. They were the first British players ever to be sent off at Wembley but when the game finished 1-1, something else happened . . .

Leeds goalkeeper David Harvey missed the 11th kick of the penalty shoot-out after the sides were tied at 5-5, and Ian Callaghan scored the next to clinch victory for Liverpool.

David Harvey, did someone say? Wasn't he the goalkeeper? Correct. And he took a kick ahead of me, Leeds' new £250,000 signing who had scored 26 goals for Nottingham Forest the previous season. And the reason was that Clough was protecting me.

I was cocky enough to want to take one and expected that I'd be given the chance in the first five. It wasn't to be. Clough had sent word on to Norman Hunter that I was not to take one. His reasoning was that because he was having a tough time and I was his new signing, I'd be crucified for ever if I missed the all-important kick. Clough didn't want to expose me to that so early in my Elland Road career. He was protecting me, even though it probably ended up costing Leeds victory that day.

I still think about that and what must have been going through his mind. But it does say a lot about his relationship with players when he looked after me at his own expense that day.

He didn't want me saddled with some of the baggage he was having lumped on him and went out of his way to make sure I didn't cop a load of stick before I'd even kicked a ball in the league.

❛ I've decided to pick my moment to retire very carefully . . . it's in about 200 years time ❜

170

Journalist KEN LAWRENCE had a 40-a-day smoking habit. But only when he went to Forest . . . the rest were ones John Robertson tried to hide from the boss.

95

SMOKE SCREEN

KEN LAWRENCE

Cloughie loved John Robertson. I don't think there's a single player who has passed through Clough's keeping who has given him as much pleasure – or as much material.

Cloughie would crucify Robbo for his appearance, his physical condition, you name it. But the one thing he was always on Robbo's case about was his smoking.

I was quite pally with Robbo at the time despite the fact that I used to spend half my time in Forest's Jubilee Club lighting fags for him and leaving them in an ashtray at some convenient distance.

I'd nip to the bar and buy us a drink and then light a fag and leave it just far enough away so that if the gaffer came striding in, he could deny any knowledge of it. I'd pick it up and Clough would supposedly be none the wiser – I suspect he knew all the time. Clough wasn't stupid – he'd have noticed Robbo and me never smoked a cigarette at the same time!

Looking back on it, it was all quite strange. Here was a top international player who had made the goal for Trevor Francis' 1979 European Cup winner and a year later scored the goal that won it and he was terrified of Clough giving him a hard time for sneaking a crafty smoke!

But make no mistake, Clough thought Robbo was a magician with a football and he wasn't far wrong.

I remember returning home with Forest after they had won the second European Cup with the win over Hamburg and watching yet another bizarre Clough press conference.

He got Robbo to sit on his knee like it was some strange old-time music hall ventriloquist act.

'You don't really like me, do you?' Robbo said with a mischievous grin cracking his face.

'Don't be silly, young man,' Clough replied.

❛ . . . Whenever I felt a bit off-colour I'd go and sit next to John Robertson - then I looked like Errol Flynn ❜

Flying winger FRANZ CARR spent six years under Clough at Forest and recalls a terrified team-mate facing up to the fact that he might have to give the boss some very bad news.

96

IN THE DOGHOUSE

FRANZ CARR

We were never short on laughs during my times at Forest but one of the funniest things I remember was the time Gary Charles lost the gaffer's dog.

When I first arrived at the club, the apprentices would be picked at random for dog-walking duties. That involved taking Del Boy, the gaffer's golden retriever, for a good, long walk, usually along the banks of the Trent.

So one day, Charlesy had the fantastic honour of taking the dog, much to the relief of everyone else. Well, quite a bit later, Charlesy returned out of breath and with a kind of haunted look on his face. Hardly surprising when he explained his predicament.

'The dog's disappeared,' he exclaimed, looking down at the collar and lead in his hand.

'He just shot off the lead. Has anyone seen him?' he asked hopefully. Ian 'Bomber' Bowyer was one of the more senior members of the squad but could offer little comfort.

'Bloody hell Charlesy, never mind walking by the Trent, you might as well chuck yourself in it if you don't find the gaffer's dog. I should go and have another look.'

Charlesy gulped and set off on another desperate search mission. He went off back down the embankment, just praying that Del Boy would somehow magically turn up.

Eventually he returned after giving up any hope of finding him and reluctantly decided that the only way was to go and knock on the gaffer's office door and break the bad news.

Charlesy stood outside Cloughie's office with Del Boy's collar and lead in one hand and sheepishly knocked the door with the other.

'Come in!'

As he entered the office he saw Del Boy sitting there in the chair.

'What can I do for you, young man?'

'Oh, err. I've just come to return the dog's lead, gaffer.'

6 No one ever really gets the hang of me. I don't want them to - I like to keep people guessing 9

Trevor Francis is officially acknowledged as the first ever £1m footballer. But veteran football boss JIM SMITH says that all was not exactly what it seemed with the deal that stunned soccer.

97

POUND STRETCHER

JIM SMITH

Trevor Francis quite rightly regards himself as Britain's first ever million pound footballer but in fact his historic transfer came to a quid less than that!

I should know because I was the manager at Birmingham City of the time and therefore had a unique insight into the somewhat reluctant sale of our star player.

It was February, 1979 when it became clear that hanging on to the sublimely talented Francis was no longer going to be an option open to us.

The transfer went on for quite a while because there were complications over Trevor going to America in the summer to play for Detroit Express. There were other things going on, but to cut a long story short we had finally come close to wrapping up a deal which took Trevor to Cloughie's reigning champions and League Cup holders for what was then a massive, transfer record-shattering deal.

But the crux of the matter was that Brian didn't want Trevor to carry the burden of being the first million pound footballer and he also said he didn't want it to make the player big-headed!

So eventually we arranged a deal where the actual fee for Francis was £999,999 – a pound short of the magical million mark. Of course when you slapped taxes and various things on it then the transfer of Francis did cost seven figures.

On many occasions I've crossed paths with Brian and I count myself fortunate to be one of the people he got on with.

People are left with all sorts of different impressions of Brian depending on the circumstances of their meeting. But life was certainly never dull with him around.

One of my biggest feelings about him was that for all the bluster, he was a very kind man.

He once helped me out by letting me sign Colin Todd when I was in charge at Oxford. That gave us a real boost and I will always be grateful to him for that.

One of the loveliest stories I tell people about Brian was the one when he kept his players waiting for well over an hour on a frosty, winter's day on the pretext of having a team meeting.

Apparently the players were baffled to be told there was to be a meeting and they should be ready and waiting at 10 am for the gaffer to arrive.

Brian eventually turned up an hour later and then offers the players an excuse that, by his standards, left them shaking their heads in disbelief.

'I'm late because I've been feeding the ducks. It's important to feed the birds at this time of year because it's cold and they're struggling,' he assured his baffled players.

'So, I want you all to feed the birds when you get home and if I found out that anyone hasn't he'll be fined. Tara!'

Pure Cloughie. Pure madness - but also pure kindness. It's little things like that I will always remember.

' I'm always amazed when managers allow players to go away and think about a proposed transfer. Let them out of your sight and the chances are they'll go and sign for somebody else '

When the manager told Tranmere's ROY McFARLAND he'd be an England player within the 12 months, he thought he was barmy. The stylish defender did play for his country, but Clough was a month out.

98

A CLOSE CALL

ROY McFARLAND

'We'll make you an England player within 12 months,' Cloughie insisted as he desperately tried every last trick in the book to get me to sign for Derby. Me? England? 12 months? I was working for a tobacco company in Liverpool and playing Fourth Division football with Tranmere. What kind of crackpot was this man?

He got it wrong . . . by a month. Thirteen months after signing for Derby I got the call to play for England Under-23s against Holland at Birmingham. Incredible.

Over the years, so many people have asked me what was Clough and Taylor's special strength. They had too many to mention, but without doubt, as that story shows, they had an uncanny knack of being able to see something in players long before anyone else could see it.

That was certainly the case with me and I also recall when John McGovern joined Derby he barely looked a player at all at that level.

'You wait and see,' the gaffer insisted. 'You just wait and see.' He was right – again.

When John came to the club he was always last or next to last in training runs. He was a skinny little thing and looked like one good gust of wind would blow him over.

Two years down the line and he was bigger, stronger and was up there with everybody. He wanted to be first in everything. We couldn't see that he was developing, but Cloughie and Taylor could and were convinced that he had everything it took to be a top player.

And that skinny kid went on to lift the European Cup as captain of Forest, not once but twice.

❝ When I first won the League Cup in 1978, I stuck the trophy on the telly and just sat there eating fish and chips and gazing at it ❞

Striker ROGER DAVIES had been plucked from part-time football and so wasn't used to negotiating contracts when he went into the bear pit with two of the game's masters.

99

IT'S GOOD TO TALK

ROGER DAVIES

I was so scared doing my first proper contract talks with Cloughie that I'm pretty sure I agreed to take a pay cut! The thing with me was that I was a bit different from most of the other lads. I was a young guy who had joined the club from non-League Worcester City and so I had no comprehension of what to do. Add to that the fact that I was petrified of the gaffer and it's hardly a recipe for standing your ground and negotiating a deal in your favour.

I'd made my first team debut at the end of the 1972 championship season. In those days, all the players would sit in the dressing room and wait to be called into the manager's office. Then you would be able to discuss terms for the following season. I hadn't a clue what to do – this was all completely new territory. Arguing with Brian Clough didn't bear thinking about. Roy McFarland tried to guide me in the right direction and said: 'Just say to them (Clough and Peter Taylor) that you think you've done well this season and for that reason you think you are worth a pay rise. That's all you need to do. Nothing heavy-handed.'

'Great,' I thought. 'I can cope with that,' and rubbed my hands at the thought of them agreeing to give me a nice little rise into the bargain. The call came. It was my turn. To say I was a touch anxious would be an understatement . . .

'Come in.'

Peter Taylor was sitting there alongside the gaffer and the 'negotiations' started virtually from the off.

'We have decided to offer you a drop in wages,' came the opening gambit. My jaw must have hit the table but I was struck dumb.

'But, given the circumstances, we will give you a small rise, just to stop you moaning.'

'Thank you very much,' I said and walked out. That was it, my first successful contract talks – and hardly all my own doing!

> ❝ I've found generally in life that people who say 'money isn't everything' have loads of it ❞

Taylor, Clough and young Nigel Clough sit pitchside at the 1980 World Club Championship clash with Nacional in Tokyo. Forest lost 1-0.

NOTTINGHAM FOREST 1978: Back(from left): Ian Bowyer, Viv Anderson, Tony Woodcock, Kenny Burns.
Centre: Jimmy Gordon(trainer), Frank Clark, Larry Lloyd, Chris Woods, Peter Shilton, Colin Barrett, Brian Clough(manager).
Front: Peter Withe, David Needham, John McGovern, Martin O'Neill, John Robertson.

DERBY COUNTY 1971-72: Back(from left): Jimmy Gordon(trainer), Peter Daniel, Kevin Hector, John McGovern, Colin Boulton, Terry Hennessy, Frank Wignall, John Robson, Brian Clough(manager). Front: Peter Taylor(assistant manager), Alan Durban, John O'Hare, Archie Gemmill, Roy McFarland, Alan Hinton, Colin Todd, Ron Webster.

MANSELL CRASHES: Nigel Mansell crashes attempting a passing manoeuvre at the City Ground in 1992.

Ball control: Cloughie larks about with the world champion.

HOLDING HANDS: Cloughie and Terry Venables lead their teams out at Wembley FA Cup final between Forest and Spurs.

WE LOVE YOU: Forest fans say farewell to Clough.

IT'S A STICK UP: Cloughie relaxing in his retirement.

Picture: Nottingham Evening Post

FITTING TRIBUTE: The European Cup takes centre stage among the trophies Clough won in front of the stand that bears his name.

UNITED
IN
GRIEF:
Forest fans' tributes.

UNITED IN GRIEF: Derby fans pay their respects.

PAYING TRIBUTE: *Forest European Cup winning heroes (from left): Peter Shilton, John O'Hare, John Robertson and Tony Woodcock walk out on the pitch before the home game against West Ham on September 26, 2004.*

Picture: Nottingham Evening Post

PAYING TRIBUTE: Ex-Derby players (from left): Barry Butlin, Roger Davies, Ron Webster, Henry Newton, John McGovern.

HIS WAY:
Making sure Cloughie
is never far from
people's thoughts.

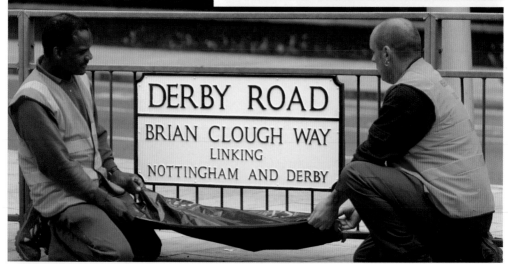

He's behind you . . . ex-Forest players at the unveiling of Brian Clough's statue in Nottingham in November 2008.
Back (from left): Kenny Swain, Nigel Jemson, Chris Fairclough, Colin Barrett, Steve Sutton. Centre: Archie Gemmill, Gary Mills,
Garry Birtles, Frank Gray, Tony Woodcock. Front: Liam O'Kane, Franz Carr, John McGovern, Kenny Burns, Viv Anderson.

DYNASTY: Barbara Clough at the unveiling of her husband's statue in Nottingham with (from left): son Simon, daughter Elizabeth and son Nigel.

*Derby Evening Telegraph sports writer STEVE NICHOLSON
recounts the afternoon when he received a shock
phone call in the office from an
'anonymous' well-wisher.*

100

GOOD LUCK CALL

STEVE NICHOLSON

Back in April 1988, I received a phone call which still leaves me somewhat bemused and stunned to this day. I covered Nottingham Forest for the Derby Evening Telegraph, but obviously, they were very much our second club. Derby County were the major team for us – always was and always will be. But Forest were only 16 miles up the road and so needed to be covered.

I'd been to every Forest game, home and away, that season but to Cloughie I was basically not really on the radar. I suspected that he would be familiar with what I wrote if only for the fact that his family home was in Quarndon, a beautiful village on the outskirts of Derby city centre.

The previous weekend I had been to see Forest lose to Liverpool in the semi-final of the FA Cup and they were due to play at Anfield in a league match on the following Wednesday. I was set to miss my first game of the season because I was going into hospi-tal for a routine operation on my nose. I'd broken it playing football a few years before and it was causing problems which needed sorting out.

I was due into hospital on the Tuesday but I was at my desk in the office the day before. At around 4.30pm my direct line rang.

'Hello, sports desk.'

There was no introduction from the caller who said: 'Hello young man. What are you still doing at your desk when you've got a big day tomorrow?'

I recognised who it was immediately, but I was absolutely stunned because he'd never rung me before and, like I said, I was really of no significance to him at all.

'Get yourself home – and good luck.' The phone went dead before I'd even had time to say thanks.

I just sat there with the phone in my hand, hardly believing what I'd just heard. It just showed a kind and considerate side to him that I'd never witnessed.

❛ Resigning at Derby was a piss-poor decision on my part - infact it's the worst I've ever made ❜

When the taxman called threatening to close Nottingham Forest down, a secret benefactor came to their rescue by digging in his own pocket, as ALAN HILL reveals.

101

CHEQUE MATE

ALAN HILL

Not many people know that Brian Clough saved Nottingham Forest from closing down by taking decisive action.

His actions on the pitch are well documented, but I recall the day he took matters into his own hands to stave off a catastrophe.

I was in the office at the City Ground when club secretary Paul White came in and delivered a bolt out of the blue.

'The Customs and Excise are coming in to close the club down tomorrow. There's an outstanding VAT bill for £35,000 that can't be paid,' he informed us.

'Are you joking?'

It was clear he wasn't so Brian asked him who he'd spoken to and I'll always remember the name because it just stuck in my mind. I suppose given the enormity of what was happening, it's hardly surprising.

'It's a Mr Barber, I spoke to,' Paul said.

'Well get Mr Barber on the phone for me,' the gaffer said.

'Mr Barber . . . Brian Clough speaking. I understand you are planning to come here to close MY football club down.'

The guy on the other end must have confirmed that's exactly what he was going to do, but I'll bet he's never heard anything like the response he received.

'If I signed you a cheque for £35,000 now, would that do the trick?'

'Is it YOUR cheque?'

'Yes, it's my personal cheque,' Cloughie assured them.

They were obviously happy enough, so the gaffer gave Whitey a cheque for thirty five grand and then went and sold Peter Davenport to Manchester United for £600,000 so I'm assuming he got his money back pretty sharpish.

> **❛I miss having the privilege of being the worst timekeeper in the business with the power to bollock anyone who was late! ❜**

*Forest won the 1990 League Cup final over Oldham
with a single Wembley winner from NIGEL JEMSON
who tells the tale of his wife's chance meeting
with the boss at the shops.*

102

SO, YOU'RE THE ONE

NIGEL JEMSON

My wife Mandy bumped into Cloughie in West Bridgford and he made a fuss over our young son Charlie, saying: 'He looks like trouble!'

Mandy said to him: 'You know his dad – Nigel Jemson.'

'No wonder then. So you're the unlucky bugger who got lumbered with him are you?'

Typical Cloughie, who I got on great with despite him continually insisting that I'd got an even bigger head than him. I was a young striker with a lot of confidence and I think he kind of liked that, although he'd always try and knock you down a peg or two. He was very generous and had a warm side to him that some people never get close enough to see.

I've got so many warm memories of him – like the time when we were on a pre-season tour of Sweden and I was one of the substitutes. The gaffer gave us some money to go and get some hot dogs and there we sat on the bench scoffing these huge hot dogs, when one of the players got injured. The Swedes must have been wondering why we played for a while with only ten men but it was because the gaffer was worried that if one of us went on we'd be doubled up with indigestion.

When I scored the winner at Wembley, he didn't show the slightest bit of emotion. I've watched the highlights again and when my goal has gone in, I swear his head never even moved.

You know something, he even had us in training the following morning. He was running us hard and we couldn't believe it. I remember Des Walker grinning and saying: 'He can run me as much as he likes I've got an eight grand win bonus in my pocket!'

It was just typically unpredictable Clough and he's sorely missed.

❛ I was never particularly close to Alex Ferguson, but I do have a great deal of affection for him because I saw lot of myself in him ❜

179

Welsh international ALAN DURBAN helped steer Derby County to the title but found when it came to trying to negotiate a new deal, Clough and Taylor were in a different league.

103

A CUT ABOVE

ALAN DURBAN

Clough and Taylor were like the archetypal 'good cop, bad cop' and they played their roles to perfection. To see them in action was brilliant. You'd get the impression that it was all off-the-cuff knockabout stuff, yet I suspect when it came to given situations, they'd already discussed exactly how they were going to play it.

Cloughie could be funny, but Taylor was extremely funny. But never mind the pair of them having you in stitches – they could tie you up in knots just as easily.

I went in for talks knowing that this was going to be my last contract and adamant on getting a £30 rise. I was on £100-a-week, but after the part I'd played in a very successful side, that seemed more than reasonable to me. Bad cop Clough immediately set about his part of the routine.

'Well, to be honest, we've got an attractive package to put to you. It's not so much on your basic but it will be well loaded on appearances,' Clough assured me. I wasn't having that! Contracts loaded to appearances usually mean only one thing – you don't get too many appearances. That was no good to me at this stage of my career. This was probably going to be my last deal and I needed a good increase – in the region of thirty quid sounded more than reasonable to me. Introducing . . . good cop, Taylor, who rounds on Clough.

'I can't believe you're trying to treat that lad like this,' he says, looking at Clough.

'After all he's done for you. You ought to be ashamed of yourself. This lad has run his balls off for you.'

I puffed out my chest and suddenly felt like I was back in the driving seat as negotiations proceeded. Now I had Taylor in my corner. I got my rise.

As I left the office I did feel like I'd won hands down. I'd certainly shown Cloughie that I wasn't going to be trampled on and the fiver-a-week rise would come in handy too!

❛ Who's been the biggest single influence on my career? That's easy. Me ❜

Leeds United's Scotland international PETER LORIMER lifts the lid on Clough's explosive impact during his ill-fated 44-day spell as manager at Elland Road.

104

WRONG MOVE

PETER LORIMER

I'd love to be able to come up with a funny anecdote from Brian's time at Leeds but it was all pretty serious stuff from the minute he walked through the door.

He had a terrific career but it was just marred by one episode – his brief spell in time at Leeds.

The first thing he did was ask for all the furniture that had been in Don's office to be taken away. He wouldn't sit on the chair he'd sat on and he wouldn't have the desk there that Don had there. Then we realised he really did hate Don and the set-up at Leeds.

Despite what a lot of people might think, he never said an awful lot. People might find that hard to believe, but I think he realised almost straight away that he had done the wrong thing coming to the club he'd criticised.

And when he did speak it hardly endeared him to people who had been totally shocked he'd been named manager in the first place.

When he eventually got round to talking to us he explained that he'd wanted to form his own impressions of the club rather than listen to what other people might tell him, which sounded reasonable.

Then he famously said: 'Before I start working with you lot – he called us 'a lot' – there's something I've got to tell you what I think about you all,' and he then launched into a personal attack on every player.

His finishing gambit was: 'And finally you've won all the trophies, the domestic trophies and the European competitions, but as far as I'm concerned you can throw all your medals in the bin because you haven't won one of them fairly.'

After that he was always struggling. He just handled it all wrong and he admitted that afterwards.

If he'd had a couple of years who knows what would have happened? Given what he went on to do at Forest, what he could have done at Leeds is one of the great unanswered questions.

❛ I wouldn't say I was the best manager in the business, but I was in the top one ❜

England keeper PETER SHILTON can't help but
smile as he recalls a seaside rendezvous when
the Forest players made waves and took
the risk of a little light poisoning.

105

SCARBOROUGH FAYRE

PETER SHILTON

I can reveal the revolutionary diet which helped Brian Clough conquer Liverpool to win the League Cup final – prawns, crabs, cockles, winkles, a few beers and a large dose of salty sea air. How half the Forest team didn't go down with food poisoning is still a source of some amazement to me, but who can argue with something that seemed to work?

As preparation for the 1978 final against Kenny Dalglish and Co, Cloughie had taken us away to Scarborough for a few days to do a bit of training and get some bracing sea air through our lungs.

I couldn't play because I was cup-tied so Chris Woods was the man between the sticks. The gaffer was a master at trying to get players relaxed and he didn't mind how unconventional he had to be to achieve his aims. We walked up the front and went into a pub with Cloughie asking if anyone wanted a beer. I declined the invitation even though I wasn't playing but a few of the players had a beer.

As we were coming back, he made us take our shoes and socks off and told us to go and have a paddle. It was freezing! It's a wonder some of the boys didn't go down with frostbite. If the Liverpool boys could have seen us they would have thought we were barmy.

Anyway, after we'd put our gear back on, we walked back along the promenade. Cloughie spotted a seafood kiosk which was surrounded by a group of disabled kids.

The gaffer greeted all the kids and made a fuss of them all and we stopped to sign some autographs.

'Anyone want some seafood?' shouts the gaffer.

I couldn't help thinking what a risk it was. You don't need to be Jamie Oliver to know that eating shellfish can be a risky business at the best of times.

'Have some crab . . .' I could hear him saying.

'Have some prawns . . .'

Suffice to say not one of the lads was ill. Oh yes – and Forest went on to beat Liverpool and win the cup after a replay.

It's just something that I remember about how totally unconventional Clough was but it's just part of the magic that made him what he was.

Some managers would send you to bed with a head full of stuff they had tried to put across in diagrams or on a blackboard. Clough was having none of that. If he wanted to relax his players, he'd often send them to bed after a couple of beers. That way you weren't being kept awake worrying about the game. You always knew to expect the unexpected when Cloughie was around. If people could have seen some of the things he had us doing before matches they would just think you had made them up. Like running through stinging nettles . . .

We used to run from the City Ground along the Trent to a park area we used for training. In spring and summer, tall nettles would grow alongside our training pitch.

If results were going WELL, Clough would make us run through the grass and nettles, round a tree and back to him. The players didn't used to relish running through the nettles but I think it was Clough's way of keeping our feet on the ground and not letting a sequence of good results go to our heads.

That was all part of the Clough magic formula for getting the best out of everyone. Forest was never considered to be a star-studded side but we really worked for each other. We were a side that gelled in every sense of the word and that was largely down to Clough and his 'all for one and one for all' attitude running through the club.

Anyone who even hinted that they might have ideas above their station was quickly brought into line. And it didn't matter whether you were a youngster fresh into the first team or a big money signing, you were made to muck in.

Small details were important to Clough. I didn't escape having to make the tea – neither did Trevor Francis, despite being Britain's most expensive player.

Yet I can honestly say the dressing room atmosphere at Forest was one of the best I ever experienced.

❝ Where I was brought up in Middlesbrough wasn't the nicest place in the world - but to me it was heaven ❞

106

WHO TOLD YOU THAT?

AUTHOR

My back page exclusive that morning stated that Forest striker Peter Davenport was set for a big-money move to Manchester United. I knew my informant was spot-on and in a great position to know what was going on, but to protect them the story was littered with 'an insider said' and 'I understand.'

I knew my source was impeccable, and if I hadn't been sure, confirmation was to come in the form of an early morning phone call from Cloughie's secretary Carole. Clough rarely, if ever, rang you. It's just something he didn't do. Was I in for the biggest bollocking of my life? I'm guessing it would have been about 9.15 because I recall, it hadn't taken long for Cloughie to first, see the story, and then decide to make some urgent enquiries. It either had to be spectacularly wrong or spot-on to spark such a reaction. I was still confident. It caught me completely off guard – another well-used Clough tactic – and I needed to clear my head and be very careful what I said.

'David? It's Carole . . . the boss would like a word.'

'Hey shithouse! What's all this bollocks in your paper this morning?'

'The Davenport stuff?' I said rather unconvincingly.

'Course, the Davenport stuff,' he snapped back.

'Well . . '

'Let me just ask you something,' Cloughie continued.

'Course.'

'Have you been speaking to my player?' This was a difficult line of questioning from the off because to keep answering 'no' to everything he asked could eventually point him in the right direction.

'Look Brian, I don't think you'd respect me if I told you who I had and hadn't been talking to.'

'Have you been speaking to my player?' he repeated.

'No, but that's as much as I'm prepared to say.

'Was it a director then?'

'Brian . . . I've got to protect my sources.'

'Are you convinced it's right, though?' he chipped away.

'Yes, I am.'

Cloughie's parting shot told me

everything I needed to know.

'Hey, well done. Tara.'

I couldn't help feeling good about it. Cloughie knew it was right and probably deep down didn't have a problem with that. What really niggled away at him was that someone on the inside had been prepared to tip me off.

Now that really got under his skin and though I never found out what lengths he went to to try and uncover the 'mole' I know darned well he would have.

And the other thing is, Clough had a strict set of values. He wouldn't have expected me to reveal my source. I never would have done. But if I had even considered it thinking it might get me some favour with the manager, I'd have been dead in the water.

He, quite rightly, would have immediately marked me down as someone totally untrustworthy – and he'd have been right. So he was mad with me for a while, but there would have been a sneaky little bit of regard thrown in there too.

6 Sometimes you win football matches in unusual places - like before you have even set foot on the field 9

When FRANK CLARK joined Forest from Newcastle he couldn't have imagined that not only were his glory days as a player still in front of him but that he'd eventually follow Clough into the manager's seat.

107

HOW'S THAT GAFFER?

FRANK CLARK

The night of Tuesday, April 25, 1978, saw another Clough masterstroke at its best even though the tremors weren't felt too far outside of the Clark household. It is a night that should go down in footballing folklore – well, it's certainly a night I'll never forget. There were scenes of mass hysteria at Ipswich's Portman Road ground. Not because Nottingham Forest had won the title and not because Ipswich had a date in the FA Cup final. No, it was something much more rare than either – I actually scored a goal.

I'd played around 400 games for Newcastle and never managed a league goal and when that historic night came around I'd chalked up around another 100 for Forest.

The season was in its final throes and we were already in cruise control having done the unthinkable and won the title. That Tuesday night's encounter was never going to be a blood and thunder affair with Ipswich's players desperate to stay fit for their FA Cup final date with Arsenal.

I was substitute that night for a game where we had been short of fit players. Little Archie Gemmill had started up front alongside Peter Withe in a match that developed into an awful game.

At half-time the gaffer went berserk and announced that he was taking Big Peter off.

'It could have been anyone, Withy,' the boss assured him. 'But you were the worst!'

I got warmed up and just presumed that with Ian Bowyer playing left-back, I'd slot in there and he'd stick Bomber up front.

The bell went in the dressing room to alert us to get out for the second half. Big Larry Lloyd's smirk developed into full-blown laughter as the gaffer said nothing at all. And so, without a word being said, it turned out that our front two for the second half was Archie and yours truly. It was hardly a pairing to strike fear into the opposition but as the game kicked off and we took up our positions, Ipswich's international centre-half Allan Hunter let me know in no uncertain terms that he wasn't planning to get too involved with a big day at

Wembley around the corner.

'You keep away from me and I'll keep away from you,' he said. That was all right with me as I was playing a position totally alien to me.

Anyway, we won a corner midway through the second half and the ball fell straight into my path. The goal was gaping in front of me and for a split second it occurred to me that even I couldn't miss this one. The ball hit the net and all our lads went wild. Cloughie and Taylor went berserk on the bench at the absurdity of it all. Around 500 League games and this was the first time I'd ever managed to score!

After the match Peter Taylor went into the Ipswich dressing room and asked if he could have the match ball. Their manager Bobby Robson could not believe it, but after a lot of persuading handed the ball over.

It felt so good, but there was a whole lot more to come. Who would have thought when I left Newcastle to join Forest for nothing that I would go on to win a championship winners' medal and then lift the European Cup. It truly was the stuff of fairytales.

When Newcastle gave me a free transfer, I was looking for a move that would prolong my career. I certainly could never have imagined I'd be an integral part of a side that was about to conquer Europe.

Clough had the knack of extracting the maximum out of people. He developed a style of playing that HE understood and, more importantly, his players understood.

He was a master manager and was someone never afraid to try the unorthodox. I had a lot to be grateful to him for, giving me a fantastic ending to my playing career – one I could just never have dreamed of.

He stands with the greatest ever. He was a football man in every sense of the word and his achievements are up there to stand comparison with anyone in the game.

❛ We liked a soft pitch. I used to water ours more than the groundsman. Half the time nobody knew I was doing it because I went back at night ❜

*Former Newcastle, Spurs and England winger CHRIS WADDLE
reveals how his big-match routine of scampi and chips
washed down with three pints of Guinness would
probably have found favour with Clough.*

108

SCAMPI AND QUIPS

CHRIS WADDLE

I happen to think I was a Brian Clough type of player – and he once told me he thought so too. It was one of the biggest compliments I've ever been paid and I've never forgotten it. I was playing for Newcastle against Forest and I'd made one and scored one. I was in the tunnel afterwards, just making my way to the dressing room when I came across the great man himself. Our eyes met and just as I was wondering what the hell he was going to come out with, he surprised me.

'Hey, you could play for Forest you could,' he said.

I was a little bit shocked but then realised that was some compliment coming from the guy who had made John Robertson, a winger like myself, such an integral part of his success.

And I'm sure my pre-match routine for night games would have met with his approval too because one or two players have told me that he wasn't averse to players having a beer before games. He believed that having your mind clear and not playing with tension was crucial – and I couldn't agree more.

When I was at Spurs and we had a night game, I would go to my local at lunchtime have three pints of Guinness and a meal of scampi, chips and peas! Some people find that unbelievable but it worked for me.

I'd go home and have a good sleep in the afternoon and then I was ready to go! In one great spell, I scored for four games running.

Terry Venables pulled me aside and said: 'What is that you are doing on a Tuesday?'

I came clean and told him: "I'll be honest boss, I go to my local have three pints of Guinness along with scampi, chips and peas, then take two or three hours kip and that sorts me.'

Terry looked long and hard, smiled and said: "Keep doing it – and take five or six of the lads with you next time!'

❛ The River Trent is lovely. I should know, because I've walked on it for 18 years ❜

There's no getting away from the gaffer as JOHN O'HARE reveals. The Scotland international is synonymous with Clough, playing under him at Derby, Leeds and Forest.

109

GIVE ME A BREAK

JOHN O'HARE

If ever you needed to get a break from Brian Clough, it was like he was never far away. I found that out when I slipped off to Blackpool for a get away from it all weekend!

I remember it wasn't far into the season, but Peter Taylor said to me that he thought I looked a bit jaded and needed a break. I jumped at the chance and decided that seeing as I'd never been to Blackpool, the wife and I would treat ourselves to an enjoyable weekend there.

We got there on the Saturday and hadn't been there long when I took a phone call in our room to be downstairs to meet the boss and his wife Barbara for dinner! It was just amazing. I don't think he was stalking me – there was a Labour Party Conference in the town that weekend and I presume bumping into us was purely co-incidental!

But I didn't have too many breaks from him during my career. I'd known him as a young lad at Sunderland and even then when he took training it was always just so much more enjoyable. I'm sure that career-ending injury there was what drove him on. There was a desire burning so deep within him, you could see it. The injustice of having to finish his career early was instrumental in lots of things he did. He had an aversion to hospitals and crutches. He just hated them.

When I joined him at Derby, I came purely because of him. I just knew this guy was going to be a good manger. I couldn't have known how good, but I knew he had the ability and ambition to succeed.

I even followed him to Leeds for his ill-fated spell there before eventually linking up again at Forest.

At Leeds he was always struggling. There was real animosity right from the off. The players were okay with me despite my obvious Clough connection but I went along to the players' meetings during what could be described as his eventful 44 days in charge at Elland Road.

I knew from early on that he'd had it there.

Leeds were a great team but they had been used to Don Revie's dossiers – Clough kept things simple and had no time for all that. He gave players phenomenal amounts of rest time – he was quite revolutionary in that way.

I remember him giving Frank Clark a few days off and someone spotted him training. The gaffer went crackers at him!

Majorca became like a second home to us. Off we'd go if a gap in the season allowed it and he never minded his players having a beer.

He was an absolute one-off whose philosophy on football was to boil everything down to bare bones and keep it all simple. He instilled great spirit in his teams and that can go a long, long way. It worked for him and his players.

But most of his players loved him for all his little idiosyncrasies. He had an attention to detail which had to be seen to be believed. He spotted things on and off the pitch. He had good players and he and Peter Taylor were a fantastic double act. Peter was the funny guy, without a doubt, but together they were just fantastic. Infact, together they were much better than when they worked apart. They made things work which other people would have steered well clear of. They just did – and it was magical to be a part of it.

❛ I paid for that stand and I bribed the erectors because we built it in winter. They said they couldn't work on it because of ice, so I provided coffee and brandy and sent their wives hampers and all sorts! ❜

110

OPENING SHOT

EDDIE GRAY

I still believe Brian Clough was one of the truly great managers despite being on the receiving end of one of his most famous putdowns.

'Young man, if you'd been a racehorse, you'd have been shot,' was Clough's much-quoted observation on my injury record.

I wasn't hurt by it as some people have suggested over the years. I took it as a joke and just put it down to it being the way he was. Yes, it was a bit insensitive but I ended up playing for another 10 years anyway.

Some people have said maybe it was the right man, wrong time, but I don't go along with that. He was quite possibly the right man at the right time but he just went about it completely the wrong way. Clough stormed into Elland Road like a bull in a china shop and I'm positive that if he had been given his time again he would have handled things much differently. I really genuinely believe that.

Hey listen, my brother Frank won the European Cup with him, so there has to be something about the man. Even now he still can't pinpoint exactly what it was.

There's absolutely no doubt in my mind that he was a great manager, I just don't think he should have conducted himself the way he did.

Clough's first meeting with Leeds' multi-talented bunch of internationals has become the stuff of folklore. Even accepting Clough's penchant for a bit of mischief-making, no one could have anticipated his opening line.

'Gentlemen, the first thing you can do for me is throw your medals and pots and pans in the dustbin because you've never won anything fairly. You've done it by cheating!'

It was a disastrous start and one from which Clough never fully recovered. He brought it all on himself and it was unnecessary because there was not much wrong with the team.

❛ It was a swanky do with lots of photographers. Roger Moore was there with his wife. I gave him a kiss - he looked a bit surprised! ❜

BBC soccer pundit and former England skipper JIMMY ARMFIELD played with Clough and recalls how, in an early encounter behind the Iron Curtain, he showed he wasn't one to take things lying down.

111

EARLY POINTERS

JIMMY ARMFIELD

I'll say one thing about Cloughie – forget any notion that somehow his forthright manner and inclination to speak his mind, was some kind of act. I'm in a better position than most to judge that and I can tell you straight that he never changed from being a young man.

I played with him for England and many years later followed him into the manager's chair at Elland Road. Our paths crossed many times from the early days when I first came across this headstrong young man.

In the late 50s, we went on an England U-23 tour behind what was then the Iron Curtain. Bill Nicholson was the manager of the team for the tour which went to Romania, Czechoslovakia and Bulgaria.

We checked into the hotel, which was a boarding house type of place. It was certainly not much better than that. I always remember the very first meal we had there because it comprised of what looked like a soup bowl of Bovril and then a guy came along and just broke an egg into it!

Jimmy Bloomfield was with us and he'd been in the catering corps during his national service, so I remember him going into the kitchens and knocking us all up some scrambled eggs and things to eat.

In our rooms they had set us out in alphabetical order. I was in with Alan A'Court of Liverpool and in the next room were Cloughie and Blackburn's Bryan Douglas.

The rooms were dreadful. They were basically made up of two camp beds. There was a flex dangling from the ceiling with a bulb on the end of it. There was a rather primitive washbasin in the corner of the room.

We left our room to go and see if next door was any better. Cloughie was in there. It was exactly the same except in the middle of the rug was a beetle the size of a golf ball looking up at him. He went berserk.

'I'm not sleeping in here,' he yelled. He created merry hell about it and that was when I first became aware that he had an inner confidence about himself that set him apart. The rest of us were basically quite quiet young men, a bit hesitant to take on authority. Things were different in those days, but Cloughie would speak his mind. And before long he was making his views known right at the very top!

Cloughie had scored our only goal in a game against Bulgaria which we were always going to lose because a ref from behind the Iron Curtain was in charge.

The next match was against Romania when some players from the senior England side, who were still eligible to play, came and joined our party. The great Duncan Edwards was one, along with West Brom's Derek Kevan. They went straight into the team with Derek taking Clough's place.

Cloughie was furious and just couldn't get his head around this at all.

'I can't believe it,' he said as I tried to calm him down a little.

'You can't do anything about it,' I assured him.

'We'll see about that,' he growled before marching off defiantly to see England manager Walter Winterbottom to tell him exactly what he thought about the decision.

All the players were amazed because, like I said, we were young men who were reluctant to speak up against authority and Cloughie had no qualms about confronting the England manager.

'This is absolutely ridiculous that I've been left out!' he exclaimed. We were stunned, but that was what he was like even at an early age.

There was a sense of injustice that burned within him and that never became stronger than when his career was so cruelly cut short by injury.

He was a good player with a terrific first touch – not the quickest. But he had that knack of being in the right place at the right time and he scored goals for fun.

I remember ringing him up after the injury and asking him how bad his knee was. 'It's a mess,' he said somewhat forlornly.

'That bad?'

'Yeah, it's a right mess.'

I don't know if he knew he was finished but you could tell he knew it was a bad one.

Our paths crossed throughout our entire lives really and when my career as a journalist with the Daily Express took me to Trent Bridge cricket ground I took the opportunity to ring him when play was stopped by rain.

'Come over, come over,' he said. I made the short walk to the City Ground and he invited me to meet the players. We went into the dressing room and he told them all to stand up!

'This is the first time we've had a really good player in this dressing room for ages,' he declared much to my embarrassment.

'Hey Viv,' he said pointing to his England international full back Viv Anderson and putting his arm around me.

'Now this is what you call a good right full-back, young man.'

❛ I fight lost causes. It's just the way I was brought up - the way I am ❜

*One of Cloughie's most trusted players,
IAN 'Bomber' BOWYER spent eight years
at Forest as a player and later became first
team coach at The City Ground.*

112

THEY'RE IDIOTS

IAN BOWYER

One of the funniest things I ever remember about the gaffer showed his razor sharp wit and his ability to defuse a situation. Let me first say, before even telling this story, that Cloughie could be a lot of things – awkward sod, know-all, whatever, but he wasn't a racist.

His big musical heroes were the Ink Spots and Nat King Cole among others and he loved the likes of Viv Anderson and Chris Fairclough.

I only pre-empt this story by saying that because in these days of political correctness, it would be too easy for someone to take this particular story out of context.

Forest had a young black player called Calvin Plummer who was on the verge of the first team and was substitute for a match at West Ham.

Hammers' fans decided to barrack him and were throwing fruit towards the touchline.

Brian told Calvin to go and do his warm up but less than a minute later he was back in the dugout.

'What the hell do you think you're doing? I told you to go and get warmed up properly.'

Calvin was clearly ill at ease and explained that when he'd gone down to the touchline, the fans had tossed fruit at him.

The gaffer ordered him to go and do another warm-up and show them that he wasn't scared of pathetic stuff like that. Cloughie said to go and show them he was above all that and to get ready to come on.

'Hey, and do me a favour! When you come back bring me a banana!'

❛ If anyone should be grateful for their upbringing, for their mam and dad, then I'm that person. I was the kid who came from a little part of paradise ❜

Forest full-back VIV ANDERSON says that if anyone had seen the club's unique preparations for the 1980 European Cup clash with Bundesliga giants Hamburg, then all bets would have been off.

113

SUP FOR THE CUP

VIV ANDERSON

No one who saw us stumbling around the streets of Majorca in the early hours of the morning could ever have dreamed that we were professional footballers about to play in the biggest game of our lives.

There are certain dates that go down in Forest folklore with the players – and the week before the 1980 European Cup final is right up there with the very best of them.

It's fair to say our preparation for the big clash with Hamburg in Madrid was, to say the least, a touch unconventional.

Cloughie made us train every morning and then once afternoon time had come around we were free to do anything we wanted. People to this day find it hard to believe, but the boss put no curfews on us at all. His only rule for the week was that we were fit to train first thing. After that, it was a case of anything goes.

It's not something that you could even think of getting away with in this day and age. But what a time we had! We must have had some astonished looks from people out there who couldn't possibly have imagined we were preparing for such a huge game. It was Cloughie's way of relaxing his players. Had we lost, then the theory would have a major hole blasted in it and the week in Cala Millor would be dismissed as one big disastrous mistake. We won. We beat Kevin Keegan's Hamburg and made sure the European crown we'd won 12 months earlier was going nowhere. Mind you, I swear it would have been a case of 'All bets off' if any bookie could have seen the state some of us were in at times.

The gaffer believed that there was no greater benefit to players than letting them get away from it all with some sun on their backs and let their hair down. If he hadn't been so successful he would have been dismissed as an idiot. There aren't too many people who think that!

❝ There's nowt wrong with a place being run by a dictator - just so long as that dictator is me ❞

The sight of the world's greatest goalkeeper Peter Shilton thumping a tree before a big European game might give most managers a heart attack. GARY MILLS explains exactly what was going on.

114

PUNCH TRUNK

GARY MILLS

It's a good job the men in white coats weren't around when Cloughie had his Nottingham Forest players punching hell out of a tree trunk while preparing for a big European game. You couldn't make it up.

We were in Austria in 1984 for a game against Sturm Graz in the UEFA Cup. Graz is a pretty village and the gaffer had decided, which certainly wasn't unusual, that we should go for a walk along the river. It was his way of keeping us occupied and gave everyone a chance to stretch their legs.

Cloughie was, I'm guessing, some 50 yards ahead of the party of players when he suddenly ordered us over to where he was standing by a large tree. He was getting quite excited about this tree and one or two of us, I think, started to wonder whether he had finally flipped. Our worst fears seemed to be confirmed when he made us all gather around it in a big circle and announced that this is what is known as 'a punch-ing tree.'

'Right come on you lot, give it a good punch,' he ordered us all.

We were all gobsmacked as we braced ourselves to give it a whack, because even the likes of our star goal-keeper Peter Shilton had been ordered to give the tree a good thump.

Anyway, we either all trusted the gaffer beyond belief or were too scared to disobey orders, that we all started beating hell out of the tree. I don't think we dared do anything else. No one argued.

But the upshot was that he was absolutely right and the bark of this very big tree was in fact as soft as can be. He'd obviously been told about it by someone there and decided to try and spot one on our walk.

I still can't even begin to imagine what the headlines would have been back home if Shilts had bust a couple of fingers because the boss had told him to give a massive tree a punch!

> ❝ Some people liked to think it was a flash in the pan. It lasted 20 years - some flash in the pan ❞

So what was the reason for an off-the-cuff team bonding session in Scarborough? KENNY BURNS discovered the real truth when the bus driver told him about a secret load in the hold.

115

MAGIC CARPET

KENNY BURNS

You never knew what was going to happen next with Clough and you just knew he liked keeping everyone on their toes.

I remember once, it was February time, and we'd had about three days off training. I came in and was getting into my training gear and Cloughie said: 'Don't bother.'

He promptly got us on the team bus and we went to Scarborough. We had a 20-minute walk, a couple of beers, then another 20-minute walk followed by steak and chips.

I said to Albert our driver that the whole thing had been a waste of time and he said: 'Well . . . it hasn't been a complete waste of time.'

I asked him what he meant and he told me they'd dropped some carpet off at Peter Taylor's flat!

As for team talks, we rarely had them. People will find that hard to believe, but honestly, they were rarities. If anyone had seen our dressing room they would have been incredulous.

John Robertson would be having a fag in one of the cubicles. Clough knew exactly what was going on. He'd give Robbo a hammering for his smoking, his scruffiness, anything at all, but he loved him.

And yet, I've seen the time when Clough would come in with a big, fat cigar and plonk himself right down next to big Larry Lloyd. He'd then deliberately proceed to blow big puffs of smoke all over him.

Lloydy would be flapping away trying to get rid of some of the smoke and would end up coughing and spluttering in protest.

All of the players would be glancing across and once he knew he'd done enough to get right under Larry's skin, the gaffer would wink and say: 'I only do it to annoy that big bastard.'

❛ Our team is so young that away trips are like school outings. Our biggest problem isn't injuries - it's acne ❜

Clough's bid to ban swearing at Forest's City Ground seemed like a decent story for Manchester radio journalist Tom Tyrrell - until he tried to pursue the matter.

116

SWEAR BY IT

TOM TYRRELL

Even by Cloughie's standards it was extraordinary. Dismayed by some of the language coming from the Trent End of the ground, he'd had a big placard made pleading: 'Gentlemen – No Swearing Please! – Brian.' Not only did he do it, but the fans responded by singing songs with the expletives either changed or taken out! It was a great story and had been all over the papers.

Soon after, Manchester United were playing at the City Ground and in those days I was working for Piccadilly Radio. United had won and this was in the good old days when I was actually in the tunnel after the game doing live interviews for the show. Cloughie knew who I was because I had been the compere at a few sports forums where he had been a guest and so, though our paths only crossed occasionally, we were on nodding terms.

I'd covered United for years and had such a good relationship that after a game, I'd usually be successful in calling a player over and asking him for his observations on the game.

The way it worked in these circum-stances was that if I caught the attention of a player and he agreed to come over, I would alert the guys in the studio, who might just be talking away over the airwaves.

So, for example, I'd shout a player and then alert the studio who I was about to be talking to. Anyway, like I said, on this particular occasion United had won. My job principally was to get reaction from the United players, but sometimes if the opportunity arose you would get someone from the opposition – particularly if they were a big enough name. Then I spotted . . . Cloughie.

Given that there was no bigger name in football and that he'd had all this publicity over the swearing sign, I couldn't resist chancing my arm as our eyes met across the passageway. Like I said, he knew who I was and of my United connection and – just as impor-tantly – he would have known I was going out 'live.' Cloughie had a work-ing knowledge of how all aspects of the media operated.

'Brian, can I just do a piece with you?' I said and I was chuffed to see that he started to walk towards me.

What a coup this would be.

I hurriedly told the studio to alert them to the fact that it looked like I was going to get a few words with the one and only.

I hadn't a lot of time to prepare for such an event, but that didn't matter. I was experienced enough not to be thrown off track and, anyway, I could ask him about the placard. That would make a nice line. Anyway . . . he was here. I nodded, smiled and was poised with the microphone, waiting for his words of wisdom.

'Hey, and you can fuck off for a start!' he said pointing his finger. Oh my God!!!!

It went out live on air. The studio certainly heard it but it happened so quickly that I'm pretty sure it would have been missed by most of the listeners.

I never did get chance to ask him about that placard.

6 One of the few ambitions I have left is to return to the Wailing Wall and show my three children the notes I wrote and left for each of them. As with tradition you tuck them into the cracks in the wall and I know almost precisely where I left mine 9

*What's in a name? England star TEDDY SHERINGHAM
found out when he joined Nottingham Forest that
there was only one man who would end up
having the final word - and it wasn't him.*

117

NAME GAME

TEDDY SHERINGHAM

From the first time I met Cloughie I was quickly made aware that he was the boss – and not just in name.

I was walking around Forest's City Ground with my then agent Frank McLintock and Alan Hill. I became aware of people scarpering all over the place and was told that the gaffer was obviously about.

No matter who you were at Forest, Cloughie had this aura and reputation that could have people running for cover at the slightest mention of his name.

He was the main man at the club and woe betide anyone who ever suggested differently – not that anyone dared!

Cloughie was different. He was a complete one-off and whatever anyone may think of him he had won things in the game and built a reputation on keeping things simple.

Anyway, we were standing by the entrance to the ground when Cloughie suddenly clocked us and boomed: 'Ah, I see this is our new signing Edward Sheringham is it?'

I couldn't remember the last time someone had called me Edward. Cloughie had this thing about people being called what they were christened or the name that was on their passport. It was just one of those little foibles of his.

I said: 'Well yes, I am the new signing, but I would rather you call me Teddy. The only person who calls me Edward is my mum – and that's only when she's mad at me.'

'Oh that's right is it? Well, welcome to Nottingham Forest, Edward!'

I just smiled because it was clearly his way of letting me know who was the boss and I could sense I would get nowhere by labouring the point.

**‘He was the slowest player on the staff.
Probably because of all the nightclubs he told
me he didn't visit -** *on Teddy Sheringham* **’**

Drowning some of your players isn't listed in any of the manuals as the ideal preparation for a new season. FRANZ CARR recalls how some Forest stars got in a flap at a summer training camp.

118

GETTING IN A FLAP

FRANZ CARR

The gaffer had some pretty different ideas on preparing his players for a new season, but I didn't realise drowning half of them was a particular favourite of his!

We were in Holland at a training camp and it was a huge, very impressive place. Part of the complex housed an Olympic-sized swimming pool and the gaffer, being as ultra-competitive as he was, decided we should have a relay race. Some of the lads weren't great swimmers to be fair. Infact some couldn't really swim at all and the thought of lining up in two teams for a race with Cloughie screaming at them, was their idea of hell.

Anyway, there wasn't any time to argue and the 'race' descended into chaos as players flapped about in the water, just falling short of having to toss the lifebelts in. Hardly the standard expected in a pool the British Olympic swimming team would have felt quite at home in. There was never a dull moment with the boss, that's for sure. But talking about things coming to an unexpected halt . . .

I recall coming back from an away game when the team bus spluttered and ground to a stop just outside Nottingham near the massive power station - a well-known local landmark.

The gaffer wasn't renowned for his patience and when enquiries revealed a replacement coach and driver would take some time, he took matters into his own hands.

'That's too long,' he snapped and proceeded to step out into the road and start waving down cars. You could literally see disbelieving passengers mouthing, 'Hey look, that's Brian Clough!' as they slowed down.

'Hey, can you take a couple of my lads back to my football ground?' he'd ask. And, invariably, they did whether they were planning on going anywhere near the City Ground or not. And so in no time at all we had all been fixed up with lifts back into the city without too much problem at all.

❛ I'm the shop window - Taylor is the goods in the back ❜

Local radio journalist MARTIN FISHER has a story to cap them all when he was invited into the manager's office only to get more (or far less) than he bargained for.

119

CAP-IT-ALL PUNISHMENT

MARTIN FISHER

When Cloughie was good he was very good – but he could be brilliant at being bad. Clough had a profound instinct for exactly what made good radio, but equally, he had the ability to send you away with absolutely nothing on your tape. You never quite knew which Clough you were going to get, but one thing was for certain – it didn't take you long to know if you were in for a fruitless interview.

One day I always remember was going down to his office and thinking I was going to get a decent interview for Radio Nottingham. As we sat down, I had a full tape to fill and I had prepared myself with plenty of questions. They say 'fail to prepare – prepare to fail' so I was ready. Within seconds it was clear that despite all my preparation, I might as well prepare to fail.

Cloughie, for whatever reasons, had decided that he was more interested in doing a James Bond-type act of launching his cap at the coat-stand in the far corner of the office. He was replying to my questions with one-word answers, only straying from that if the cap successfully managed to land on its target!

My tape was running its course and I was getting nowhere. He knew that and was having a bit of a laugh at my expense.

He was just being pig-headed and he knew he was in control and I ended up with a totally unusable tape. He knew what he'd done.

But, as I said, you never knew which Clough you were going to get and people largely forgave him his idiosyncracies because he was such a fascinating character. He knew he could do anything on his own terms.

Some time later, when he was receiving the Freedom of the City of Nottingham, I was treated to a different side of him. This was quite a big story in the city and working for the local radio station it was important for me to get something decent.

I was in the council chambers waiting for him when I suddenly seized the opportunity.

'Mr Clough, could I have a quick word please?'

'Son, because I'm in a good mood, you can call me Brian.'

'Oh, err, thank you. How's your

day been, Brian?'

'It's been very nice, thank you.'

'I bet it's been a bit of a hassle though, being chased all over the place by journalists, trying to have a word with you,' I said.

'Journalists? You're one of them. You've been having a go at me all day as well!'

'Guilty, Brian,' I said with a knowing smile.

He proceeded to give me some fantastic stuff for my radio station and went on about how honoured he felt to be recognised in this way.

So he did reveal his warm side, but it was inevitably on his terms. He liked to keep people on their toes and he certainly did that with me.

The thing about it was that he knew his worth in terms of the quality of material he could give you and sometimes made you fight for it.

But when he was on form there was no one better and some of the modern day managers just wouldn't hold a candle to him. Yes, he could be totally infuriating, but then he would come up with a gem and everything seemed worthwhile.

❛ I don't even know when they make the FA Cup draw these days, but I do know one thing - you'll never beat its appeal when it was done on the radio on a Monday lunchtime ❜

Loyal secretary CAROLE WASHINGTON reveals why something with a very sharp bite acts as a constant reminder to the only time she ever dared answer the boss back.

120

LOYAL SERPENT

CAROLE WASHINGTON

I'll never forget my boss – I've got a little snake to give me a sharp reminder should he ever be too far from my thoughts!

Whenever I look at the charming snake ring on my finger the memories flood back of the one and only time I ever answered him back and thought I might get the sack.

I was his secretary for 12 years and a regular visitor to his family home after his retirement. He was like a father figure to me at times – often listening in when my own dad died and when I needed occasionally to get things off my chest during my divorce. For one who built his reputation on sounding off, he was an amazingly good listener.

There was one day I remember well when he just pushed me too far and I answered him back – something I had never, ever done before.

At home that night, it whirled around in my mind and I honestly thought I was in for the high jump when I reported for work as usual the next day.

'He'll sack you!' I told myself.

It wasn't that he was an ogre, it was just that I respected him so much and had probably even surprised myself that I'd actually stood up to him.

I had it in the back of my mind that I'd be in bother. He would never have said 'sorry' to me, so it was a fair assumption that a frosty silence and just being told to get on with my work might be the best result I was going to get.

When I got in he was there and, I recall, he had a pair of jogging bottoms on. He looked at me, reached into a pocket and pulled out a £50 note.

'Here, go and buy yourself something nice,' he said.

Like I said, he wouldn't have said sorry. That was as near as I'd get – and I was still in a job!

I bought the ring, which I'd liked for some time, and now whenever I look at it, I can see him.

❝ Trevor Francis should have advertised instant coffee because he was an instant footballer ❞

Radio show host and newspaper columnist STAN COLLYMORE reveals how a meeting with Clough at Wembley left him regretting not teaming up with the soccer legend.

121

WHAT MIGHT HAVE BEEN

STAN COLLYMORE

I got a big hug and a kiss off Cloughie at Wembley. What a pity we hadn't embraced each other as boss and player a couple of years earlier. I can't help thinking things might have turned out differently for both of us if my proposed transfer to Forest had come about.

Now, I was playing for England having been signed for Forest by Frank Clark not long after the great man had retired. Perhaps my goals could have helped save him from relegation in his final season and I'm sure he could have helped me with one or two of my troubles. Cloughie was not only a master manager he was a psychologist of the highest order. I honestly believe he could have been really good for me. Sometimes managers like him are what players with a bit of edge need. He certainly worked his magic with the likes of Larry Lloyd and Kenny Burns, who were hardly shrinking violets.

The man's aura is legendary. I admit I was frightened to death of him, but our meeting was as warm as could be. I was in the Centurian Bar at Wembley having just played for England when he grabbed me and said: 'Well done. How are you?'

It's one of my biggest regrets not playing for him because I know it was that close to being a reality.

People talk about his maverick personality but there was so much more to him than that.

I think by the time he came to watch me playing for Southend, he admitted he didn't know whether he could trust his judgement. It's a shame, because I was absolutely on fire. He came to watch me play at Notts County and I didn't have the best of games. I wonder if that was what finally convinced him not to bother?

I wish he had. I think if I'd played for Brian Clough, my career might have taken a completely different path. From the warmth of that Wembley hug, I suspect he thought so too.

‘ I'd have loved to have been Muhammad Ali - that big, that quick, that talented . . . that famous ’

Long hot days and cold beers . . . Derby midfielder
WILLIE CARLIN remembers how a special guest
to his Spanish bar was always guaranteed
to give custom a welcome boost.

122

CHAMPION OF CHAMPIONS

WILLIE CARLIN

It was funny how whenever a certain Brian Clough visited my bar in Spain the takings would go through the roof. In the mid-80s, I had a bar called Champions in Cloughie's favourite Spanish getaway spot – Cala Millor. He always used to pop in and see me when he came to Majorca. In fact, he was the best PR man you could ever have because the number of customers would quickly double just because people had seen him sitting there having a quiet beer.

The bar was located down in the German end of the town and so while he wouldn't have been a massive hit with that lot, the Brits loved him. It didn't seem to matter what anyone's club allegiance was, everyone loved the gaffer.

He was brilliant with the customers. He would just sit there in the sunshine looking as happy as could be and you wouldn't have known he wasn't just any other tourist getting a bit of sun.

But the punters soon spotted him and would sidle in to either just have a peep or ask for an autograph. He was absolutely brilliant with them, chatting away or posing for pictures.

There were sides to him that people never saw. When I was at Derby and my wife was pregnant with our son David he always made a point of making sure everything was okay. In fact, Peter Taylor had taken us away on a break to Guernsey and Brian came around to take my missus Marie out to do all her shopping.

I hear experts who never even met him droning on about how he ruled by fear yet nothing was further from the truth. You were only frightened of not pleasing him.

I remember a six-week spell when I was rubbish. I couldn't pass water, let alone a football. I was waiting for the mother of all rollockings but it never came. He left me to sort it out. When I got my form back, he just said casually: "By the way, it's nice to see you earning your wages again!' Class.

❛ When I get on my high horse about Yorkshire, my kids say they are Midlanders ❜

123

MOTORWAY MADNESS

PETER DAVENPORT

Cloughie used to joke he could walk on water. While that might be a bit beyond even him, I have to admit his sheer presence meant he could remove obstacles from his path where lesser mortals would have found themselves in all sorts of bother. I admit I was terrified of him at times, but it was nice to know his powers stretched far outside the dressing room.

One of the funniest things I've ever seen came back in October, 1983, when we were on the team coach driving down to a game at Tottenham. It seems hard to believe now, but this was the very first 'live' match to be shown. It wouldn't have been screened at all but for Cloughie's powers of persuasion and a policeman who went above and beyond the call of duty.

We had set off down the M1 only to find we were losing a desperate race against time because of horrendous roadworks. The motorway was down to one lane and all the lads were commenting that we weren't going to make it. The whole situation seemed so much more desperate because of the fact that the game was on live – one of ten scheduled for that season.

But the gaffer wasn't used to having obstructions put in his way and hatched a cunning plan. Poor Albert, our much-loved and loyal coach driver, almost had a heart attack when Cloughie set about his novel way of speeding things up.

'Just stop here, Albert,' he barked and the bus came to a halt. What happened next takes some believing, but there were too many witnesses for it to be anything but the truth. . .

Cloughie got off the coach and started removing some of the cones so that we could get into one of the off-limits lanes and instructed poor Albert to take his alternative route!

No one on the coach could believe it as we made our way down one of the other lanes and when a policeman flagged us down, we could just imagine the press having a field day. All the cars were slowing down to take a look as the copper put his hand up and ordered poor old Albert to stop.

'What the hell do you think you're doing?' asked the copper as Cloughie immediately got out of his seat and jumped off the bus.

'Hey, we're live on the telly down at Spurs and we're going to be late. Can you help us please?' asks the gaffer.

You could tell the policeman was just gobsmacked the minute he realised it was the one and only Brian Clough and just as we were all contemplating the prospect of the boss being handcuffed and led away, we realised the extent of his powers!

The policeman agreed to give us an escort as far as he was allowed and we ended up dodging loads of the traffic to get to White Hart Lane with about 10 minutes to spare. We got changed in an instant and dashed out onto the pitch without anyone realising that but for Cloughie, we wouldn't have got there at all!

❛ Some kids I'd been at school with would say: 'You're dead lucky, you are, being a footballer because I was always a better player than you.' I'd smile and remind them 'Well you're not now!' ❜

*When Clough wasn't convinced Forest's man-mountain
LARRY LLOYD had fully recovered from an ankle
injury, he decided there was only one thing for
it - he'd carry out his own special fitness test.*

124

I GET A KICK OUT OF YOU

LARRY LLOYD

Cloughie had his own special way of trying to establish whether I was fit enough to play in the 1980 European Cup final – he kept kicking my injured ankle to see if I squealed or not. It hurt – but I didn't react. And somehow, I managed to pass Clough's unique fitness test to face Kevin Keegan's Hamburg.

I'd declared myself fit, but the gaffer didn't believe me. He didn't think I could have recovered so quickly – and he was right.

I'd been nobbled a couple of weeks earlier by the late Terry Yorath. No, he's not dead, just always late. My ankle went right over and I had damaged ligaments. Cloughie and the lads went on a pre-match trip to Majorca while I was forced to stay at home to undergo intensive treatment which in those days meant having a fair few cortisone injections.

I had injections all week before joining the rest of the players in Madrid. On the morning of the final we had a light work-out and a small-sided game between ourselves. Clough kept close to me and kept giving my ankle a rap and staring me full in the face.

'No problem, boss,' I said, even though I was in bits. When we'd finished I went back to my room at the team hotel, took off all the strapping and stuck it in a bucket of ice. It virtually sizzled!

There was just no way I was going to miss a huge game like that . . . and the rest is history. I got through the game, largely on pure adrenaline and cortisone, and we went on to see off mighty Hamburg to make us back-to-back kings of Europe.

❛ . . . Hey, big head. Just win the ball and then give it to someone who can play with it - *to Larry Lloyd* **❜**

*One of the greatest sports writers of his generation,
BRIAN GLANVILLE'S fluency in Italian helped a
raging Clough get his uncompromising message
over on one of his blackest nights in football.*

125

CHEATING BASTARDS

BRIAN GLANVILLE

Before Brian reveals how he became a piece of Clough folk-lore, it's worth just shaking off the dust surrounding Derby's controversial European Cup semi-final first leg in Turin. To his dying day Clough was convinced his men were robbed, saying: 'Juventus bought that ref – of that there is no doubt.

'We could have won it that last year at Derby if it hadn't been for the shenanigans away to Juventus. And we would have done. We had the players.'

Legendary Wales and Juventus centre-forward John Charles had travelled with the Derby party to the game after being hired as the club's ambassador and advisor for the tie. And it was he who warned Clough and Taylor of suspicious activity. Juve substitute Helmut Haller had twice been in to see the referee – fellow West German Gerhard Schulenberg.

Archie Gemmill and Roy McFarland were the only two Derby players who would miss the all-important return leg if they were booked. And both were booked for trivial offences in the opening 15 minutes.

At half-time, instead of following his team mates to the dressing room, Haller was spotted by Taylor walking away with the match official.

Taylor ran after them asking if they minded him listening to their conversation and was promptly elbowed in the ribs by Haller before being pinned up against a wall by burly men, presumed to be Juve security staff, until the second half started.

Derby lost 3-1 before being held to a 0-0 draw at the Baseball Ground and it was an elimination which stuck in Clough's craw for ever. But it was anger which erupted on that night in explosive fashion.

Brian Glanville reveals just how his words appeared in newspaper headlines all over the world:

At the end of the game in Turin, I'll never forget it, Clough was beside himself with anger. He was raging. Cloughie was expected to do a press conference after the match but could not bring himself to do it.

'No cheating bastards will I talk to. I will not talk to any cheating bastards,' he yelled. The door opened again and there was Clough looking at me saying: 'Tell 'em what I said Brian!'

I'm sure they had probably got the gist of it anyway but I dutifully acted as Clough's interpreter and promptly launched a thousand headlines.

I had lived in Italy for some years and worked for many of the Italian publications so I was well known for my command of the language.

He had probably seen me talking it out there at some point, I don't know, but he certainly knew who to turn to when he wanted to get his message across. I suppose it's not everyone who can give a fluent translation of 'cheating bastards' but I was just the man and was happy to oblige!

❛ Some people didn't get it. I was ranting on about 'cheating, Italian bastards.' And they were - we got done. Which part of 'cheating, Italian bastards' is so difficult to understand? ❜

Respected radio commentator TOM ROSS hasn't missed a single one of his Friday night phone-in programmes in 30 years. But when he compered a Clough forum, he wondered if the outspoken boss might just have got him the sack.

126

A FUNNY THING HAPPENED . . .

TOM ROSS

I remember once thinking Cloughie's unpredictability might just have cost me my job! I was hosting a live forum for BRMB with Clough as the main guest and he was ripping into people, swearing like a trooper and generally being his outspoken self with a bit stuck on top just for good measure.

The audience absolutely lapped it up because there was no one quite like Brian Clough in full flight. He had that God-given knack of being able to insult people and they'd end up feeling privileged! Clough could tell you to 'piss off' and people loved it. My only problem was this was live on radio and the whole episode ended up being front page news in the Daily Mirror. Normally a radio station would give anything to get front page coverage in a national newspaper, but this was for slightly different reasons.

Myself and George Gavin the presenter were called in to give our version of how it had all gone wrong. We had every reason to think we were in

for the high jump but the listeners loved it and Clough had them eating out of his hand.

The feedback was incredible and we went from a situation where we thought we were in really hot water to getting pats on the back for such an evocative show, which had quite literally hit the headlines.

There was an aura about Cloughie. To me, he's the nearest thing to a kind of footballing Pope. In terms of charisma there was only Bill Shankly who came close. He had supreme confidence and he somehow managed to get that into his players.

Cloughie was magnificent. There was a crackle in the air every time he got near a microphone and though he could turn the air blue, people seemed to just love him all the more for it. You never knew what was coming next with Cloughie, which did cause one or two anxious moments but there's never been anyone like him before or since – and there won't be.

'I've lost count of the number of referees who said they just loved refereeing my teams'

Former Derby Evening Telegraph reporter GEORGE EDWARDS got a swift rebuke when he thought he was on the scent of a story Cloughie didn't want anyone to know about.

127

TWY-CROSS!

GEORGE EDWARDS

I very rarely, if ever, fell out with Brian but I do recall him looking at me daggers one day for suggesting something which ruffled him slightly.

Not long after moving to Derby he hired a large minibus and took a group of under-privileged children to Twycross Zoo for the day. I think there would have been around ten to a dozen of them. Brian dropped in on a local children's home, orphanage as it would have been known then, and whisked the kids off for a day out. He was no stranger to driving larger vehicles having been known to drive the team bus in his early days managing cash-strapped Hartlepool. So a minibus certainly couldn't come up with anything he couldn't handle – unless it was full of excited kids!

Anyway, I got wind of this lovely gesture and told him that it would have made a great picture for the newspaper had he told us about it in advance.

If looks could have killed. He told me it was just something that he liked to do and the thought of getting any publicity from it was the furthest thing from his mind.

He told me in no uncertain terms that he didn't need people accusing him of trying to buy popularity by doing things like that.

'I didn't do it for publicity and I don't want people to think I'd use kids that way. Please don't write a word about it.'

I didn't and neither did I raise it with him when I later learned that he was regularly dropping off baskets of fruit at the Derbyshire Children's Hospital on his way home from the ground.

I came to realise spontaneous acts like this were something that shouldn't have surprised anyone.

❝ Football academies worry me. They're grabbing kids almost before they've lost their milk teeth and if you're not careful you coach the individuality out of them ❞

128

BLANK LOOK

PETER THE GARDENER

Cloughie often joked that I was the 'most expensive git' he'd ever employed . . . but it could have been so much more costly!

I'd done some extra work around the place and when I'd finished it was time to talk money.

'How much do I owe you?' said Cloughie. I told him what work I'd done and how many hours I'd put in and it was agreed that £150 should do the trick.

Brian went into the house and as he came out I could see he was popping a cheque into an envelope before passing it to me.

'Cheers,' I said and proceeded to make my way. When I got home, I found a blank cheque signed by Cloughie with a brief note saying: 'Put in the amount you require – all the best, Brian.'

To this day, I don't know whether it was some kind of test, but regardless, I printed out the agreed sum of £150 and submitted it to my bank.

On my next visit, Brian looked at me in that slightly perplexed way he did so well and I wondered if something was the matter.

'Hello Brian, how are you?'

'Hey, you're a fool you, aren't ya?'

'Pardon?' I said.

'You.'

'What?'

'I sign you a blank cheque and you write £150.'

'Yeah, that's what we agreed.'

'No, that was the figure you mentioned. You just missed the biggest chance of your life to pay off your mortgage!'

I hadn't of course. Brian was no fool when it came to money, but I think he respected the fact that I hadn't taken any liberties.

> ❛ Ali is the only person to make me feel insignificant. Old Big Ead was reduced to the size of a pinhead and I'm not too conceited to admit it ❜

Midlands radio legend TONY BUTLER got more than
he bargained for when he found a favour he'd
done for Clough returned in full with
a close-up of the master at work.

129

BEST SEAT IN THE HOUSE

TONY BUTLER

Sitting on the bench with Cloughie and Peter Taylor in full flow is something I will take to my grave.

How it came about was I had done a sports forum he was at with a host of other big names like Ron Atkinson and Trevor Francis and the whole night went down very well. Cloughie asked me if I'd do him a favour and do a couple for him in Nottingham. I said I'd be delighted to and he said: 'Hey, if you do that for me, I'll come on your programme.'

'For free?' I said.

'Yes of course,' came the reply.

The following season had just got under way and I left him alone because I thought I'd better give him a month or so to get his feet under the table as it were. One morning, out of the blue, the office phone went. It was God himself!

'I thought I was coming on your show?' he said.

Anyway, he came on the show, did his piece which was brilliant as always, and said: 'Be my guest at the game tomorrow.'

Forest were playing Everton and I went to Nottingham and when I got to the ground was surprised to find that all the stewards and suchlike seemed to know I was coming and kept directing me through different corridors.

Suddenly, there was Cloughie and it crossed my mind I'd got a bit nearer the inner sanctum than was wise when he pointed me towards the bench and said: 'Sit there and keep that big gob of yours shut for 90 minutes. Don't say a word.'

It was a revelation. To see them work that close up was just fantastic. And let me tell you, they had their disagreements out there.

It was an absolute education and one I will just never forget. And I did manage to keep my mouth shut for 90 minutes, which would surprise anyone who knows me!

❛ I don't speak foreign languages. I find F*** off is understood by pretty much anyone ❜

*Former Luton boss and TV pundit DAVID PLEAT was
left sweating on landing some crucial transfer
cash when Clough suddenly laid into
the player and 'pinched' his watch.*

130

BLACK MAGIC

DAVID PLEAT

Brian and myself had been friends for years when our paths crossed over a transfer. I had just gone back to be manager at Luton for a second time and because of a desperate financial situation, I had been left in no doubt that money needed to be brought into the club – and quickly.

The big saleable asset we had was Kingsley Black and with Brian showing an interest, I was keen to try and get something sorted.

Don't get me wrong – selling Kingsley was the last thing I wanted to do in a perfect world. He was a super player and a really lovely fella. But this wasn't a perfect world and Luton had to get money in fast. A figure of around £1.5m had been agreed.

I'd warned Kingsley that Brian could be a bit unconventional. He made him stand back to back with him and remarked: 'I'm taller than you!'

He was testing Kingsley out to see what he was made of. He was browbeating him a bit, to be honest, to the point where I told him to go easy.

'I've heard you're a coward!' Brian said.

'No. No – I'm not,' Kingsley said.

'Right son, I want an agreement now then. Let's get you signed.'

'I can't possibly do that right now,' Kingsley said firmly, standing his ground and insisting that he needed to discuss things with his family before making a decision.

'That's a nice watch,' says Brian. 'What make is it?'

Kingsley said that it was an Omega, and then looked shocked at Cloughie's next request.

'Hey, give it me!'

'What?'

'You give me the watch and when you come back up to the City Ground tomorrow to get the forms signed, you'll get your watch back.'

Brian got his way. He got the watch and he got his player. Hardly the normal way to conduct negotiations, but that was his way.

> **❛ I've tasted most things, but if there's owt better than family life then let me know ❜**

Merseyside journalist MIKE ELLIS is a doyen of the Liverpool football scene. He re-lives the night he had a ringside seat as Cloughie threatened to walk out of a big soccer bash.

131

DINNER JACK-IT

MIKE ELLIS

I ended up sitting next to Cloughie at the Bells' Manager of the Year dinner in Glasgow – and the night nearly went off with a bang!

It was 1974 and I couldn't have know what was in store as I wondered who, if anyone, would be occupying the spare seat next to me. Clough arrived late to find there wasn't a seat left in the house – well, apart from the one right next to me.

I smiled and nodded as he took his seat at my side. His presence certainly didn't faze me after working so closely with the great Bill Shankly at Liverpool for so many years. Clough leaned over towards me.

"Is Revie going to win this award?'

Clough's hatred for Leeds boss Don Revie and what he considered the dubious and rule-bending way they won things bordered on obsessive.

'Well, he's the favourite,' I replied.

'I'll tell you summat now, if Revie wins that fucking award I'm walking straight out.'

My ears pricked up at the thought of having a massive story dropped, quite literally, into my lap. Clough was one of the most famous people in the country and his outspoken views had already led to him being one of the best known faces on British TV.

Sensing his agitation at the prospect of Revie standing up there, I leant back across and whispered:

'If you do walk out, would you mind giving me a quote?'

'Quote? Believe you me, if I bugger off out of here, you won't be needing a quote off me!'

The great man was right of course and as it happened a pearl of wisdom from him wasn't required.

Jack Charlton became the first manager from outside the top flight ever to be given the honour after steering Middlesborough to promotion in his very first season in charge.

Cloughie, being a Middlesborough lad, could hardly argue with that now, could he?

❛ Ground rules apply just as much to millionaires as they do to someone who's got nowt ❜

217

Former Coventry and Wimbledon boss BOBBY GOULD
remembers how he panicked the day Cloughie
got himself in a spot of bother with the police
and ended up being taken into 'custody.'

132

COPPING IT

BOBBY GOULD

It might well have been April Fools Day . . . but this was no joke. I was manager at Wimbledon and we had a big problem with Cloughie that I just knew was going to get out of hand. It was April 1989 and his Forest side were visiting our 'compact' Plough Lane ground around a week before they were due to play Luton in the League Cup final at Wembley.

This visit had a slightly different edge to it because Brian was serving a touchline ban after whacking a supporter. The problem we had was that our directors' box was so near to the touchline anyway that a seat there was not going to prove too prohibitive to Cloughie with his unique communication skills! Our chairman Sam Hamman had warned the police there might be a problem and that proved to be spot on when we really got at Forest and scored a couple of goals on our way to a 4-1 victory.

Cloughie started lambasting his players from his position in the directors' box and Sam asked him to be quiet. Well, as you can imagine, he wouldn't and so the police ended up removing him.

My missus told me that something had happened and so I went racing down the tunnel to the away dressing room where the chief inspector was reading him the riot act.

I said to Sam that it was all totally unnecessary and that Cloughie was an institution in British football who should be respected. Sam told me to go and concentrate on my football team while Cloughie was promptly escorted outside the ground to a police box that actually overlooked the pitch. He was 'detained' in there for the entire game and the whole business was kept in house. No-one got to know about it.

But there was an odd twist to the whole story a few months later when we went up to the City Ground for a match. Most of the coppers who had been responsible for keeping Cloughie under wraps at Plough Lane had been given special invites and free match tickets for our game up there! He'd obviously taken the time and trouble to find out the names and addresses of his captors and decided to treat them to a VIP day out on him! Sheer class.

But he was like that. I remember

going up to Forest's ground with Don Howe who was just up on his feet again after suffering a heart attack. We were just having a look at a player but Cloughie must have seen a list of the names who were visiting.

Don and myself left with about 10 minutes to go to avoid the bulk of the traffic and just as we were making a hasty exit, we were stopped mid-tracks by Brian's secretary Carole.

'There's a present for your good lady from Mr Clough,' she said handing something to Don.

It was a cut glass vase for Don's wife Pauline. It was totally unsolicited and totally unexpected, but I knew what it meant to Don.

‘ Trevor Brooking was upset with me because I adapted one of Ali's phrases about him. I said he floated like a butterfly and tackled like one. He asked me why I'd said it and I said: 'Because it's true' ’

Ex-England boss GRAHAM TAYLOR reveals why his wife Rita always had a vested interest in whether he had chosen to include Nigel Clough in his national squad.

133

FLOWER POWER

GRAHAM TAYLOR

I'd always got on really well with Brian ever since first crossing paths with him during my time as an extremely young manager at Lincoln City. I loaned Tony Woodcock off him in fact, so I had plenty to be grateful for even in those early days.

We came across each other on many occasions after that during my spells at Watford and Aston Villa and I have to say, I always found him an enthralling personality. The word genius is tossed around far too readily these days, but when it comes to Cloughie I think it's an apt description. Geniuses are few and far between in any era, but the term would rest easily on Cloughie's shoulders – he'd make sure of that!

He was a complex man. Much has been made of his cruel side, but he could be a kind, generous and wonderful man. He was a maverick – one of the most bewitching and interesting characters you were ever likely to meet.

A couple of things that did make me chuckle about him came about during my time in charge of the England team. When I first picked his son Nigel for the national side, my wife Rita received an absolutely gorgeous bouquet of flowers delivered to the door with the simple note 'With love from Brian.' It was a lovely gesture. Then when I didn't pick him, sod all arrived; when he was picked again, she'd get another lovely bouquet delivered.

It's one of the few occasions I can remember my wife taking an active interest on who I was going to name in my England squad!

The other thing was that when I became England manager I went around to all of the clubs who had players in the set-up. Brian had the likes of Neil Webb, Stuart Pearce and, of course, his own son Nigel at Forest and so he was one of my ports of call. The purpose of the exercise was to create some dialogue with the club bosses and to find out a bit more about the players from people who worked with them every day.

I went up to the City Ground accompanied by Lawrie McMenemy who had known Brian years and had a wealth of experience in the game. But when we got there to get a bit of an insight into some of our England boys,

I couldn't help wondering if Brian perhaps thought I had taken the Republic of Ireland job. All he could talk about was a young lad called Roy Keane.

I tried to coax Brian back on track.

'I was wondering what you thought about . . .'

'Graham . . . what a player I have just signed. This young boy is going to be some player, you mark my words.'

I felt like telling Lawrie to try and tell him to shut up, but he was having none of it. Our England fact-finding mission was turning into a bit of a waste of time. Anyway, to cut a long story short, the inside information we had gleaned on our England lads could have been written on a postage stamp. Brian just wasn't playing ball. If Roy Keane had been English, the advance warning of an emerging talent would most certainly have been useful. As it was, it had been something of a waste of time.

Now, as it happened, I was at Anfield when Keane was thrown into the side for his debut and I have to admit I couldn't see anything in him. I watched him carefully and wondered if Cloughie was guilty of grave misjudgement. I've followed Roy's career quite closely ever since that first bizarre warning of a force to come.

Hands up Brian . . . you were right. That skinny kid with the mop of black hair became one of the true modern greats of the game and in no small part down to the footballing eye and instinct of the great man himself.

> 6 Robbo didn't look anything like a professional athlete when I first clapped eyes on him In fact there were times when he didn't resemble a member of the human race 9

When one of his players was coming in for what he felt was unfair criticism, Clough went to extraordinary lengths to get to the bottom of it. Ex-Nottingham Post journalist IAN EDWARDS explains.

134

RADIO GA GA

IAN EDWARDS

Clough was never short of verbal ammo, but if he needed to get some background information to arm him for an argument, he would go to extraordinary lengths to make sure he got it.

Martin Fisher, a reporter for a local radio station, had been giving the team a bit of stick on air and had been singling out Gary Crosby for some special attention.

The suggestion which had riled the gaffer was that Crosby wasn't justifying his place in the team and that maybe he was only in it because he was one of Cloughie's favourites! Red rag to a bull or what?

Because the criticism was taking place in live broadcasts from matches where Clough was otherwise engaged, he hadn't heard the remarks first hand. So, unbeknown to anyone other than his closest associates, Clough decided to get the broadcasts taped.

One morning there were three of us hanging around hoping for an audience when Clough came stalking down the corridor, clearly bristling about something.

He had the capacity to scare people when he wasn't even in the same room, let alone coming face to face with them.

'Which one of you little lot is Martin Fisher?' he asked.

'So you're the one who's been giving me stick and having a pop at Gary Crosby saying he's only in the team because he's one of my favourites are you?'

'Well err . . .'

'I think I'm going to sue you,' Clough declared.

'Well, the thing is . . .'

'Hey, who's your producer?'

'Well, that's me as well actually, Mr Clough.'

'Oh good! I'm going to sue you twice! You two go into my office and you . . . fuck off!'

❛ I never froze a player with fear in my life. I sent them out thinking they were the best since Stanley Matthews ❜

*Liverpool journalist and broadcaster JOHN KEITH
has worked the Mersey beat for decades and
recalls Cloughie being left gobsmacked by
a little Scouse diamond called May.*

135

BUTTON IT

JOHN KEITH

How many people can say they've seen Cloughie get a dressing down and be too dumbfounded to answer back.

I was lucky enough to be close by on that occasion many years ago and it still tickles me when I think about it.

Cloughie was one of the special guests at a Liverpool Supporters' Club forum. In fact, with Denis Law and the great Bill Shankly to accompany him, it was a pretty special line-up full stop.

There was a lovely lady called May Devine, a typically forthright Scouser who was part of the furniture at Anfield. Anyway, May had been asked to come along early and look after the catering or whatever, when she came close to Cloughie.

'Just look at the state of you!' she said clearly addressing a somewhat startled Clough. 'You've got a button missing off your jacket. You can't go up on the stage like that. It looks awful . . . give me a minute.'

I honestly don't think Cloughie knew what to say as May, bless her, set off in pursuit of a suitable button and some needle and thread.

Soon she was back and sewing away industriously with Cloughie, still in his jacket, open-mouthed.

'There you go,' said May, biting off the surplus cotton. 'That's better.'

I just recall Clough with a massive grin, gratefully telling her how wonderful she was and saying a polite 'Thank you very much.' I think he knew he'd met his match that day.

Working the Mersey 'patch' my dealings with Clough were few and far between but I do remember a perplexed Bob Paisley revealing a bizarre chat with the Forest boss once.

I was sitting in Bob's office one day when he told me a lovely story about Clough and his typically unpredictable behaviour.

Paisley told me: 'I was in my office when the receptionist said that Brian Clough was here to see me. It was completely out of the blue and I was a bit surprised. Anyway, he came up and he asked me how I was doing and said that he was going to watch Tranmere and thought I might like to accompany him.'

Paisley insisted that his wife had got his tea waiting for him and that there was no way he could go, but seemed rather pleased with his pay-off line to Clough.

'So, I said to him . . . how you getting there Brian. Not planning to walk across are you?'

6 I constantly doubt my ability to manage.
I think I'm right but I'm not infallible.
If Hitler had sat down and thought for a minute,
we wouldn't be here today 9

It might have been his big day out at Wembley but master showman DUNCAN McKENZIE was left wishing he hadn't asked the question when Clough gave him a withering put-down.

136

TICKET TURMOIL

DUNCAN McKENZIE

How many players make their club debut at Wembley? Not many, I'd guess, but I joined that elite band when Cloughie signed me for the great Leeds United.

I'd never even seen the famous old stadium, let alone played there, when I became Clough's first signing for Leeds at the bargain price of £250,000!

Don't laugh . . . that was quite a few quid then and my move from Nottingham Forest came to the rescue for me personally because I was skint.

I had been absolutely crapped on from a great height at Forest and, if you'll pardon the French, I hadn't got a pot to piss in when Cloughie signed me.

Anyway, he picked me for the game, so I knew that my very first match for my new club I would be at Wembley and I tried to get a couple of tickets so my proud parents could come along.

I asked Cloughie if there was any chance of a couple of the club's complimentary ticket quota and stood back in astonishment as I received my rather curt reply.

'What on earth do you want with complimentary tickets young man?'

'Err . . . they're for me mam and dad,' I assured him, knowing his views on family values.

'For your mam and dad, eh?'

'Yeah.' I nodded.

'Hey, well tell me something young man.'

'What?'

'If your mam and dad won't pay to see you play at Wembley how do you expect anyone else to fork out good cash to watch you?'

> **❛ I climbed trees for all sorts of reasons other than bird-nesting, mainly nicking apples and pears from the posh areas of the neighbourhood ❜**

So, if there's anyone out there wondering why half their flowers were missing but there was cash put through the letterbox . . . former Forest keeper MARK CROSSLEY reveals all . . .

137

MUM'S THE WORD

MARK CROSSLEY

Somewhere near Derby there's someone who once came home to find their flower beds raided and a pile of notes pushed through their letterbox. It's probably remained a puzzle to this day, but as someone who was on the Nottingham Forest team bus that day, I can finally unravel the mystery . . .

The whole team witnessed the astonishing sight of Brian Clough wandering around a garden right near where we used to pick him up for away matches.

We always picked him up at Sandiacre because it was the most convenient place for him to get on. The players had all boarded at Nottingham and Albert, our trusty coach driver, was pulling up at the designated spot when someone spotted the gaffer in a neighbouring garden.

What in heaven's name was he doing? All was to become clear. It was Mothering Sunday the following day and I can only imagine that the boss had admired the flowers in this particular garden and almost certainly knocked the door to ask if he could have some.

Anyway there he was picking some of them before going up to the letterbox and sticking a fair few quid through by way of thanks.

You couldn't make it up could you? Brian Clough, one of the most recognisable faces in the country, picking flowers from someone's garden while the Nottingham Forest team bus waited for him before heading off to an away match.

The gaffer gets on and informed us that just in case any of us didn't know, it was Mothering Sunday, next day.

He started to dish out the blooms, saying: 'Give this to your mother, your wife or your girlfriend and make sure you say it was with love from Brian.'

What a complete one-off. How do you compete with that?

❛ I'd tell players if they couldn't get into work by 10.30 in the morning then they weren't worth bothering with ❜

There was no love lost between the two but Scotland international star WILLIE JOHNSTON tells just what it was that sent Cloughie absolutely ballistic when he showboated at West Brom.

138

BUM RAP

WILLIE JOHNSTON

I once got a foul-mouthed blast from Cloughie and couldn't have been more delighted! Boy, did he go ballistic and I loved every minute of it. I was playing for West Brom in an FA Cup Sixth Round match against Forest. We were 2-0 up with probably 10 minutes to go when I spotted my moment to really wind him up. I had a problem with Cloughie because he thought Forest's John Robertson was a better player than me and would have had him in the Scotland team at my expense at the drop of a hat. Needless to say, I had a different take on that.

Anyway, with 38,000 in the ground, an FA Cup semi-final place there for the taking and me right in front of Cloughie's dug-out, my moment came. A long 50-yard crossfield ball came sailing towards me and I trapped it with my backside and sat on it. Well, Clough went absolutely bananas and just hurled a torrent of abuse at me. I smiled at him, which just made him even angrier.

Albion boss Ron Atkinson recalls: As he did it, I've leapt out of my dugout to go mad at him because we're two-up with time ticking away. But Cloughie was out of the blocks before me, giving it the pointed finger, and I just start pissing myself laughing. I said to Willie after 'By the way, Cloughie's fined you for that!'

West Brom legend Tony 'Bomber' Brown remembers: It was hilarious at the time. It just stunned everybody. That's the way Willie was. Cloughie went mad – and understandably so, but Willie was a showman through and through.'

Former England and Manchester United skipper Bryan Robson also played in the game and recalls: The Hawthorns was rammed and our fans loved it but I just remember Cloughie going barmy about it. He was pointing and screaming at Willie. He just thought it was disrespectful and you can see his point but Willie was lapping it up.

❛ Ali's handshake took me by surprise - my hand just disappeared into his ❜

*Clough's close friend JOHN SADLER remembers the
incredible tale of how Benfica officials had to be
told why it had rained only on the pitch
and not anywhere else in the town!*

139

WATER STUNT

JOHN SADLER

Clough at his innovative best still makes me chuckle as if he was sitting just across the way telling the story. When I sat with him to ghost write his autobiography *Walking on Water* the stories came thick and fast. He was an endless source of mischievous quips and anecdotes. The one I do remember with such fondness was the night he stole into the Baseball Ground in the dead of night to water the pitch the night before a massive European Cup game with Benfica. The Portuguese side, the great Eusebio and all, were at a loss to understand how the pitch could be so sodden when it hadn't rained since they had arrived in the country. It's best, coming straight from the horse's mouth . . .

'We liked a soft pitch at our place. It wasn't soft enough for my liking the night before Eusebio came to town with his Portuguese mates from Benfica. I knew what was needed to get the likeliest winning performance from that team of ours at home. Those were the days when Brian Clough took more water with it!

I used to water our pitch more times than the groundsman did. Half the time nobody knew I was doing it because I went back at night. I had the keys to just about everything and everywhere at the ground. If I needed to see, in the interests of accuracy, I knew how to switch the floodlights on, but the night prior to the Benfica game I did it in the dark.

We didn't have sprinklers; we had two big hosepipes that were equivalent in power to the ones firemen use. I would switch them on, sit back on the terrace steps and let them do their job. Usually, I'd leave them for no longer than 20 minutes because the pitch couldn't take any more than that so quickly. Unfortunately, or fortunately as things turned out, on that night I dropped off. Hey, I was a busy man working a lot of hours in a week, and I had three small children at home. Life can get tiring even for somebody who believed he was a genius.

I don't know how long I slept while the hoses gushed their gallons. All I know is that I woke up drenched and with enough water on that ground to have staged an Olympic diving event from the top board!'

Derby went on to win the game

emphatically 3-0 but not without the mystery of the heavens opening over just the ground coming under closer scrutiny from none other than the FIFA President Sir Stanley Rous.

He'd expressed surprise that the pitch was inches deep in mud when half a mile away in town, there hadn't been a drop of rain. It was one of the wonders of Mother Nature, Cloughie explained. Derby defended for their lives in the famous Stadium of Light to send out one of the truly big names of Continental football.

Said Clough with that naughty grin: 'We'd survived and prospered partly because of what I'd done in the dark. Don't ever try telling me there's nothing to be gained from falling asleep on the job.'

❛ Misinformed people say fear was my biggest weapon with my players. That's crap. My teams couldn't play the kind of football they did if they'd been frightened ❜

Former Forest and England midfield ace NEIL WEBB was as surprised as anyone when a late night call got him out of bed to come and listen to a pianist the night before a big game.

140

THE PIANO MAN

NEIL WEBB

I always remember one night before a league match, all of us players had gone to our hotel beds when we received phone calls.

'The gaffer wants you down in the lounge. There's a guy playing the piano and the boss says it's absolutely lovely.'

We had no choice, though I'm sure the rest of the boys would have been quite happy to settle down and relax. It was not to be. We all trudged downstairs to where the boss was listening to the piano man.

'Does anyone want a drink?' he said, glancing at me. I said: 'No, thanks.'

'You never say no, you Webby,' he said with a laugh.

So about 10 of us ended up having a pint before we all, literally, had to ask if we could go to bed.

Once we travelled up to Bradford for a game that evening and at lunchtime we stopped off at a pub and had a pint of lager! I'm sure the landlord must have thought we were imposters

It was just his way. He was a master psychologist who didn't miss a trick. He was a great manager who turned me from an ordinary player into an international. I still can't help but smile at so many of the little things he did.

I recall picking up a hamstring injury and at that time it meant that about six of us were having treatment. Cloughie shut down the treatment room!

'You lot are depressing me,' he groaned. 'Bugger off home and I'll see you in a few days.'

That was the way he was. He'd got a group of injured players, so what did he do? Shut the treatment room.

He always kept you on your toes. You never knew what was coming next. There was never a dull moment that's for sure.

❝ I'm not sure who Fergie regards as his best ever signing at Old Trafford but there can't have been one better than Roy Keane ❞

Journalist GEORGE EDWARDS found himself labelled a disgrace to the neighbourhood when he went on holiday and let his lawns grow longer than deemed acceptable.

141

THE LAWN ARRANGER

GEORGE EDWARDS

Covering Derby County for the local evening newspaper and living, quite literally, a stone's throw from Brian Clough could quite easily have been a recipe for disaster.

I can honestly say that in all that time, Brian became a close friend and never interfered or passed undue comment on anything I'd written in the newspaper – either about him or the team!

The very first time we met he outlined exactly how he was going to do things and said something to the effect of: 'I will trust you until the minute you let me down and then you'll get nowt off me ever again!'

And in fairness to him, that's exactly the way it was. My main trouble on occasions was being too close. Often he'd tell me things in secret knowing that I couldn't break a confidence. He was clever that way. He'd tell me stuff, knowing I couldn't use it and sometimes left me wanting to say 'please don't tell me that!'

He wouldn't interfere – well, when I say that, I must say that was in a professional capacity. On the domestic front he once gave me a timely prod in the ribs.

As I said, I lived not a minute's walk from his house in Darley Abbey and on one occasion my wife and I returned from holiday to find the front lawn looking remarkably trim.

I thought: 'That's funny, I don't remember mowing the grass before we went away.'

I hadn't – but a good neighbour had. Brian informed me he'd done it, saying: "Hey, I've mown your lawn because you're a disgrace to the neighbourhood!'

❛ When Gazza was carried past me on a stretcher, I turned to our coaches and said: 'He's finished as a player if he's got what I think he's got.' I wasn't far wrong ❜

Clough's abrasive nature often disguised the warm
and generous side to his character. 'Mr Derby'
GORDON GUTHRIE reveals how he was
a hit with the ladies - young and old.

142

THE OTHER SIDE

GORDON GUTHRIE

Brian's brash and outgoing nature shouldn't be allowed to disguise the fact that he was actually, at times, a very warm and generous man.

I've seen first hand acts of generosity such as always sending flowers to the wives of players and staff on birthdays. Boxes of chocolates at Christmas, just the same. He'd just come in and give the backroom staff a couple of days off on a whim to give them a break. He could be headstrong, yes, but his attention to detail on things such as that were legendary.

I know for a fact that one day he was in the supermarket, behind a dear old lady who was holding a basket with some groceries in.

She was fumbling around in her purse, trying to find the right money, when Brian tapped her on the shoulder.

'Shut your purse, darling – I'll see to those,' he said. That was typical of him, though some people would have you believe differently. That wasn't a one-off occasion either.

For such an outspoken, brash sort of guy, who made out that he couldn't give a monkey's, he'd always see that wives and girlfriends weren't forgotten on special occasions.

When it was your wife's birthday, you'd get home and there'd be a wonderful bouquet of flowers there. The note would read, 'All my best wishes. Have a happy birthday. Brian.'

You'd go in the next morning to thank him for the flowers and he'd just reply: 'Hey, those are between me and your wife!'

In the day when I was club physio, there was only a small squad of players so it was sometimes a 24-hour-a-day job trying to get them all out for a game.

Brian appreciated that and, when he could, would come in and tell us to have a break.

'Get out of this bloody place and spend some time with your families,' he'd say. 'Come back Thursday.'

❛ I've always loved Western films. I was brought up with cowboys who could shoot with both hands ❜

Charismatic former Manchester United boss
TOMMY DOCHERTY reveals some of
his most amusing conversations
with Old Big 'Ead himself.

143

TELL THE DOC

TOMMY DOCHERTY

The last time I saw Brian, I was privileged enough to be doing a dinner in recognition of his services to football at the Grosvenor Hotel in London.

It was incredible really because it was not that long after he'd had his liver transplant and so, understandably, he wasn't 100 per cent.

But he was magnificent that night. He was sensational and ended up bringing the house down before getting a standing ovation from 1300 people at that dinner.

I've known Cloughie over 40 years after first bumping into him at the Midland Hotel in Derby when I ended up having a champagne breakfast on the house!

I've got to say that in all of those 40 years, I've never seen anyone quite like him. Who has? Brian was a one-off. People have been kind enough to refer to me as being charismatic but I'll tell you something, Clough had it in spades.

He could walk into a room and simply command people's attention just by his presence. He didn't have to say anything, but when he did, you could see the jaws drop even further.

Brian only had to snap his fingers and people jumped. He was a master at it. That night at The Grosvenor just underlined for me the esteem he was quite rightly held in.

But the funniest thing I remember about that night was something he said to me in the VIP lounge afterwards.

He gave me the: 'Hey, young man,' routine before thanking me for what I'd done and he was great company.

I asked him if everything was well and how he was feeling after the operation and he leaned over and whispered in my ear. 'There's only one slight worry, Tom. I just hope they haven't given me George Best's old one!' Priceless.

* * *

I never had cross words with Brian but I'm pretty sure I must have told him nicely to 'fuck off' when he tried to get Tony Hateley off me for some ridiculously low amount.

I was manager at Chelsea when I broke the club record to sign the big striker for £100,000. Hateley was

233

absolutely terrific in the air though, to be fair, I told him his passes ought to be labelled 'to whom it may concern!'

Brian was in charge at Derby and called me to say he quite fancied making a proper centre-forward of Hateley and all that kind of stuff.

'Hey, he traps the ball further than I can kick it, but I reckon I can teach him a thing or two, Brian insisted asking me if I was prepared to sell the big bugger. It hadn't quite worked out for Tony as we'd both have liked and so I was prepared to listen to offers – just not Brian's!

He offered something ludicrously low which I turned down flat and it got to the stage where we just could never agree a fee.

He thought I was trying to rob him – infact he knew I was trying to rob him! But anyway, Tony eventually moved on to Liverpool for about the same price and so Cloughie missed out.

I always got on well with him. He called a spade a shovel. He was a great manager for sure and I know when I took over at Derby not that long after he'd gone, he was just an impossible act to follow.

He's arguably the best ever because of what he did at Derby and Forest because they are comparatively small clubs and I mean that most respectfully.

❛ Football's full of people who think they can be managers, when they haven't got a cat in hell's chance. Infact, a cat would have a better chance than most of 'em ❜

Why does ex-Forest centre-half
CHRIS FAIRCLOUGH find his old gaffer is
never far away when he plays his CD
of 40s songbird Nellie Lutcher?

144

NOT ON YOUR NELLIE

CHRIS FAIRCLOUGH

I was 17 and in the apprentices' dressing room when I got the dreaded call to go and see the gaffer. What could it be?

The boss had sent his assistant Ron Fenton to come and get me and there was little or no time to even give much thought to what was going on. I just presumed I was going to get earache off him for something trivial that I'd done. The lads all looked at me with that mixture of curiosity and overwhelming relief that it wasn't them. You can always enjoy it so much more when it is someone else. And this time it was me.

'The gaffer wants to see you,' Ron assured me.

'What about?'

'Dunno.'

I was a bit scared as I made my way to the office, took a deep breath on getting there, and gently knocked on the door.

'Come in.'

The boss was sitting there in his chair with his legs up on the desk. From his old record player came the haunting strains of a female bluesy type singer. He was tapping his fingers and singing along with it.

'Listen to this,' came the instruction. I sat there, reluctant to speak until spoken to.

'Do you like it?' he asked.

'Yeah, err . . . who is it?' I said.

'That, young man, is Nellie Lutcher. She's an old-time jazz singer. Magnificent.'

'Yeah it's really good,' I nodded, not quite sure what to make of the rather odd episode.

'Now that's what you call real music,' he said. I just looked at him and waited.

'It's good. It's really different,' I assured him

'Okay, you can go now,' he said.

I didn't know what the hell to make of it. I went back and explained what had happened to my inquisitive young mates, who were just open-mouthed.

It wasn't until later that I realised he was just keen to introduce me to something I'd never heard before. He obviously wanted to share that with me and as the years have passed, it has become a really lovely moment I will remember for ever. Infact, the songs stayed with me.

When I heard that he'd died I became fascinated with what I'd heard that day and I went out to see if I could track down anything by Nellie Lutcher. I was lucky enough to come across a compilation disc of her best songs.

She has a very distinctive voice that I could still remember from that day when I thought I was going to go into Cloughie's office and get a right dressing down for something or other.

I was so young that I didn't know anything about her – and there was no real reason why I should I guess. It turned out that what I'd heard that day was one of the top artists of the 40s and 50s. She was an African-American rhythm and blues singer and pianist who was hugely popular at the time.

Anyway, I love it. If only the gaffer could see me listening to it occasionally. I think he'd have a wry smile. I play it every so often and when I do I get a real lump in my throat as this picture floats back to me of the gaffer sitting there behind his desk with his feet up, tapping his fingers as he introduced me to an artist that clearly meant so much to him.

He obviously thought one day I might come to appreciate it . . . and, as usual, he was right.

❛ Larry Lloyd was a big lad. When he finished playing he took on a pub and he became the only landlord I know who was actually bigger than his pub ❜

145

TRIUMPHANT RETURN

PAT MURPHY

A year before Brian died I was lucky enough to be alongside him as he made a triumphant return to Leeds' Elland Road ground for the first time in a non-managerial capacity.

He had been concerned beforehand that he might get a hostile reception but emerged from the stage to rapturous applause admitting to me later: "Phew! I sweated more in one night than I did in all my 44 days there back in 1974!'

Not bad for a man who steadfastly refused to moderate his comments. Brian had asked me if I would be the man with the mic at a packed convention centre where he was due to speak about his life and his turbulent time at the club.

I was basically redundant on that stage. All Brian needed was the occasional conversational tickle and he was off with some hilarious and provocative comments.

He gave no quarter with his observations about the Leeds side he inherited but still emerged totally overwhelmed by the warmth of the audience.

He was particularly pleased to meet up with one of his football heroes, John Charles. It was touching to see the legend of Leeds and Juventus yarning away with a managerial legend for a good 15 minutes. At one stage Brian held John's hand, aware that the big Welshman was not for long in this world. It's poignant now to remember that cancer claimed these two giants of football within six months of each other in 2004.

I prefer to remember Brian's reaction to the way he was treated that evening. 'I couldn't get away till one o'clock, you know,' he gasped appreciatively.

An enormous queue formed after he had sat down to thunderous applause and it didn't shrink for a couple of hours. Cloughie had time for every well-wisher, signing every scrap of paper thrust in his direction and posing happily for endless photographs.

No one chided him for his remarks 29 years earlier about the sharp practice of the Leeds players. Yorkshire folk appreciate blunt speaking even if some players can be a bit precious. And that was Brian – a man who defied forensic analysis. He was quite simply a force of nature. Some folk work at being characters in public life, but only a few are naturals when taken away from the orchestrated ad-libs. Brian Clough really did march to a different drumbeat from the others.

A couple of years before he died, and well into his retirement, he did a fascinating programme with me for the BBC's World Service, in which he picked his favourite XI. It was a great team, but when I asked him who should be the manger, he replied in a flash, without any false modesty: 'Well, it would have to be someone who had played a bit, could talk about it clearly without waffling on as if he was Albert Einstein, and wouldn't be afraid to tell that Cruyff bloke to pass the ball a bit more. I suppose it had better be me then!'

That's why Cloughie is missed by so many who never met him and aren't remotely interested in football. Can you say that about many in sport in this conformist age?

❛ Kenny Burns was capable of cutting you in two and came with a bit of a reputation, yet he turned out to be as nice a lad as I've ever managed ❜

Comic capers at the hospital. When News of the World journalist DAVE HARRISON went to visit Cloughie he could never have realised he'd be at the centre of a bizarre escape bid.

146

NURSING A GRUDGE

DAVE HARRISON

I once had to 'grass-up' Cloughie and he was far from pleased about it, I can tell you.

I had arranged to do a column with him but it hit an obstacle because he'd gone in to hospital to have an old knee injury cleaned up.

He was staying in a private hospital in Mickleover, just on the outskirts of Derby, and I drove there to go and see him. Clough and hospitals made for uncomfortable bedfellows and from the minute I got there it was clear he had hatched an escape plan. His greeting was spectacularly friendly.

'Hey, David. Brilliant to see you. I'm so glad you're here.'

I was delighted to have been so warmly received, but quite possibly my suspicion was etched over my face.

'Nice to see you too. How are you?'

'I'm bloody fed up. I'm sick of this place. Come on – give us a lift up to the house. We'll do it there.'

'I can't do that,' I said, well aware that Cloughie wasn't used to people disobeying his instructions. This was different – it was a hospital for God's sake and I was not of the mind to start upsetting nurses and specialists and whoever else had a vested interest in keeping him there.

By this time, he was out of bed and hobbling down the corridor. He was not very good on his feet and I followed him, informing him that he would have to abandon his plan.

It was just like a scene from the Keystone Cops. I was left with no choice but to signal to a nurse and before long, he was gently placed into a wheelchair and told in no uncertain terms that he was going back to bed.

He was far from happy and I was in a bit of a quandary having been put in such an awkward position in the first place. Clough looked at me with a sense of resignation and perhaps just a little betrayal.

'You shithouse,' he grumbled.

❛ When I read some of the stuff Glenn Hoddle came out with, I didn't know whether to reach for the dictionary or a calculator ❜

Just how did Clough get his hands on legendary Argentinian star Diego Maradona's signature? Here ex-Daily Mail journalist RAY MATTS recalls a poignant meeting after Clough's retirement.

147

FROM THE HAND OF GOD

RAY MATTS

It's one of football's best kept secrets, but Argentinian superstar Diego Maradona once signed for Brian Clough. I know because I was the middle man – it's just that no one told Maradona!

Actually, how Brian got the legendary No 10's signature is the culmination of a quite emotional meeting I had with him at his house. I'd always got along just great with Brian, although he could also be the most awkward man on earth at times. It's just what you got with him.

I went to see him just after he'd had his new liver and he seemed really delighted to see me. Our paths had crossed for 30 years and I'd been in his company on many occasions and in many locations. We were just reminiscing and there was this vulnerability about him. Anyway, so where does Maradona come into this? Well . . .

Brian did a column with me and steadfastly refused to take any money for it. He always used to charge a thousand pounds for a special exclusive interview and then give the money to buy an electric wheelchair for a disabled child. He did that for years and

God knows how many wheelchairs he must have purchased. That was a side of Brian few people got to see.

'It'll cost you a wheelchair,' was his stock answer if asked to do anything beyond the norm. Anyway, on this occasion he just wasn't having it and I think he'd been genuinely pleased to pass a couple of hours with me talking about the old times. During the chat he revealed how, despite the fact that he wasn't a well man himself, he was still doing one or two charity appearances. He'd mentioned that he was shortly to attend a charity auction and so, by way of thanks, I told him I had just the thing to attract a few juicy bids.

Before my retirement I had spent many years covering the Formula One grand prix circuit for the Daily Mail and had collected a number of prized momentoes along the way. But one kind of stood out. I had been in Monaco and had just bought myself a fabulous designer t-shirt with the 'Monaco Grand Prix' logo on. I'd still got it in the bag when someone pointed me in the direction of a Rothmans reception and so in I went.

I couldn't believe my luck – there on the next table was Maradona and so I asked him if he'd mind signing the shirt for me. Because he had time and was in a relaxed environment, he really gave it the works. He emblazoned the shirt with a really big proper signature and a 'No 10.' Everyone around me was saying how lucky I'd been to get such a lovely item signed by the great man himself.

On returning home, I put it away tidily in a drawer and planned to just leave it there as some kind of family heirloom, I suppose. It was a really lovely shirt and signed in such a way that I could only guess it would fetch quite a lot if someone wanted it. There was only one thing for it. I gave it to Brian for his charity auction and hoped that some child would benefit from it.

If it hadn't been Cloughie, I would never have parted with it. Anyway, we got chatting and he revealed that he felt like people didn't come to see him anymore since he'd retired.

I tried to explain that the reason for that was that people didn't know whether they could just turn up or what kind of reception they would get what with him struggling with his health and everything.

'People aren't bothered about me any more, Ray,' he said and he had tears in his eyes.

'Brian, the trouble with you is that you don't realise how much people love you,' I said. He smiled.

You know what? For all the memories I have of him – European Cups, having a drink, having a laugh – that moment lingers.

He wasn't in the limelight any more. There was a kind of vulnerability about him. And even though I can't explain why now, that moment is my abiding memory of him.

❛ I was a keen bird's-nester when I was a lad and became a bit of an expert on which bird laid which colour eggs and how many ❜

A lovely tale with a haunting twist as ex-Nottingham Post sports editor TREVOR FRECKNALL remembers a conversation and one thing Cloughie said to him . . .

148

A SPOOKY TALE

TREVOR FRECKNALL

Brian once said something to me that took on a spooky ring when I heard the sad news that he'd died. We'd been having a drink and a chat and I told him that I was absolutely knackered, tired of working, and thinking of calling it a day.

He nodded in agreement and said that he too was worn out and feeling the effects of it all. To use Brian's terminology, I'd just about 'shot it' and was ready to hang up my notebook. When I told him I wasn't going to be able to carry on, he said to me:

'Well, I'm going to have a go. Life catches up with all of us Trev, but you have to give yourself a target.'

We were both in a rather sombre frame of mind. We were both probably feeling a bit unloved and taken for granted. Just weary, basically. He poured me another drink and I asked him what targets he had left.

'Hey Trev, I'll tell you what I'd like to do. I'd like to live long enough to see this club back where it was when I found it.'

It wasn't that Cloughie was wishing any bad on his beloved Forest, it was just that I think he felt the staggering success he'd brought there wasn't always fully appreciated by those in power. I got the impression that he felt it had all started to be taken a bit for granted. The magnitude of what he had done at a provincial club had been truly staggering. To take a club like Forest to the championship and then back-to-back European Cup wins is a feat never to be repeated. It was a monumental achievement then – it's an impossible one now.

When he died I couldn't help noticing that Forest were one place below where they had been when he took charge . . .

❛ I love the smell of live sport. My missus reckons I smelled of embrocation for more than 20 years. She thought I bathed in it! ❜

This story remains anonymous though the names of several culprits have been put forward over the years. A classic Clough story that the Forest boss told against himself on many occasions.

149

CUP UPSET

ANONYMOUS

This story has to remain anonymous though I've heard several different names put forward by people claiming to know the individual's identity!

Cloughie could hear the apprentices returning to the Derby ground after training and knew a piping hot pot of tea would be waiting for them in the dressing room. The manager's office was only just across the way and so he decided to make a call to the dressing room and get one of the lads to bring him a welcome cuppa. What happened next is etched in Clough folklore. The youngster picked up the phone on the dressing room wall.

KID: 'Hello.'

BC: 'Young man, I'd like a nice cup of tea bringing up to my office straight away please.'

KID: 'You what?'

BC: 'A cup of tea. To me. Now. Please.'

KID: 'Fuck off!' and the phone was slammed down. An irate Clough rings back immediately.

BC: Do you know who this is?'

KID: 'Yeah! Do you know who this is?'

BC: 'No.'

KID: 'Well, fuck off again then!'

Rumour has it that Clough, even with his dodgy knees, made the dressing room in around fifteen seconds flat but that an entire team of muddy, sweaty, apprentice footballers, somehow managed to mysteriously disappear in less than half that time.

And though he never discovered the identity of that particular rascal, he had a sneaky regard for the culprit and was big enough to tell the story against himself with a mischievous cackle.

❛ We were brought up on vegetables from my dad's garden. We ate that many and that often, they were coming out of our ears ❜

And finally. . . secretary CAROLE WASHINGTON describes Clough's emotional final hours at the City Ground and the very last thing he said before vacating his office for the last time.

150

AUF WIEDERSEHEN PET

CAROLE WASHINGTON

I will never forget the boss's last words as he walked away from his office at Forest for the very last time. I had some truly lovely times working for him but I sobbed my heart out at the sight of him walking out of the City Ground for the last time.

It was well past midnight on a Thursday night when he made his final exit, turned to me, kissed me on the cheek and walked towards the car waiting for him. His great friend Colin Lawrence, who he thought the world of, was waiting to drive him home.

You'll notice that I still call him the boss, even though after his retirement I still went to see him as a friend not an employer. That's the way it was – I had too much respect to call him anything else. I never, ever called him Brian.

The boss hadn't been due at the ground at all that day. His wife Barbara had called earlier and asked if all his personal stuff could be carefully packed away in boxes and someone would be down to collect them the following day.

I was in tears as I gently placed some of his personal belongings, pictures and stuff into bags and boxes. I packed every last thing. His pictures of the Ink Spots and Sinatra were taken down off the walls. The picture of Del Boy his faithful dog, sitting in the chairman's chair, was removed from his desk. It was heartbreaking. I sobbed as, bit by bit, piece by piece, I carried out a task that I'd rather not have been doing. But I was the only one who could, should and would be doing it. It was funny really because even though the walls and his desk were bare, while the boxes were there, you had the feeling that he hadn't actually gone.

Unexpectedly, at around 6pm, he turned up and as he was looking around his office, I was consumed by a strange feeling of guilt as if he might be thinking that I couldn't wait to get rid of him or something.

'Where's so-and-so?' he would ask and I would point him in the direction of whatever it was he was looking for. The reserves were playing later on and he stuck around to watch the match. The dust surrounding the news of his leaving had settled but as word got around that he was at the game, people started to queue up wanting to say one final farewell and maybe try to get an autograph. It wasn't just me who was feeling a sense of real loss – you could feel it among the fans.

He signed every last autograph even though it took him to well past midnight. My son Justin and his friend had been banished to a guest room while I oversaw things. Colin helped with ushering the fans away as they passed through. In the end there was just the boss and me in the offices and his white shirt was covered in my mascara! I sniffed away trying to muffle my sobs as he made his way through the door.

You didn't need to be told that a piece of history was walking through those doors with him.

'Well, this is it pet,' he said giving me a last kiss on the cheek, looking around one last time before making his way to the car.

❛ Don't tell me I would have failed as England manager. Me? Working with the best of the very best. I couldn't have failed ❜

Also by Dave Armitage

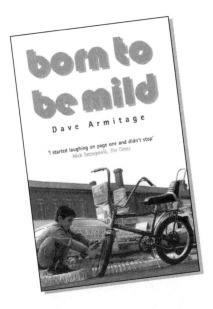 

BORN TO BE MILD

It's Christmas, 1969 . . . a pint of bitter is 2s.4d(12p) and a new Ford Escort costs
£703.13s.11d. Paul Dunn is 11 and more important issues lie ahead - like getting a good
signal on Radio Luxembourg and the beautiful, but out of reach, carnival queen Belinda.
Santa has brought him a Chopper and Dunny takes a rocky ride through the 70s
- Pan's People, puberty, Slade and T.Rex.
Thirty years later he meets Belinda and she's available, but so much has changed since those
days. She is the size of a house, Donny Osmond is a grandad and Gary Glitter is facing the
firing squad for something other than his records.

'Stingray, sex and the 70s . . . superb' - Daily Mirror.

'I started laughing on page one and didn't stop' - The Times.

PAST AND PRESENTS

A self-made billionaire receives a shock 50th birthday present - a photograph
relating to the blackest day of his life when he was 16.
Could this now be the best present he's ever had? As he thinks back
a fascinating and funny story unfolds as he recalls all of his birthdays - past and present.

'Outrageously funny' - Daily Mirror.

'Laughtastic' - The Sun.